P9-CQG-925

STREETWISE®

INDEPENDENT CONSULTING

STREETWISE®

INDEPENDENT CONSULTING

A Comprehensive Guide to Building Your Own Consulting Business

DAVID KINTLER
with BOB ADAMS, M.B.A.

adams media

Copyright ©1998, F+W Publications, Inc. All rights reserved.
This book, or parts thereof, may not be reproduced in any form without permission from the publisher; exceptions are made for brief excerpts used in published reviews.

A Streetwise® Publication.
Streetwise® is a registered trademark of F+W Publications, Inc.

Published by Adams Media, an F+W Publications Company
57 Littlefield Street, Avon, MA 02322. U.S.A.
www.adamsmedia.com

ISBN: 1-55850-728-0

Printed in the United States of America.

J I H

Library of Congress Cataloging-in-Publication Data
Kintler, David.
Adams Streetwise consulting / by David Kintler and Bob Adams.
p. cm.
Includes index.
ISBN 1-55850-728-0
1. Business consultants. I. Adams, Bob, 1955- . II. Title.
HD69.C6K52 1997
658.4'6–dc21 97-35172
CIP

Cover photo: © Rob Gage/FPG International Corp.
Inside photos: Photodisc™ Images ©1996, Photo Disc, Inc.,
Image Club Graphics StudioGear™, and BodyShots™ ©1994.

This publication is designed to provide accurate and authoritative information with regard to the subject matter covered. It is sold with the understanding that the publisher is not engaged in rendering legal, accounting, or other professional advice. If legal advice or other expert assistance is required, the services of a competent professional person should be sought.

–From a *Declaration of Principles* jointly adopted by a Committee of the American Bar Association and a Committee of Publishers and Associations

This book is available at quantity discounts for bulk purchases.
For information, call 1-800-289-0963.

CONTENTS

CONTENTS

CONTENTS

CONTENTS

CONTENTS

CONTENTS

CONTENTS

CONTENTS

CONTENTS

CONTENTS

CONTENTS

CONTENTS

INTRODUCTION

INTRODUCTION

Your ultimate success as a consultant is going to depend more on how well you manage and run your consultancy as a business, (than as opposed to) the specialized consulting skills and background that you bring to the business. Many extremely knowledgable and talented professionals have not succeeded in consulting because they did not view consulting as a business in itself and did not develop the skills necessary to succeed at this business. On the other hand, many people with only average skill in their particular profession, have developed thriving consultancies–because they did a good job of running their consulting business.

This book is designed to show you all of the in's and out's of starting and successfully running an independent consulting business. It is designed to fill the gap between the skills you have learned in your particular profession and the information that you need to know to turn those skills into a flourishing consultancy. Like any other business, you will more likely succeed at consulting if you carefully develop a plan and a strategy for your business, than if you just start trying to land clients.

Landing clients might at first seem like a formidable task–but as you will learn in this book there are many proven techniques that enable you to develop a steady flow of new clients. You'll learn how to solicit potential clients, how to to get potential clients to contact you, what to say on the phone with potential clients, and how to make an in-person presentation. You'll learn how to create all kinds of different proposals–and what the key elements are that make a proposal much more likely to win an assignment.

There are many other facets of the consulting business that you need to know–and this book covers them all. From pricing your services, to renting an office, to legal issues–you'll get the inside story from David Kintler, the primary author of this book and a highly successful consultant. You'll learn how to run your consulting business right! And you'll soon be consulting your way to success!

Bob Adams
Founder and President
Adams Media Corporation

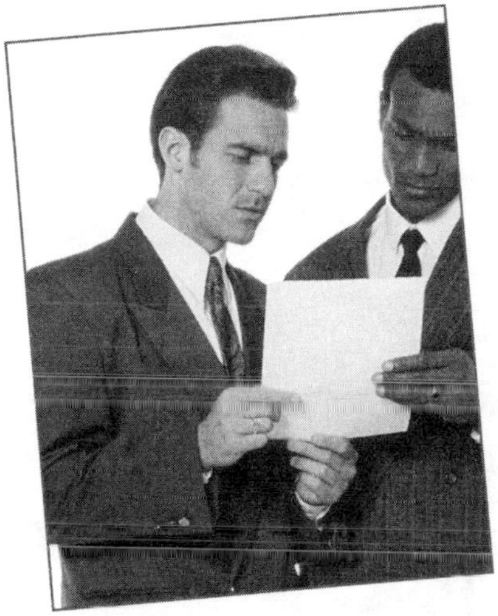

CHAPTER 1

GETTING STARTED

Because of downsizing, com
panies are increasingly ou
sourcing for services an
exper r availabl
from n staf
Consu their tim
and e elp fill i
the g e neede
becau ve skills
experience, or knowledg
not perceived to be availab

Getting started in consulting is like building the foundation of a house. The key is to build a solid foundation in order to build a strong business. Some of the very important starting steps include: developing a mission statement; writing up a target market profile; identifying your competition; doing a service benefits analysis; and creating a unique selling proposition.

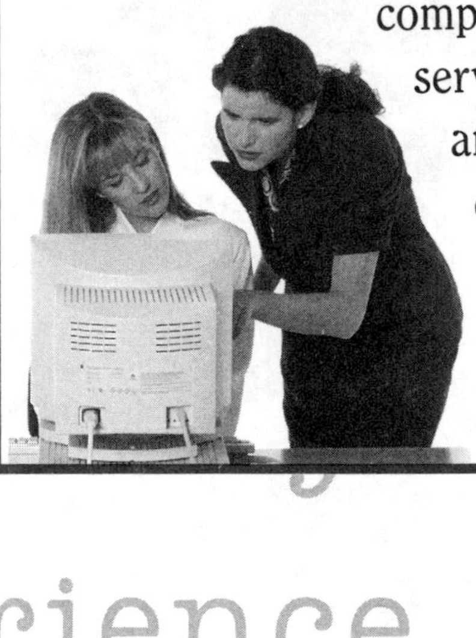

TO BEGIN

Congratulations! After all those years in corporate life, you've decided to start a consulting practice. This is a new era—and that means corporations are continually downsizing and rightsizing. Whatever you want to call it—things are not the same. The opportunities that used be present in corporate life—the security, the path to advancement, and the ability to build a future are just not what they used to be.

Perhaps you're at a place where you've had it with corporate life. Maybe your company has merged with another, and you've been reengineered out of the new organization. Perhaps you've been asked to move to one of the worst cities in the U.S. at a lesser position. It could be that you don't believe in the company you work for—or your boss is a total turkey. You know there has to a better way—and consulting seems like the answer.

The Good News

A consulting practice can be all that you dream it can be. Just some of the things that it will provide you are:

- The opportunity to put to work the knowledge that you've accumulated in your years of industry experience
- The ability to enjoy the freedom and independence of doing your own thing
- The possibility of achieving excellent financial rewards
- The flexibility of living wherever you want

GETTING STARTED

Consulting firms are fast becoming an essential outsource service for downsizing companies.

- The freedom to take on those assignments you feel are stimulating and rewarding–and the option of walking away from opportunities you don't intrinsically enjoy
- The chance to meet new people in other companies and industries
- The satisfaction of working with the best resources you can find to get the job done

YOUR SERVICES ARE IN DEMAND

The career opportunity you've chosen is one of the most rapidly expanding areas in business today. As reported in *Management Constant International,* published by Lafferty Publications, Ltd., "Combined revenues [in 1995] at the top 30 firms grew by 21 percent to $23.2 billion in 1995."

Because of downsizing, companies are increasingly outsourcing for services and expertise no longer available from their own staff. Consultants bring their time and expertise to help fill in the gaps. You are needed because you have skills, experience, or knowledge not perceived to be available in-house. Companies or individuals may need your help to:

The consultant's objective position can help streamline and improve a company's overall performance.

- Oversee or conduct special projects because an organizational overload requires a knowledgeable outside resource
- Analyze existing organizational functions, operations, and results to recommend specific areas and actions for improvement
- Be the outside resource that acts as an 'agent for change'
- Develop and conduct training courses specific to a company's needs
- Provide an objective third-party viewpoint on strategic planning, marketing, and other operational issues to help companies avoid pitfalls and wasted effort
- Troubleshoot tactical issues, such as sales performance, to help improve a company's quarterly results
- Provide technical advice in product development or manufacturing areas

- Write articles, white papers, and technical product bulletins and manuals
- Create marketing and promotional materials
- Conduct computer consultations to help resolve MIS issues, including software, networking, and client-server applications and to assist in computer system hardware and software selection
- Bring financial background and industry resources to bear to help a company resolve financial issues
- Act as the outside resource used to provide product evaluations–including competitive analysis

This list is not all-inclusive. What's important is that you can take the skills you've developed and the experiences you've gained to add value to the companies you've worked for directly in corporate life–and now add value to the firms you consult with.

Are You Committed?

This all sounds great–so why aren't there more consultants? One reason is that in order to be successful at consulting, you must be totally committed. In fact, the four keys to consulting success are:

- Total commitment to making a success of your practice
- Meaningful differentiation of the services you have to offer
- The ability to sell yourself
- The deserved reputation for providing more value than expected

Consulting demands the complete dedication of the consultant to the practice.

What about total commitment? If it's not there–forget it. You're better off getting another job in a corporation. Don't use consulting as a way to run away from the problems in a corporation. You'll be running from one set of problems to another–with a lot more surprises! Consulting is a lifestyle you choose for your future because of what it gives you.

I've had my own consulting and training business for six years. I'm convinced that the number one reason I've been successful (and success to me is having my net worth increase every year) is that I've chosen this career lifestyle for the rest of my working life. It's so

GETTING STARTED

good I don't even think of retiring–I'm allergic to leisure. When I left corporate life as a Vice President of Sales for a Computer Systems Division, I vowed I would never work for another corporation again. This isn't an indictment of the corporation–it was the best job of my corporate career. I worked for a General Manager who was the best boss I've ever had. But I was committed to making my own consulting business a 'go.'

Here's how not to succeed. Don't just dabble in consulting or use it as a 'holding pattern' until something better turns up in a corporation. It's okay to do this if you recognize that this is your real purpose. But if you're just not sure–if you haven't made up your mind to stick with it–a divided purpose is a recipe for disaster. Someone once said, "A man without a purpose is like a ship without a rudder..." This is especially true in beginning a consulting business.

You can't just dabble in consulting and expect to succeed.

As an example, a good friend of mind was a corporate casualty and believed that companies would use him for consulting assignments because of his vast experience in the process control industry. This sounded good to me until I called him a few times and found he was watching TV or taking a nap! Thankfully, he's now out of his 'dabbling in consulting' business.

CHALLENGES AND OBSTACLES

Here are some challenges and obstacles you may encounter in launching your own consulting practice:

- Getting your first assignment
- Financial uncertainty
- Gaps between assignments
- Timing
- Lack of control
- New skills sets are required
- Developing a resource base for project assignments
- Developing strategic alliances
- Developing relationships that lead to business success

GETTING STARTED

Getting Your First Assignment

Unless you are able to connect your knowledge and experience to the needs of a contact you currently have, it may be awhile before you get your first assignment. I was fortunate to have an in-depth knowledge of computers used for real-time applications. As a result, I landed my first assignment for conducting a competitive analysis study for a computer corporation within 33 days of starting my business. You can do this too. We'll explore how later in this book.

Finding your first assignment is a sure test of your dedication to consulting.

Financial Uncertainty

There's something about a corporate paycheck that can be addicting. Perhaps this is no big deal to you, but if you're supporting a family they can get really nervous when that paycheck disappears. The only way to solve this issue is to continually hustle for business. You must be confident of the value of what you have to offer, and possess the materials and skills to help you put your best foot forward. This book will show you how to do that.

Gaps Between Assignments

Staying on top of new business projects will keep business afloat.

The biggest trap consultants get into (and that includes me) is that we get comfortable with the work and income flow from our existing client base. But they can dry up in a hurry. All it takes is a change in top management, financial belt-tightening–even the successful completion of a long-term project–and that income flow disappears. But we haven't taken the time to find and sell new opportunities because we're too busy. We often get so caught up in the tasks at hand, we drop the ball that is our future.

If we haven't done our homework, when a major project is over, it's like starting the business up all over again until we get a new contract. There's no need for this to occur. Once you learn this lesson (hopefully with this book) it won't happen again. It's no fun in the 'tween times.

Timing and Control

In a consulting practice, timing and control are quite different from what we learned to expect in corporate life. There, everything

GETTING STARTED

Consulting is a relationship business that relies on the need of the client.

Control of the situation is always in the hands of the company.

was relatively simple. It was a cause-effect environment. We issued a directive and things got done, sometimes on schedule. There was a predictability and rhythm to the culture of the company. Our actions as corporate manager or executive made things happen. Running a consulting business will give you a whole new perspective on timing and control.

First, any time-related issues are those of your client. Wait a minute, you say. I've got an unbeatable selling proposition, my promotional materials are excellent, and I've got great references. I can really help this company, and they just are not responding right now. What's up?

You may have a great story to tell to a prospective client, but they may not be ready for your services yet. It's not time–other issues are more important. In corporate life you were part of the mainstream, but here you're an outsider. That's why a successful consulting business is a relationship business. When it's time to use the services you can provide, you want to make sure they'll call you instead of someone else.

Second, let's talk about control. In corporate life, you may have believed that through the application of appropriate management techniques you were able to control the actions of the people who worked for you. In a consulting practice, you only influence, you don't control. One of the temptations to overcome is attempting to take control of a situation where you are contracted to be an advisor. I once blew a consulting contract with a major workstation supplier by attempting to run a project that was going south instead of acting as a advisor. Old corporate habits, especially management ones, die hard.

NEW SKILLS SETS ARE REQUIRED

Remember when you used to be to able dictate a letter or send an outline to the marketing department to create some visual aids? With a consulting practice, those days are gone, unless you want to spend a lot of money using outside service firms. Some of the new skill sets you'll need to develop are:

GETTING STARTED

- Computer literacy–this means learning word processing, spreadsheets, presentation graphics, database manager (for direct mail campaigns), and desktop publishing
- Positioning your services–becoming a streetwise marketing guru
- Sales skills–even if you've been a VP of Sales, it's back to square one. Most likely, you're like I was and will have to relearn the basics.
- Writing winning proposals–it's all up to you
- Handling money–why is it so easy to spend?
- Time management and discipline–this means being at your desk on time and putting in a full day–every day

Outsourcing can help you improve your services for company clients.

Developing Resource Bases for Project Assignments

By now you've figured out that you can't do everything supremely well. Other people are more gifted than you are in some areas. Don't hesitate to use them if they'll add to the success of a project. Outsourcing some of the fees you receive may be one of the best investments you'll ever make. One client contracted me to develop a new-hire training course from scratch. I immediately sought out the best I know in the business and achieved an unbelievably high 4.75 out of 5.0 rating for a pilot training course.

Here are some of the areas where you may need to have outside resources help you:

- Graphics design for preparation of marketing and promotional material
- Technical, marketing, or financial functions
- Letter writing
- Telemarketing
- Telephone answering
- Dictating and typing
- Printing
- Any other services you may need that you do not have the skills to provide

GETTING STARTED

> Successful consulting depends upon the creation of mutually beneficial business relationships.

DEVELOPING STRATEGIC ALLIANCES

Yes, there are others out there in the consulting world–the 'no man is an island' truism applies here in spades. Developing mutually beneficial business relationships with your peers in the consulting world can help you to:

- Add value to an assignment where others may require your services
- Provide referrals where and when they can't handle an assignment
- Offer reciprocity with finders fees to provide financial incentive

DEVELOPING RELATIONSHIPS THAT LEAD TO BUSINESS SUCCESS

You probably realize that your success in corporate life was not solely because of your knowledge and skills–much of it had to do with the relationships you had with your superiors, peers, and subordinates within the company or companies. Now that you've left the corporate scene, those relationships are gone (unless you get your initial consulting contract from your existing employer).

Success in the business world depends on relationships. You've heard, "It's not so much what you know, it's who you know." There's more to it than just knowing–a relationship–a mutually respectful connection must exist. And you're going to have to develop a lot of new relationships quickly! We'll share how to do this later.

HOT GROWTH AREAS FOR CONSULTANTS IN THE '90S

Virtually all industrial areas and some governmental areas in the U.S. will be using an increasing amount of consulting services between now and the turn of the century. Consulting is one of the fastest growing professions in the '90s. The following factors provide the business climate that contributes to this growth:

- Large corporations are reengineering and downsizing
- Small business start-ups are on the rise
- Specific industries are experiencing significant growth

GETTING STARTED

Two years ago, *Business Week* projected that the consulting profession would grow by double-digit rates for at least the next five years. Results currently reported in *Management Consulting International* confirm these figures. This trend has not gone unnoticed by MBA graduates–the percentages eschewing corporate management positions for consulting opportunities is increasing.

> Consultants help soften the blow of downsizing by sharing their professional expertise.

Large Corporation Reengineering and Downsizing

Layoffs create major opportunities for consultants. The quest for survival and increased quarterly profits causes major corporations to cut staff expenses to come in line with revenues and profit projections. Companies that I have consulted for pride themselves on high revenue-per-employee ratios.

Although the number of people within a company is less, the tasks still have to be accomplished; and the jobs must get done. Corporate downsizing creates consulting opportunities in large companies and the small companies that serve the corporate giants. First, consultants are engaged by large corporations to compensate for the knowledge gap created by departed employees, either through layoffs or early retirement. Second, large firms outsource to small business subcontractors, who in turn need consulting resources for expertise that may not be available in the smaller firm.

> Small companies are the sources of most of the new jobs created today.

Small Businesses

Most of the jobs being created in the U.S. today are in the small business sector. Many small business firms compete with the corporate giants, while others have large corporations as their customers. Whatever market is being pursued, small businesses typically don't have the depth of resources available to large corporations. Two types of consulting opportunities exist; providing consulting services in your functional area of expertise and working for the small company on a temporary ('temp') basis.

GETTING STARTED

Advancements in communications and software are areas of the most growth for consulting—but there's plenty of consulting demand in almost every industry.

HOT GROWTH AREAS FOR CONSULTANTS

The following table provides a capsule summary of some of the major growth areas for consulting in the '90s.

Industry	Growth Areas for Consultants
Health Care	Outsourcing human resource functions including benefits administration, outplacement, and recruiting. Outsourcing patient care functions, requiring consulting support for administration and recruiting.
Telecommunications	Software development, including security and billing products, setup and installation of microwave and satellite links. Network consulting to set up corporate Local and Wide Area networks.
The Internet	Marketing consulting in the design and implementation of Home Pages for small corporations. Technical consulting in the areas of communications software, operating systems, graphical user interfaces, and systems design.
Finance/Banking	Management and staff training and development including computer and software training and installation.
Environmental	Site testing and evaluation of toxins and other harmful chemicals for non-environmental companies. Expert testimonial consulting.
Government	Consulting to prime contractors serving the government to transition their capabilities for the private sector. Project consulting for defense-related projects.
Not-for-Profit	Management development, financial consulting, marketing and sales consulting, as well as consulting for fund-raising activities and events.

GETTING STARTED

BUSINESS AND PERSONAL OBJECTIVES

This section is designed to help you put a framework in place for offering the capabilities of your consulting practice to prospective clients. This is not a discussion on developing business plans and developing a plan to start your own business. These issues are addressed later in the book.

TYPE OF CONSULTING PRACTICE

What type of consulting practice are you considering? Are you offering a highly specialized service to a very specific market niche or are you operating more as a generalist? You could also be offering services as a "temporary executive." Describe the nature of your consulting practice below.

Questions to consider include:

- What type of consulting practice are you operating?
- What types of services and products will you offer?
- What are the business objectives of your consulting practice?
- What are your specific objectives and their schedule for accomplishment?
- What are your criteria for success in your consulting practice?

Other questions to consider include:

- What kinds of services will you offer?
- What are the types of clients that can use these services?
- Who will be your primary market? Your secondary market?
- What strengths and experiences do you have that enable you to effectively offer these services?
- What kinds of expertise do you need to acquire to more effectively offer these services?
- What types of resources do you need to more effectively offer these services?

SERVICES AND PRODUCTS OFFERED

Are you going to just show up or will you develop a series of tools to help your clients achieve the results they want? Some of the tools to consider offering are:

You'll need a concrete framework for your practice in order to attract the right clients.

GETTING STARTED

- Surveys for organizational effectiveness (your client and your client's customers)
- Tools for analysis (financial, sales and marketing, manufacturing, human resources, customer service)

List below those tools that you intend to use to increase your value to your clients. These could include: analysis tools and systems you've used in your past life as a corporate manager or executive; tools you're going to develop from scratch; or approaches and systems you can use to offer in conjunction with another consultant. Describe the tools you will be employing in your consulting practice.

The tools you used to improve your services will help create a solid client base.

BUSINESS OBJECTIVES

1. What do you want your business to be? (Describe in 25 words or less.)
2. Are you going for national market penetration or will you concentrate regionally?
3. Will your consulting practice consist primarily of your efforts or will you have a staff? If a staff, what kinds of people and when? Are you hiring employees or using the services of Independent Contractors?

SPECIFIC OBJECTIVES AND SCHEDULE FOR ACCOMPLISHMENT

What are your specific objectives?

	Five Years	One Year	90 days
Revenue			
Industry served			
No. of clients			
Specific clients			
No. of employees			
Demographics served			
Major milestones			
- Profit			
- Other			

GETTING STARTED

Success Criteria

One difference between a career in corporate life and operating your own consulting practice is that it's personal—the business is YOU! Because some degree of success is tied to your self-esteem, you need to know why the business is important to you.

What's neat about this is that you determine what goes into your performance appraisal—no one else is involved!

First, will your life be different when you achieve your five-year objectives, one-year objectives, and the things you have committed to accomplish in the next ninety days? Consider your objectives from these three perspectives:

- Financial
- Mental
- Personal

Your own personal goals help determine how successful your consulting practice will be.

Second, what has to be present for you to be satisfied with your consulting practice? What are those things that must happen for you to know that you are satisfied with your business? This is highly personal. Some consultants strive to grow a million-dollar consulting business—others do just enough consulting to have a comfortable lifestyle. Let's design how you'd like your life to work as a result of your being a consultant.

Design your practice to fulfill your ideals for success.

What are your success criteria? What has to be present for you to know your consulting practice is a success? List your success criteria below:

1. ______________________________
2. ______________________________
3. ______________________________
4. ______________________________
5. ______________________________
6. ______________________________
7. ______________________________
8. ______________________________
9. ______________________________

GETTING STARTED

Test these criteria. For each one list what's important to you.

1. ______________________
2. ______________________
3. ______________________
4. ______________________
5. ______________________
6. ______________________

SAMPLE SUCCESS CRITERIA

To help you with this process here's an example:

What are your success criteria? What has to be present for you to know your consulting practice is a success? List your success criteria below:

1. A net income before taxes of $150,000 per year
2. A wide variety of challenging assignments
3. Working with top executives in the companies I serve
4. The ability to make a difference in the results of the companies I work with
5. National prominence in the field of consulting
6. Travel to the major cities of the world

Test these criteria. For each one listed, what's important to you.

1. Net income of $150K means a great lifestyle–homes in Florida and the Northeast. The ability to help out our children when they need it and to have fantastic vacations for my wife and myself.
2. Challenging assignments mean that I stay abreast of the latest that's happening in business and that I develop my mental capacities to the utmost. It also means I'll take prudent risks. Based on my background I know I can do things I haven't done before. This means personal growth and the satisfaction of accomplishment.
3. Working with top executives: Although I'm an "outsider" now, this is the group I came from. I enjoy associating with those who used to be my peers. As a consultant serving high levels, I'm still part of the "club."
4. Making a difference means I add value to the companies I serve, which gives me a strong sense of satisfaction.
5. National prominence: I like to be recognized for the good things I do. I am driven to achieve, and being known at a national level is recognition of that achievement.
6. I like the excitement of travel and going to new places, seeing new people, and experiencing new things.

GETTING STARTED

Mission Statement

With your success criteria in mind, you have the required material to generate a Mission Statement for yourself. A Mission Statement provides a capsule summary of who you are and where you are going. It's a clear statement of what you want to accomplish with your consulting practice.

Taking the example criteria above, here's an example Mission Statement.

My name is __________. I am a nationally recognized expert in the field of consulting to the ____________ industry (or profession). I work with the top management of the corporations I serve, and add value to their operations. By accepting challenging assignments and by taking maximum advantage of my capabilities and experience, I am able to make a measurable difference in the results of the companies I serve.

Because of these results and my reputation in the field, I have an enjoyable lifestyle with a gross income of $150,000 per year. This allows me to live where I want when I want, to travel extensively, and to support my family in style.

Now it's your turn. Craft a Mission Statement of 100 words or less that includes the following three items:

- Who I am and what I do
- What I accomplish
- My success criteria

We've just scratched the surface. Revisit this section when you complete the rest of this program and periodically thereafter. It's important for you to know your current success criteria and where you stand in their achievement.

A Mission Statement helps to define the goals of your consulting practice.

You need to define your own Mission Statement to truly realize your goals for success.

TARGET MARKET PROFILE

What is your target market? Who are your prospective customers? Where are they, and what are their characteristics? The Fortune 1000; small businesses between $10 million and $30 million? Is the

GETTING STARTED

size of a company enough information to target the companies that might use the services offered by your consulting practice?

The more specific you are in focusing your services, the more likely you will be successful. The more you understand the needs of the specific person you intend to serve, the higher your likelihood of winning the business. This means rifle shooting–not a shotgun approach. Won't you lose flexibility? Absolutely not. There's infinite flexibility in the various turns a consulting practice can take. Look for options within the direction you have chosen for your practice.

By focusing your services in a clear direction, you in fact increase your flexibility and potential for success.

We've designed the Target Market Profiler to help you. It will enable you to operate with a strong sense of direction and knowledge about who you want as clients for your consulting practice. And because your practice is about people, we've included the psychographics of your prospect as well as the characteristics of his or her company.

TARGET MARKET PROFILER

1. **Industry/Product/Service Classification**
   In what industries do you have experience or prefer to work?
   What are the companies/products produced with which you prefer to consult to?
   What are the companies/services provided with which you prefer to consult to?
   From what industry or types of industries will your consulting business be obtained and in what priority?
2. **Company Size and Location**
   What is the size of the firms you have selected to target your efforts?
   - Annual revenues
   - Number of employees

   Where will you get your customers? (regionally, nationally, internationally) and where will you be concentrating the majority of your efforts?
   Approximately how many prospective companies in your primary and secondary market areas are there?

GETTING STARTED

3. **Market Analysis**
   What types of consulting requirements do your target prospects have and how do you know them?
   How is your typical prospect currently meeting his or her requirements?
   What time of year will your services be most in demand?
   What will be the typical length of one of your consulting assignments?
   What market trends or shifts do you see emerging in the next six to twelve months that could affect the type of consulting services you offer to these clients?
   What technological, economic, or social trends could emerge in the next twelve months that could affect your consulting business either positively or negatively?

4. **Competition**
   Who are your chief competitors? Do you know them personally?
   Do they have more resources and industry awareness than you? Is their perceived value high?
   How do they price their services? Are your prices higher or lower than theirs?
   What are the typical payment terms or agreements for consultants in your industry (e.g., 25 percent upon signing, 25 percent upon first deliverable, 50 percent on final delivery)?
   What are the strengths and weaknesses of each of your chief competitors as compared with the services you offer?

	Strengths	Weaknesses
Competitor A		
Competitor B		
Competitor C		

   How do your competitors obtain business now (direct mail, advertising, telemarketing, direct sales, networking)?

Knowing the positions and strategies of the competition helps to narrow your own consulting practice's focus.

GETTING STARTED

Good consultants can "read" clients to determine the appropriate focus of their services.

5. **Prospect Personal Profile**
   Who are typically the decision-makers responsible for selecting your consulting services? What are their titles within the prospect organization?
   What types of professional and personal challenges do they face that can be addressed by your services?
   What is the typical educational background of these decision makers?
   What organizations (professionals and charitable) are they likely to belong to?
   What magazines and periodicals do they read?
   What is the typical age range of each of the persons likely to decide upon your services?
   Have you prepared a list by name, title, company, address, and phone number for each of the potential clients in your target markets? If not, how will you compile such a list?

Here's a completed example provided as a model for your efforts. The consulting firm in mind (mine) has targeted high-technology companies in Massachusetts for a major marketing campaign.

GETTING STARTED

SAMPLE TARGET MARKET PROFILER

1. **Industry/Product/Service Classification**

   In what industries do you have experience or prefer to work?

   High-technology companies

   What are the companies/products produced with which you prefer to consult to? (product pop-up list):

   Computers systems
   Telecommunications
   Software
   Graphics systems
   CAD/CAM Systems

   What are the companies/services provided with which you prefer to consult to? (services pop-up list):

   Technical resources
   Health care

   From what industry or types of industries will your consulting business be obtained and in what priority?

   Computers systems companies
   Computer peripherals
   Data communications
   Applications software
   Systems software
   Graphics
   CAD/CAM
   Health care
   Industrial control

2. **Company Size and Location**

   What is the size of the firms you have selected to target your efforts?

   Annual revenues

   Priority No. 1-$50-250 million
   Priority No. 2-$25-50 million

   Number of employees

   Priority No. 1-over 200 employees
   Priority No. 2-over 100 employees

   Where will you get your customers? (regionally, nationally, internationally) and where will you be concentrating the majority of your efforts?

   Regionally–in the Massachusetts area

GETTING STARTED

Approximately how many prospective companies in your primary and secondary market areas are there?

Priority No. 1-211

Priority No. 2-178

3. Market Analysis

What types of consulting requirements do your target prospects have and how do you know them?

Competitive analyses

Sales productivity

Sales training

Organizational effectiveness

Know this from contact in the New England area and my background in corporate life

How is your typical prospect currently meeting his or her requirements?

Typically, meeting requirements with internal resources with some consulting or training contacts.

What time of year will your services be most in demand?

4th Quarter-getting ready for the new year

1st Quarter-kicking off the new year

What will be the typical length of one of your consulting assignments?

Minimum one week, typically four weeks

What market trends or shifts do you see emerging in the next six to twelve months that could affect the type of consulting services you offer to these clients?

Stock market volatility and higher interest rates suggest a slowdown beginning December 96-March 97. Sales productivity pressures will increase.

What technological, economic, or social trends could emerge in the next twelve months that could affect your consulting business either positively or negatively?

Consulting and training approaches may start to become available on the Internet. Because consulting is primarily a people business, I don't consider this to be a factor.

Computer system price-performance will continue to improve, putting competitive pressures on suppliers, especially those that don't manufacture their own CPU-chip technology. These cost pressures could reduce the funds available for consulting.

4. Competition

Who are your chief competitors? Do you know them personally?

Computer Systems Consulting-MarketSphere-know personally

Telesales/telemarketing-Multi-Track-know personally

Sales Training-Holden-Power Base Selling-do not know

Do they have more resources and industry awareness than you? Is their perceived value high?

GETTING STARTED

Both MarketSphere and Multi-Track have established a presence in New England. Existing relationships may provide a higher perceived value.

Power Base Selling is well-known nationally–some sales forces have set it up to be their 'culture'.

How do they price their services? Are your prices higher or lower than theirs?

I do not have current pricing information. Consulting prices tend to be situational (whatever the traffic will bear). Industry training prices are typically $795 per person (three-day course) for training courses like Holden's.

What are the typical payment terms or agreements for consultants in your industry (e.g., 25 percent upon signing, 25 percent upon first deliverable, 50 percent on final delivery)?

Typically 10 to 25 percent on signing, with remaining percentages allocated among the number of deliveries, with a final payment of 10 percent plus (can vary widely) with the final delivery.

Many consulting assignments are over a term of weeks, and payment for the consultant's efforts is made much the same way as the paycheck for its employees.

What are the strengths and weaknesses of each of your chief competitors as compared with the services you offer?

	Strengths	Weaknesses
MarketSphere	Established presence; Excellent contacts	Differentiated offering
MultiTrack	Established presence; Excellent contacts	Differentiated offering
Holden	National presence; Instilled in culture	Expensive; Paperwork-intensive

How do your competitors obtain business now (direct mail, advertising, telemarketing, direct sales, networking)?

Consulting competition primarily markets through word-of-mouth with some direct mail effort.

Training companies use a commissioned direct sales force, establish market awareness with books and articles, and advertise minimally.

5. Prospect Personal Profile

Who are typically the decision makers responsible for selecting your consulting services? What are their titles within the prospect organization?

Vice President (or Director) of Sales

Vice President (or Director) of Marketing

What types of professional and personal challenges do they face that can be addressed by your services?

Increased cost of a direct sales force

Lower profit margins

Lower selling price for products (means must sell more volume)

GETTING STARTED

- Technology advances accelerate obsolescence
- Products are becoming a commodity

What is the typical educational background of these decision makers?

- Undergraduate degree in an engineering or math discipline
- Graduate degree in business (for some)

What organizations (professionals and charitable) are they likely to belong to?

- Sales and Marketing Executives
- American Management Association

What magazines and periodicals do they read?

- *Wall Street Journal*
- *Fortune*
- *Advertising Age*
- *Forbes*
- *Sales and Marketing Management*
- *Personal Selling Power*
- *Selling*

What is the typical age range of each of the persons likely to decide upon your services?

- Vice President 45-55
- Directors 35-45

Have you prepared a list by name, title, company, address, and phone number for each of the potential clients in your target market? If not, how will you compile such a list?

- Used a 1994 CorpTech database to determine available market–tuned list from 1996 Massachusetts High Tech Directory

GETTING STARTED

SERVICE BENEFITS ANALYSIS

How well have you defined the consulting services you are going to provide to your target market? Have you been curiously specific or uninterestingly general? You create interest in what you have to offer when you are positioned as having something specific to offer rather than a collection of generalities and platitudes.

What if you provide financial services to small businesses? What does this really mean? Do you see them once a year during tax season, are you viewed as an extension of their finance department, or are you their entire finance department? You need to be able to articulate this quickly, effectively, and in a way that the prospective user of your services can get interested—maybe even excited—about the potential of what you have to offer.

Being up-front and personal with clients helps you to stand out as an effective consultant.

Why should a prospect choose you out of a group of consultants who are offering to perform the same services? Most consulting firms describe what they do—and supposedly do well—with general benefit information. These are comfort-food statements with no real teeth in them, such as:

- Better quality
- Faster service
- More experience
- Better this and more of that (blah, blah, blah)

When you describe what you do in specific terms and specify what benefits the client will obtain, you set yourself apart from the pack. Let's gather the data you're going to need to uniquely position your consulting services with the following Service-Benefits Analysis Interactive Questionnaire.

GETTING STARTED

SERVICE-BENEFITS ANALYSIS INTERACTIVE QUESTIONNAIRE

1. What benefits will your clients derive from contracting your services?

 ____

2. How will they measure the success of your efforts?

 ____

3. Why will your clients choose you over another consultant?

 ____

 ____

4. What is your biggest benefit or value-add to this market?

 ____

5. Prove your claim. To what do you attribute that benefit?

 ____

6. How will your clients perceive this benefit relative to your competition and your background, including work experience, accomplishments, and past clients?

 ____

7. How will your market be able to distinguish your services and practice from those of other consultants in your field?

 ____

8. How will you continue to add value after you have completed the assignment?

 ____

9. What unique skills, talents, or knowledge do you possess that your market would find critical to solving their problems?

 ____

GETTING STARTED

10. Describe the services you plan to offer and the benefits your clients will derive from those services.

11. Rank, in order of importance, the services you feel will be most in demand from your clients and why.

12. What free consulting service can you offer that demonstrates the difference you provide to your customers? Examples are: internal surveys; white papers and study results; training demonstrations

13. What types of guarantees are you prepared to offer? Examples are: money-back if not satisfied; revisions to the work until they are satisfied; no payment until results achieved

14. What will be the impact on your customers' bottom line as a result of your services? Examples are: improved time-to-market for a new product; better financial results from better asset management; increased sales productivity through sales training efforts; better market response because of better promotional materials.

15. Are you prepared to quantify the results you can provide to a customer? For example: reduce time-to-market from 6 mos. to 3 mos.; improve quarterly return-on-assets performance by 15 percent; increase sales productivity by 12.5 percent; provide 100 percent better response from direct mail campaign.

GETTING STARTED

SAMPLE SERVICE-BENEFITS ANALYSIS INTERACTIVE QUESTIONNAIRE

1. What benefits will your clients derive from contracting your services?
   - Increased sales productivity for direct and indirect sales forces, i.e., more sales volume from the same number of sales people
2. How will they measure the success of your efforts?
   - Sales results at the end of 90 days
3. Why will your clients choose you over another consultant?
   - Sterling list of referrals
   - Focus on results (will guarantee)
   - Strong industry and management background
   - Trademarked technology for sales training
   - 90-day follow through program
4. What is your biggest benefit or value-add to this market?
   - Better sales results means more profits–the training pays for itself
5. Prove your claim. To what do you attribute that benefit?
   - Have testimonials and letters as proof. Consulting and training methods are working.
6. How will your clients perceive this benefit relative to your competition and your background, including work experience, accomplishments, and past clients?
   - Guarantees reinforce the relative benefits offered. Background as a sales VP is a plus as well.
7. How will your market be able to distinguish your services and practice from those of other consultants in your field?
   - Image (carried out in literature and presentation material)
   - Focus on results–and methodology and technology to support claims
   - 90-day follow through program to ensure we deliver the results committed
8. How will you continue to add value after you have completed the assignment?
   - Continual, regular follow-up. Many opportunities arise because of what I learned in previous assignment.
9. What unique skills, talents, or knowledge do you possess that your market would find critical to solving their problems?
   - Street-smart sales and sales management experience

GETTING STARTED

- Career which mixed both sales and marketing disciplines throughout
- Strong background in high-technology products

10. Describe the services you plan to offer and the benefits your clients will derive from those services.
    - Sales training-Improved sales results
    - Competitive positioning-more wins against competitors
    - Marketing positioning-better market awareness, more leads, increased sales
11. Rank, in order of importance, the services you feel will be most in demand from your clients and why.
    - Inside sales training (many companies expanding this area and downsizing direct sales. I can provide needed skills training where currently none exists).
    - Direct sales force training in consultative and interpersonal selling skills—adds the dimension of people skills to existing product and strategic sales training.
    - Sales/marketing/product development consulting—can help companies to improve their time-to-market performance, especially required by high-tech companies.
12. What free consulting service can you offer that demonstrates the difference you provide to your customers?
    - Internal surveys
    - White papers and study results
    - Training demonstrations
13. What types of guarantees are you prepared to offer?
    - Money-back if not satisfied
    - Revisions to the work until they are satisfied
    - No payment until results achieved
14. What will be the impact on your customers' bottom line as a result of your services?
    - Increased sales productivity through sales training efforts—typically 12.5 percent or more; bottom line impact situational for each client—depends upon profit margins
    - Reducing time-to-market by 30 percent has directly related bottom line results—again, situational by client.
15. Are you prepared to quantify the results you can provide to a customer? Yes, as examples:
    - Increase sales productivity by 12.5 percent
    - Reduce time-to-market from 18 months to 12 months

GETTING STARTED

What Does It All Mean?

The bottom line is that customers are interested in their bottom line. A tough businessman I know once said, "If you make your numbers there's nothing you have to say; if you miss your numbers there's nothing you can say."

> Total commitment to the improvement of a client's operations is the greatest benefit you can offer.

General Benefits → Percentage Improvement → Dollars Saved or Profits Increased

Anything you can do to better your customer's condition–either through a measurable improvement in his/her operations or dollars saved/profits increased–will go a long way in positioning the benefits you have to offer.

Unique Selling Proposition

A unique selling proposition (USP) is your statement to the world that sets you apart from your competitors. It describes something that you–and only you–can do for your prospects and customers.

What is it about your consulting services that are different and unique? How are you different from your competition? Are you a better chess player, a slam-dunker, the old reliable, or the new gee-whiz gizmo? Are you the wizard behind the curtain or the formidable image on the screen?

Once you have figured out your target customers and how your consulting services are different from your competition, you are on your way to developing strong statements that uniquely position you and the services you perform. Your USP is critically important in positioning yourself with your current and prospective clients.

> Once your target clientele has been determined, it takes a high-impact and unique selling position to gain that clientele.

USPs must be hard-hitting. They must be integrated into your company mission. You must focus on making the selling proposition a reality, not simply another slide show, brochure, or ballpoint pen emblazoned with your company logo. You must demonstrate a commitment both behind and in front of the curtain. Show your prospects strong, creative marketing, follow-through, and attitude. Your USP asserts where you are now and where you are going.

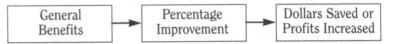

GETTING STARTED

Involve your customers. Figure out who they are and what they need from you. Make them aware of what you do well. Knowing why you deserve your customer's business is one of the most important issues you will face. Communicating that knowledge effectively is another.

Be specific. Don't generalize. Use statements that are customer-specific. To a prospect in computer manufacturing saying a processor chip 'does long division' is not as meaningful as saying it 'does long division more accurately than the Pentium chip.'

Remember, your consulting business won't stay in business for long if you can't deliver on your USP. Take a calculated risk! Be gutsy, but more importantly, be honest and deliver. Now–let's develop your USP.

1. In fifteen words or less, state what your consulting business does to benefit your customers. State the name of your company, the services you provide, and the major benefit produced. (Example: Enterprise Consulting provides sales productivity consulting for high-technology companies that measurably improves sales results.)
2. Provide the supporting information that differentiates your services from other consultants.
   (Example: We guarantee sales increases of a minimum of 12.5 percent because:
   - We conduct an in-depth survey of your sales force and major account activity.
   - We work with your sales management to put in place action plans for obtaining increased sales from major accounts.
   - We conduct on-site training and coaching sessions to enhance the sales process and make sure that results happen.
   - We provide a 90-day follow through program to ensure results over the long-term.
3. Add testimonials–information from your past experience–that supports your unique selling proposition.

GETTING STARTED

Your focus should be impressing clients with your services, rather than with your corporate office.

(Example: We helped Modcore Communications build sales by 17.3 percent. Or, when I was Vice President of Sales for Confoundit Computers, we used this process to boost our sales by 28 percent.)

SETTING UP A HOME OFFICE

If you are debating whether to set up an office in your home or lease commercial space, think quite seriously about keeping the office in your home if you can. Unless you expect clients to regularly visit your office, your face to the world will be your products, your services, your literature, and your marketing. Spend money in areas that your customers will really appreciate. Setting up a commercial office includes more expenses than just the cost of a lease. Even if you are not remodeling, you will undoubtedly undertake a few leasehold improvements. You might install additional electrical outlets, put in new carpeting, or paint the place. If you haven't previously leased commercial space, you will have to place deposits with the phone, electric, and maybe even the heating fuel companies. And your fixtures and furnishings expenses for a commercial space will probably be more than they would be for a home office.

LOCATION

Your home office should offer privacy and enough elbow room to hold the equipment and furniture you will require to effectively conduct your business. If you plan to hold client meetings in your home office, look for a room or rooms that are removed from your family surroundings. Maintain as much of a professional atmosphere as possible.

Even though you may work out of the home, try to maintain a professional atmosphere in your work area.

BUDGET

Review your finances. Determine how much you can comfortably afford to spend outfitting your home office with equipment and furniture. Don't forget to budget for additional phone lines, electrical wiring, carpentry, and supplies for the office. Before you spend a nickel, look around your home. Do you own items such as pens, paper, scissors, extra phones, tables, chairs, and desks that you can use in your home office?

GETTING STARTED

Building Permits

You will need an occupancy permit if you intend to run a business from your home in a residential area that is not zoned for business. Your local building and zoning department, typically located in your town or city hall, should be able to provide you with the necessary permits and advise you on all local zoning restrictions.

Zoning Laws

Many localities do not permit any businesses to be operated in residential neighborhoods without a specific variance, which many zoning boards are very reluctant to grant except under extenuating circumstances. Often, variances are only given after an extensive public hearing which allows presentation of objections by all nearby residents.

Just because there are already some businesses operating in your neighborhood does not mean that your neighborhood is zoned commercially or that you will easily obtain a variance. Many businesses currently operating in residential neighborhood were "grandfathered in," meaning that they were in operation before the zoning laws took effect and were therefore almost automatically granted variances.

There are literally millions of businesses operated in the U.S. out of homes in violation of local zoning ordinances. If all of these zoning laws were strictly enforced, all of these businesses would be forced to shut down and the entire U.S. economy would be dealt a significant blow.

Make sure that you research the local zoning laws before you begin your business out of your home.

Local government officials do not inspect homes to see if a small business office is tucked away in the corner. However, if a neighbor complains, then the building inspector is obliged to enforce the zoning ordinances. Furthermore, hanging out even a small sign, having commercial vehicles on the property, putting in additional parking spaces, or having a lot of client or employee traffic is likely to trigger a complaint even if you have friendly neighbors.

If your business is going to involve heavy truck or car traffic you also need to consider the safety of your neighbors. I remember one business property I considered buying in a residential neighbor-

GETTING STARTED

hood in South Boston had a commercial variance, but the variance prohibited any truck traffic after 2 p.m. because of the potential hazard to children attending a nearby school.

Insurance

Your homeowners' insurance probably provides a rider that you can attach to cover computers and office equipment including copiers, fax machines, scanners, and printers. Check out the latest pricing on the equipment you own and select coverage limits that will protect your investment. You may also need insurance for vehicles used in your business and liability coverage for accidents related to the use of your product or service.

Answering Options

Decide whether or not you want an answering machine, voice mail, or an outside service to field calls during your absence or unavailability. If it is important in your business to have a responsive human being answer customer calls, go for the service. Voice mail systems can be software-based systems that are either installed on your personal computer or purchased through an outside service provider, such as a telephone company, that offers voice mail boxes.

If you can afford it, have someone other than yourself answer your phones. Hire a receptionist, even a part-time one, or enlist the assistance of a family member or friend to help out two or three times a week. You'll be surprised at what a professional impression this makes on outsiders. You'll appear to be very well established!

Create an Image

Look professional. Create a logo, and use it on letterhead stationery, business cards, matching envelopes, four-color brochures, and sales collateral materials. Be consistent in your design. Carry the logo and color schemes throughout all of your business printing. Use good paper for printing. To get attention, sponsor a community event where your company name and logo will be prominently displayed.

Discipline

Focus on running your business. Eliminate distractions such as children, neighbors, and friends. Let your friends and family know that you are serious about your work. Tell them that they can't just pop into your office whenever they feel like it.

Don't wander into your kitchen for coffee. Don't answer your personal phone. Don't check on the dog. These diversions will hamper your effectiveness in managing and growing your business. Remember, you are at work and not really at home!

Working at home takes discipline to maintain your focus on work.

QUESTIONS & ANSWERS ABOUT HOME OFFICES

What really makes a home office appear professional?

The key is separating it from the house as much as possible. Ideally you should have a separate entrance. Living areas should not be visible from the office. At the very least, remove all non-business-related furnishings from the room you are using as an office. Another good idea is to erect internal doors to separate this room from the rest of the house. If any rooms or hallways connect from the house to the office, always make sure they are neat and kept as professional-looking as possible.

What should I give my first effort to?

Chances are, like most small businesses, you are going to do most of your business over the phone. So, one of your first concerns should be how your office "sounds." Answer your business phone with the name of your business. Have calls forwarded to an answering service if you are not going to be in your office. Try to block out any background noise that may sound like you are in a home environment. Some people try to change their voice to create the impression of being in a larger office. This is a transparent ploy. Don't do it.

Keeping your work area looking "professional" will help alleviate the distractions of home.

Are there inherent problems in having employees working in my home office?

The first obstacle may be in attracting people who want to work in a home office. Many people object to this sort of environment. But it is certainly possible to attract very talented, hardworking people who will work with you in your home.

If you intend to employ people within your home, check your insurance to determine whether or not you need additional liability coverage. You must also get workers' compensation coverage, as this is mandated by law. You need to make sure your premises are safe in every way. And you should be aware that you increase your chances of zoning problems with every employee you bring into your home office.

Do I need to notify the post office of my business name?

If you verbally tell your regular mail carrier that you will be receiving mail addressed to your business name, problems will arise each time your neighborhood is served by a substitute carrier. You should inform the post office or put the name of your business on the mailbox. Place it in very small letters, though, so as not to alarm your neighbors.

Do I need a separate business phone line?

If you live by yourself, you may want to skip the expense of another line. This means every time the phone rings, you need to answer it as though it were a business phone.

You could install a second residential line, which is generally not as expensive as business service. The phone company may call after a couple of weeks, however, to see if you are using the second line for business purposes.

CONSIDERING COMMERCIAL SPACE

Moving into a commercial office space can be exciting for a small business owner. It signals a coming of age for a business that has outlived the usefulness of a home office. More space is needed to house new employees and more equipment, and to conduct meetings, conferences, and product demonstrations. A commercial office gives a small business owner the feeling of taking the business to its next level of growth—with continued growth expected and eagerly anticipated.

Space

When considering how much commercial space to lease, add some extra space for growth to the total square footage of the space you are currently occupying. Determine how many employees you expect to be housing by the end of the next year. Determine what furnishings and office equipment you will need in order to accommodate them.

Decide whether or not you will need a reception area. Decide on the image you want to project through the layout and design of your space. Determine your need for conference and/or demonstration rooms. Try to project two or three years out from the start of the lease—will the new space accommodate your anticipated growth?

> You should lease space according to your anticipated growth.

Location

The location of your business is very important. If you locate in an upscale suburban neighborhood or a fashionable area of downtown, you may attract consumers with plenty of disposable cash. But you will also face high rents or leasing costs, and that puts you at risk for business failure. Less upscale areas may offer tax incentives or spaces with attractive lease options. However, these areas may have high crime or vandalism rates. And what about the commute? How far is it from your home to your new office? All of these considerations need to be carefully examined when deciding where to locate your business.

> When deciding on a location of your business, you have to consider the pros and cons of the surrounding neighborhood.

Parking

You should determine what your employee and customer parking needs will be. Does the space you are considering offer enough parking for your needs and the needs of surrounding businesses? Is the parking underground or on-street metered parking? Is handicapped parking available?

GETTING STARTED

TENANTS

Check out the other tenants in the building or office complex you are considering. Find out how long they have occupied the building. Ask if they are on good terms with the landlord. Find out if their experiences as tenants have been largely satisfactory. Inquire about insurance premiums, building security, and cleaning services for the building.

HANDICAP ACCESS

Check to see if the building you are considering leasing in meets with handicap access regulations, including appropriate bathroom facilities. Make sure your office space has been designed so that physically challenged employees can easily move around and are afforded an opportunity to be fully productive.

PUBLIC TRANSPORTATION

If on-street or off-street parking is limited or unavailable, locating your business in close proximity to public transportation takes on added significance. Public transportation accessibility can even be used as an advertising tool to attract customers.

EXPANSION

If you are attracted to a particular office space, but envision remodeling that space to suit your needs, such as building partitions for work cubicles or removing walls to open up a reception area—make sure the landlord has no objections. Get permission in writing. See if you can negotiate a reduction in the lease payments in exchange for doing the remodeling work yourself.

UTILITIES

Find out the typical costs for heating, electricity, and air conditioning in an office space similar to the one you are considering within the same building. Ask either the landlord or other building occupants for copies of the last six month's utility bills. Inquire about required new account deposits from each of the utility companies you will be using. If you have a prior billing history with any of the utility companies, you may not need to submit a deposit.

COMMERCIAL OFFICE SPACE PLANS

You have three basic choices in office floor plans: division by partition, open office, or individual, closed rooms. A combination of any of these floor plans is also a possibility.

PARTITIONS

Open offices divided by partitions were in vogue at many large corporations in the 1960s and 1970s. The advantage to this space design configuration is that its flexible nature offers the chance for change while, at the same time, affording a moderate level of visual and aural privacy. No one is looking directly at another employee and conversations can be conducted without fear of being overheard. A wide range of partition systems are available. They can be extremely elaborate and complex or inexpensive and simple.

The type of office floor plan that you choose can affect the overall atmosphere of your firm.

OPEN FLOOR PLAN

Another approach to organizing space is the open design. It isn't extremely common, but many newspaper offices and banks have embraced the open office concept and have their employees working openly side-by-side. This design creates a strong feeling of community among workers, but has the drawbacks of noise and visual confusion.

CLOSED ROOMS

Closed rooms can be a very expensive office design option. This option doesn't offer the flexibility of either the partitioned or open space plans. It does offer the ultimate in privacy. If you choose this plan, be sure to get the landlord's permission to complete any construction work required to meet your needs.

COMBINATION

Some combination of the partitioned, open, and closed room floor plans is another approach. You might have, for example, completely open areas for secretarial or support staff, partitioned cubicles for mid-level employees, and closed areas for senior staff.

GETTING STARTED

OFFICE DESIGN CONSIDERATIONS

FUNCTIONALITY

Functionality is an important consideration when considering office design. The first functional aspect that you need to address is noise reduction. Your employees need to be able to hear clearly in order to effectively conduct phone conversations. You need to place fax machines, copiers, and other loud equipment out of the way and out of earshot.

You also need to create nice passageways that allow employees ease of movement from one area of the office to another. These pathways should also provide efficient traffic patterns. Additionally, don't forget to group people together according to their functional need to interface with each other.

Office design has to be able to accommodate the need for both noise reduction and employee interaction.

CUSTOMER PERSPECTIVE

A customer's impression of your office space as he or she first walks in the door is critical. The same holds true for employees, and especially for new hires. Consider creating a waiting area at your entrance. It can be very simple, yet still welcoming, comfortable, and professional. All you really need is a couple of nice chairs and a table.

A meeting room may also be important in your business. This room should be as impressive as possible even if you can't afford to go all out designing and furnishing other areas of your office. Set up a nice room near the reception area with a conference table and chairs. This will give any customer a good feeling about your organization.

ASSIGNING SPACE

Assigning space to personnel can be an incredible political football, even among employees who don't typically get riled. Seasoned employees have been known to fight tooth and nail for that window spot or the biggest office space. This is an issue of prestige, of course, and many employees link space allotment to the direction of their career paths.

GETTING STARTED

The best approach is to make the assignments and have that be the end of the story. Make it clear that you have given the assignments careful thought, and this is simply the plan you have devised and will be sticking to. Do try to give each person adequate space in which to carry out his or her job. Anticipate the objections any given individual may have. Cut complainers off at the pass. If you don't assign space decisively, people will grab whatever space they can or they will whine and complain. Either way, it will be a headache for you.

Also, decide in advance to what extent employees will be allowed to decorate their space, paint the walls, or hang photographs or posters. In short, set guidelines for personalizing office space. You don't want to find yourself in the uncomfortable position of requesting the removal of decorative elements because they clash with the office design concept.

Assign office space fairly and set guidelines for personal decor.

Creating the Design

Start by making a quick, rough sketch of your office design layout and concept with pencil and paper. Then you might want to flesh out your scheme by using space layout software or creating a more detailed sketch.

Use a scale for the sketch–x inches equals x square feet–or do your layout on a gridded chart. Before you move in and start knocking down walls or dragging desks about, take out the tape measure and mark walls, corridors, partitions, and desks with masking tape. Bring your employees in to discuss the layout. This creates a feeling of community, and the group's approval on a final layout alleviates the possibility of major space wars on move-in day.

Don't get swept away by innovative technology—work within your budget to equip your office adequately.

Equipment

It is easy to get caught up in buying the latest and greatest equipment for your office. You want it to look fabulous and make a statement about your success. But don't lose sight of your budget. Your cash flow could wind up looking like the national debt. Don't despair! It really is a breeze to make good decisions about purchas-

GETTING STARTED

ing equipment and furniture, have a good-looking office, and make your business run smoothly and efficiently.

NEW VS. USED

Some people think that they have to have the latest equipment to hit the market. Cost doesn't matter. This kind of thinking can lead one to buy equipment with superfluous features or furniture that goes out of style next week. Before you equip your office, think about your real needs–what do you need to make a fair impression, work efficiently, and be able to maintain a good and continuing cash flow situation? Check into used furniture and equipment. A good bargain may be just the ticket to really fulfilling your needs!

PHONES

Do you really need all of the bells and whistles available in certain phone equipment today? Is voice mail necessary, or will an answering machine suffice? Don't get caught up in the hype. Think about your business and what you need to handle your day-to-day communications. Make a list of the types of phone equipment that you absolutely must have to run your type of business professionally. Then shop for prices at three different outlets.

SOFTWARE

Just about every business today has a computer that handles a variety of tasks, from accounting to human resource management. No matter what computer platform you are using, there are a host of programs available that will cut down on the time and expense of accounting, billing, creating financial projections, letter writing, creating graphics and drawings, and even managing your day for you. Again, determine what you need in order to adequately fulfill a function, and shop for the software package that will best meet your needs and your budget.

FURNITURE

You are projecting an image with the type of furniture that you choose for your office. Buying used furniture can certainly help offset costs, and is a recommended solution for keeping costs in check. But make sure that it is in tip-top shape. New or used, your furniture should be professional in appearance. Try for a coordinated look and a simple color scheme carried throughout your office. Good, simple, tasteful design is paramount if you intend to have clients visit your office on a regular basis.

Also, look for furniture that is comfortable and suited to working around for at least eight hours a day. If you use desktop computers, make sure your desks and chairs are ergonomically designed to minimize physical stress.

Furniture should be both professional looking and comfortable for employees.

E-MAIL

E-mail can be the bane of the business professional's existence. The decision to purchase e-mail will hinge a great deal on the culture of your company and how open you are about allowing your employees to freely communicate company information, both internally and externally.

COPIERS

If you lease a copier, make sure you have a strong service commitment from the copier or leasing company. You need to know how quickly you can get a replacement machine delivered should your leased equipment fail. Get everything regarding the leasing terms and the service offerings in writing. And keep good records of service visits and the type of work performed.

FAX MACHINES

It is nearly impossible to find a business that does not use some form of fax machine. Some businesses use stand-alones while others fax via software and modems that are a part of a personal computer. Some companies tie their networked computers into one fax machine. Whatever method you choose, you really should have some fax capability. You will quickly find a need to both send and receive information via fax, and it can also be used as a highly successful marketing tool.

GETTING STARTED

Save money on office supplies as much as possible, using those funds for the more essential needs of the company.

Leasing is a good way to get quality equipment without having to pay immediately for new equipment.

STREETWISE ADVICE ON EQUIPMENT

SIMPLE IS OK

You don't need lavish furniture or the latest equipment to run a successful business. In fact, all too many people start a business with the attitude that they are going to "do it right." They rush out and purchase the best of everything they need–and don't need. I can't emphasize it enough–this is a big mistake! You are much better off doing everything "wrong." Buy the cheapest of everything, and conserve your cash for running your business.

AUCTIONS

Bankruptcy auctions offer a terrific opportunity to acquire furniture, fixtures, and equipment. You can often pick up desks, computers, and chairs for a fraction of what they might cost at a secondhand dealer.

Remember, it is better to have cash in the till than designer desks and chairs filling the office.

LIQUIDATORS

When large corporations dispose of their furnishings, which happens when the old colors don't mesh with the new CEO's color palette, office liquidators negotiate to buy the entire lot of furnishings. They then sell it off, in smaller lots, to other businesses. Prices are higher than at auctions, but the selection is usually broader and delivery and merchandise guarantees are often included.

LEASING

Leasing is a great way to pay for equipment that is more difficult to locate secondhand than basic office furniture. Even a new business with no credit history can obtain equipment through leasing. Even if you have to pay leasing rates that are higher than you might like, you will still have cash left with which to support yourself and keep your business running while you solicit work.

QUESTIONS & ANSWERS ABOUT EQUIPMENT

Will household furniture work in an office?

A lot of household furniture will not hold up to the heavy usage office furniture gets. If you move household furniture into the office, you may be surprised to find out how soon legs break on chairs, drawers fall apart, and desks become wobbly.

Why are some file cabinets so cheap and others so expensive?

Much of the furniture designed for home offices is junk. File cabinets are an excellent example. The cheaper file cabinets feature drawers that jam even before you leave the store. I am surprised the warrantees don't promise breakage before you even get home! A good filing cabinet that really holds up can be quite expensive. It is preferable to buy a better-quality used item than a cheap new one.

Should I rent furniture?

The rates that furniture rental companies charge are usually exorbitant. It is better to buy.

Whom can I arrange to lease equipment from?

Consider the leasing options available from the manufacturer first. Then check the options available from a leasing firm. Banks also offer leasing, but this may affect your borrowing limits in the future. You can also approach any friends or relatives who helped you finance your business—and even those who refused. They may be willing to purchase your furniture and lease its use to you while retaining title. It may be viewed as less risky than actually lending money.

What about buying through the mail?

You can usually negotiate a better price with a local dealer than you can get through a mail order house. But check it out. Mail order may be your best route, especially if you don't live in a major metropolitan area where furniture pricing can be highly competitive.

> Ordering equipment through the mail may be advantageous, but make sure you research the company before you order.

While I certainly have purchased furniture and equipment through the mail, I offer one caution. One prominent cut-rate electronics mail-order dealer I once used went bankrupt. If you prepay for merchandise and the company goes belly-up after you have sent your check but before they have shipped your merchandise, then you are a general creditor. In other words, you have no special claim on the item you ordered and the check you sent is no longer yours. You are merely one of many on a long list of creditors, and you would be extremely lucky to get a full settlement on your claim. To avoid this situation, ask to be billed or pay with a credit card.

QUESTIONS & ANSWERS ABOUT STARTING OUT

What form of business do you recommend for anyone interested in starting his or her own consulting business?

I recommend Subchapter S incorporation. A corporation name conveys a more substantial image (SalesWinners, Inc. versus David Kintler and Associates), makes it easier for your client to pay for your services (no Form 1099s or withholding to be concerned with), and it does provide you with limited liability. Incorporating as a 'C' corporation is also a possibility, but the tax provisions for smaller companies may not be as beneficial as a Sub S option.

What do you need to know (legal issues, taxes, etc.) about starting your own business?

When starting your business, explore the advantages and disadvantages of the type of business entity you will be forming (sole proprietorship, partnership, or incorporation). I recommend doing this by consultation with an accountant and an attorney. Taxes for a sole proprietorship and Sub S corporation are at individual income tax rates. Be aware of tax requirements for payment of the employer portion as well as the employee portion of FICA. Also, explore the costs of business licenses you will need for your state, county, and municipality.

How do you know when you're ready to open your own firm?

You're ready when you are totally committed to making a success of your consulting practice. Other factors are:

GETTING STARTED

- You have the financial wherewithal to start and sustain your business for one year
- You have formulated the services you will offer to a specific target market
- You have thought through the specific reasons why someone will choose to use your company

Is it possible to start your consulting practice part-time, when you still have your regular, full-time job?

Yes, it's possible. You can begin to lay the groundwork–financial and marketing analysis, preparation of literature, etc. Recognize that time spent doing actual consulting work will detract from your full-time job–and you'll be dividing your efforts.

Though consulting can be started as a part-time venture, true success demands your complete commitment to it.

Is it possible to start part-time to "test the waters," or is it best to just jump in full time?

Yes, it's possible to "test the waters" by taking on an assignment that can be handled outside of normal working hours. This may give you some idea of what the work is like. However, it won't give you an appreciation of what the work environment and pressures are like. For example, it's one thing to enjoy a hobby, it's quite a different feeling when you try to make a living at it.

If you do start part-time, how do you schedule clients around your regular work? Is it in bad taste to suggest meetings outside of traditional work hours or on weekends?

If you do start part-time, you'll need to schedule your consulting activities outside of your normal work hours to avoid a conflict of interest with your current employer who is paying you for services rendered.

Selling and communication skills are important foundations for consulting.

Where do you find those initial clients and referrals? Do you just call up your old business contacts?

Most people who succeed in consulting have built a network of people who can be either a source of business or a source of referrals. In addition to calling contacts you've established in the business, direct mail and networking for new contacts can help to introduce you to some new prospective clients.

GETTING STARTED

How important is selling to consulting? What should you do if you don't have any previous sales experience?

Selling is absolutely mandatory to consulting. If you can't sell the benefits of your consulting practice, you won't win any new clients. Most people have previous sales experience, even if they haven't labeled it as such. Communicating your ideas within a corporation and making presentations to groups to get action are part of most people's career activities. What's necessary is to transpose these skills to your consulting practice. If improving your sales confidence will help, take a basic selling course, such as the one offered by Dale Carnegie. This is what I did when I began my career in sales–it helped to provide a good foundation in the basics.

What types of clients should you focus on getting? If you are new, is it better to take all jobs with every potential client that comes your way, or is it better to be more selective and build a more "elite" client base?

Be true to the mission of your business. If you provide marketing consulting to high-technology firms, don't take accounting assignments with a real estate company. When you are starting out–and beyond–it's important that you establish yourself as the authority in your field instead of a jack-of-all-trades and master of none. "Elite" can be a misnomer–you are looking for clients that match the profile of your target market.

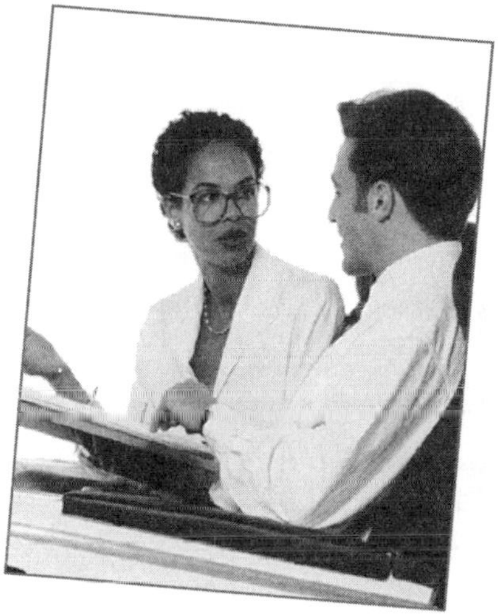

CHAPTER 2
BUSINESS PLANS

Even a one-person consulting business should create a business plan and create it in writing. Developing a formal written (if brief) business plan gives your business a solid blueprint for success. It gives you a sense of direction, it gives you benchmarks against which to compare your progress. It's quite likely that some aspects of your plan will change once you get started, but with a business plan, you'll at least have an initial path with which to compare your changes in direction.

Once you have identified your personal and professional objectives for your consulting business, the time has come to draft a plan for your business. Business plans and annual plans are by far the most common types of overall plans for small businesses. Annual plans are assembled each year, primarily to help chart a course for the upcoming year. Business plans are typically used by start-up businesses to attract investors. Business plans and annual plans share a number of the same elements and are similar in many ways. But there are typically two crucial differences: the objective of the plan and the audience of the plan.

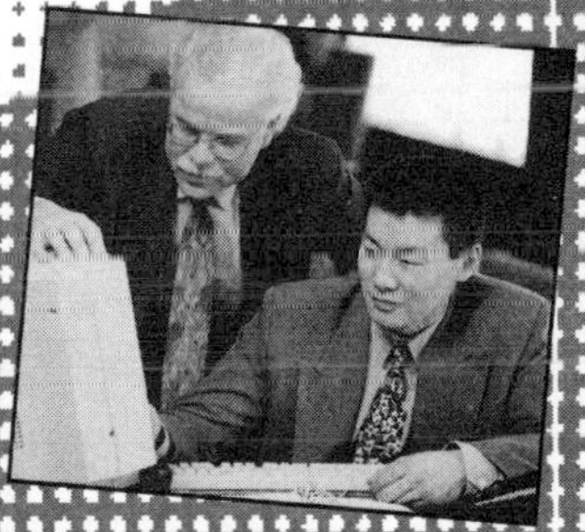

BUSINESS PLANS

Business plans are used primarily to attract capital. The primary focus of such a plan should be to interest investors or lenders. If your plan is being used to borrow money, you need to write the plan in a manner that will attract lenders as opposed to equity investors. *Lenders want to be assured that they will be paid back.* Projected profits mean nothing to lenders. They will not be sharing your gains. In fact, lofty projections may make them nervous because, typically, very high potential returns are often accompanied by very high potential risks. *Equity investors, on the other hand, are looking for a much higher return than they could get by investing in a more established company.*

BUSINESS PLANS

Business plans should assert your well-defined goals for success for clients.

Whether your audience is venture capitalists or bank lenders, *a "spiral" approach will really deliver your message, because it conveys information in order from most important to least important.* This approach is particularly effective when seeking the financial aid of outside investors such as venture capitalists. They review hundreds or even thousands of plans for every one they decide to invest in, and they generally give only a cursory look at most submissions. Get your primary message across immediately! Potential lenders will also be able to easily discern the key elements in your plan.

There are two keys to the "spiral" approach. First, position a brief summary of the plan at the beginning. This allows the reader to discern the most important aspects of the plan up front without reading through the entire plan. Second, save your financial projections for the end of the plan. Potential investors or lenders will assume your numbers look great. They are more interested in the assumptions behind the numbers. Even if you do not wish to attract outside capital, (as is the case with the majority of independent consultants), a business plan is essential to help you manage the course of your business. A business plan with your professional and business goals and strategies clearly outlined can also help ensure that you stick with your plan and keep your business on track. In short, think of the business plan as the "nuts and bolts" version of the mission statement you developed in the chapter on business and personal objectives.

Annual plans help to guide the business from the inside for the course of the year.

ANNUAL PLANS

Annual plans are generally used by the managers of a business to help guide the business in specific directions over the course of the year. Because an annual plan is intended primarily for internal use, its form and scope can vary dramatically from one company to the next. Adopt a format that works best for you.

Start with a brief summary of your overall goals for the year. If they are not obvious, explain how these goals support your business strategy and build on its competitive strengths. *Goals may be achievement-oriented,* such as raising profitability, decreasing costs, increasing your client base by X%, or expanding the type of services offered. *Goals may also be process-oriented,* such as reducing the time it takes to generate a proposal or improving client satisfaction.

You should also have a detailed budget in your plan, including what it is going to take to support the overall goals of your business. You also need to create monthly profit and loss, cash flow, and balance sheet pro formas.

Of course, if your business is experiencing trouble or if your market or industry is experiencing rapid change, you may want to consider producing a full-blown business plan like the one that's described earlier in this section. If you are preparing to expand your business and offer new services, consider producing a marketing plan, as described in the marketing and promotion chapter, as part of your annual planning as well.

DEVELOPING A BUSINESS PLAN

OBJECTIVE

Throughout the process of creating a plan, you need to keep in mind the objective of the plan. Why are you writing the plan? Is it to manage your business? Or is it to raise money? Most often, annual plans are used to manage a business, and business plans are used to attract capital. But there are exceptions and often the difference between annual plans and business plans becomes muddled. Banks and other lenders or investors may require a copy of each year's annual plan. And you may use the start-up business plan as the basis for operating your business. Since independent consultants rarely seek outside investors to contribute capital to their business, consultants most often use business plans as a way to secure a small business loan or simply as a means to guide their business.

No matter which plan you are developing, you need to be clear on the primary objective of the plan.

Keeping a clear distinction between annual plans and business plans is not important. What is important is being clear about the primary objective of and the primary audience for the plan. As a rule of thumb, if the plan will be used to attract investors or lenders, this is the primary objective, and outsiders are the primary audience. If the plan will help manage the business, this is the primary objective, and insiders, such as yourself or any employees you might have, are the primary audience. Some or all of the following elements should be a part of your plan, depending upon your objective.

Summary

Summaries should be short and concise–one page is ideal. The summary should cover the following points:

Summaries hep to direct the audience toward the most pertinent aspects of your plan.

- **Strategy overview.** Start with a brief overview of your business strategy. Describe the particular service on which your business will be based in the introductory paragraph.
- **Strategy logic.** In the next paragraph or two explain why your strategy makes sense or why your service has promise. Are you entering a fast-growing market or providing a unique service that distinguishes your business from existing companies?
- **Business development.** Describe the current stage of your business.
  - Do you already have clients?
  - Have you done test marketing?
  - Has market research been performed?
- **Business development.** Name the key people in your organization and briefly describe what special talents, expertise, or connections they will bring to the business. Most often, you will only need to talk about yourself and your experience.
- **Financial objectives.** If your plan is being developed to raise capital, be clear about the loan amount you are seeking and how you plan to use lender funding.
- **Business organization.** Describe the form of business organization you will take (or have taken) and where the company will be located.

Remember to keep your summary short and easy to understand. Avoid technical jargon and details. Don't try to summarize all the major elements of your plan. Just focus on the key elements that you think will be of most interest to your audience. Skip the pie-in-the-sky profit projections and outlook generalizations.

BUSINESS PLANS

Concept

The concept is a clear explanation of the strategy for your consulting business. It is not a definition of the business or a summary of its markets, rather, it is a quick summary of the one or two key factors that set your consultancy apart from the competition.

- **Product (service) description.** Your business strategies are most likely tied to your particular service. If this is your situation, include a clear and substantive description of the service. Follow this with a focused discussion of what will make your service stand out from any similar offerings in the marketplace. Focus in depth on just a few of the most competitive attributes of your service.
- **Impact factors.** You should also describe any other aspect of your business that is fundamental to your strategy. Areas that might have a significant impact on your strategy are marketing, research and development, or strategic alliances with other firms. For example, if everyone else in your industry is marketing themselves only through ads in the Yellow Pages, but you are ready to take out ads in trade publications as well, then you should discuss this in the concept section.

The concepts of your consultancy is the "personality" that makes your business unique from your competition.

Market conditions and the competition should be included as points of reference only when necessary. An in-depth analysis of these factors will be included later in the plan.

Stating the current economic situation of your business helps to define the need for financing.

Current Situation

This section is most appropriate for plans being used to seek financing. Within this section you will describe what stage of development your company is in and what the sought-after financing will be used for. There are three basic reasons for seeking outside financing: start-up financing, expansion financing, and work-out financing.

- **Start-up financing.** If you are seeking start-up financing, you will need to list specific milestones that have been achieved and emphasize all positive developments without being mis-

BUSINESS PLANS

A more developed company will receive better financing than a company in the beginning stages of development.

leading. You should anticipate the questions your lenders or investors may ask.

- Has the market research been done?
- Have facilities been leased?
- Is the management team in place?
- Are marketing plans finalized?

Whether or not you are receiving financing, as well as the terms of that financing, will depend upon the stage of development of your company. The more fully developed your company is, the better your financial arrangements will be.

- **Expansion financing.** If your business is already up and running and you are seeking expansion financing, you need to give clear evidence that you are not, in reality, seeking financing as a way to solve existing problems, or to cover losses or extraordinary expenses such as might be experienced during a start-up.
- **Work-out financing.** Many investors and lenders do not like to offer work-out financing. Those who are willing to consider it will want to see a plan that clearly identifies the reasons for current or previous problems and provides a strong plan for corrective action.

Financiers who are comfortable with the capital already secured are more likely to invest more.

No matter what type of financing you are seeking, financiers like to be apprised of the source and amount of any capital that has already been secured. They will expect key executives to have made substantial personal equity investments in the business. They will feel even more comfortable if they recognize any other investors who may have participated in earlier stages of the financing process.

The Market

A good business plan requires that you have a clear and well thought out marketing plan that specifically targets your markets and customer base. Aspects of your markets that should be addressed in your business plan include:

BUSINESS PLANS

- How large is the potential market?
- How many businesses have used a competitor that offers the same or similar services that you plan to offer?
- How many prospects potentially have any possible use for your consultancy?
- Is the market growing, flattening, or shrinking?

Market Segmentation

Almost every market has some major and distinctive segments. Even if it is not currently segmented, the probability that it could be or it will be is great. This is particularly true if the marketplace for your consultancy is multi-regional or national. If this is the case, segmentation is almost necessary, especially for a small firm, if you hope to be competitive.

You will need to discuss segmentation within your specialty and describe how you intend to cope with any positive or negative effects it may have on your business. Almost all markets are segmented by price and quality issues. Generally, however, price and quality do not provide the most clear or definitive market segmentation. Much stronger segmentation can usually be found through an evaluation of product or service uses and importance to various consumers.

Customer/Consumer Analysis

In your business plan, you will need to evaluate the typical clients within the market segments you are targeting. There are countless variables to consider when analyzing consumer behavior. Try to focus on those behavioral possibilities that best determine how viable your service will be in your target markets. Look at the following variables:

- Which services will most appeal to clients?
- Why does the market choose one particular service over another?
- Which marketing promotions or media avenues seem to offer the best vehicles for reaching the client base?

A good business plan takes into account market segmentation when stating business goals.

And ask the following questions:

- How much does the target market have to spend on this service?
- How do your target customers reach purchasing decisions?
- What characteristics influence the purchase of one service over another competing one?

Competition

Include an overview of those firms and their services that are in direct competition with yours. Identify the market leader and define what makes it successful. Emphasize the characteristics of the firm or their offerings that are different than yours. Don't dismiss this section because you don't have any current competition. If there isn't a service similar to yours on the market, identify those firms that provide services that perform essentially the same function. You should also make an attempt to identify any firms that are likely to enter the market or are in the process of developing services that will be competitive with those you are offering.

Outlining the strengths and weaknesses of the competition helps illuminate the unique concepts of your company.

Consulting Strengths and Benefits

You briefly described the key factors of your service in the concept section of the plan. In this section you should explore features and benefits in-depth. It is essential to be clear not only about the distinguishing features of your service, but also to delineate any strong consumer benefits. What makes your service significantly better than your competitors?

Competitive Analysis

In this section you need to do an in-depth analysis of the competitive advantages and weaknesses of your firm. When exploring weaknesses, you should include information that will help allay any concerns that may arise as to their ability to significantly hinder your success. This section is particularly important if your company is a start-up. You will typically be competing with established companies that have inherent advantages such as financial strength and name recognition.

BUSINESS PLANS

Positioning

Positioning can be thought of as a marketing strategy for your consultancy. Positioning defines how you are going to portray your service to your targeted marketplace. Your first step is deciding who your target market will be. It will consist of those potential customers toward whom you will direct most of your marketing efforts. Often, this group will not be the sole or the largest market for your service, but it will be the market that, based on competitive factors and service benefits, you feel you can most effectively reach.

Fledgling consultancies are more successful when they concentrate on a narrow market.

Start-ups are more likely to be successful if they focus on a highly specific, very narrow specialty. General markets are usually dominated by large, well-established firms. Once you have determined who your target market is, you need to decide how you want consumers to perceive your service.

- Are you the premium quality leader?
- Are you a low-cost alternative?
- Are you a full-service firm?

If you have a one-service consultancy, your marketing strategy may coincide with your overall business strategy. This doesn't have to be the case, but, it is extremely important that the strategy for your specific service is in sync with your overall business strategy.

Advertising and Promotion

Use this section to provide an overview of your general promotional plan. Give a breakout of what methods and media you intend to use and why. If you have developed an advertising slogan or unique selling proposition, you may mention it, but it isn't strictly necessary. You should outline the proposed mix of your advertising media, use of publicity, and/or other promotional programs.

Outlining advertising strategies is important to a successful plan.

- Explain how your choice of marketing vehicles will allow you to reach your target market.
- Explain how they will enable you to best convey your service features and benefits.

BUSINESS PLANS

Be sure that your advertising, publicity, and promotional programs sound realistic, based upon your proposed marketing budget. Effective advertising generally relies on message repetition in order to motivate consumers to make a purchase. If you are on a limited budget, it is better to reach fewer, more likely prospects, more often, than too many people occasionally.

Sales

Most independent consulting firms do not need or have a sales strategy. If you do elect to write one, your sales strategy needs to be in harmony with your business strategy, your marketing strategy, and your company's strengths and weaknesses. For example, if your start-up company is planning to sell products to other businesses in a highly competitive marketplace, your market entry will be easier if you rely on wholesalers or commissioned sales representatives who already have an established presence and reputation in the marketplace. If your business will be selling high-tech products with a range of customized options, your sales force needs to be extremely knowledgeable and personable.

Sales strategies need to be compatible with the general business strategy of your consultancy.

Research and Development

A discussion of research and development is obviously not germane to all companies. Most consulting firms make use of existing technologies and products to fulfill their services, rather than developing their own products. If it applies, though, financiers will want to know that research and development projects are aimed at specific, realistic objectives. They will want to be assured that an undue portion of the company's resources is not plowed into this area. Remember that banks generally lend money to businesses on a short-term basis, and venture capitalists and other first-round investors generally want to cash out in just a few years.

Operations

Operations is a catch-all term used to describe any important aspects of the business not described elsewhere. In addition to discussing areas that are critical to operations, briefly summarize how major business functions will be carried out, and how certain functions may run more effectively than those of your competitors. Don't get into long descriptions of any business or operation practices that will not sell your business plan to financiers.

People

If you have asked other key people to join your company, such as an additional consultant, mention it here. Primary attention should be on key people who have already committed to joining the firm. Elaborate on their relevant past experience and successes and explain what areas of responsibility they will have in the new company. Resumes should be included as part of an appendix or exhibit at the end of the plan.

If any important positions have not been filled, describe position responsibilities and the type of employment/experience background necessary to the position. Fill as many positions as possible before you seek funding. Many financiers reject plans if the management team is incomplete. Naturally, if you are the only member of your management team, you should describe your own past experience and background.

Have as complete a management team as possible before seeking funding.

Payback and Exit Plan

Both debt and equity lenders will want to know how they can expect to receive their investment back and realize interest or profit from the company. Most private investors and venture capitalists will want to be able to exercise a cash-out option within five years. They will be concerned that, even if the company becomes highly profitable, it may be difficult for them to sell out their share at an attractive price. This concern is particularly true in the case of minority stake holders. This is why you must provide an exit strategy for investors.

Ideally, investors hope a firm will be so successful that it will be able to go public within five years, and their shares will become highly liquid investments, trading at a hefty multiple of earnings. But, often, a more realistic goal is to make the company large and successful enough to sell to a larger firm. State what your plan is and be sure it appears realistic.

BUSINESS PLANS

Financials

In this section, you need to show projected, or "pro forma," income statements, balance sheets, and cash flow. Existing businesses should also show historical financial statements. How far into the future you need to project and the number of possible scenarios you can anticipate depends upon the complexity of the business. Three to five years for financial projections and three years for scenarios are average.

Scenarios should be based on the most likely course your business will take, a weak scenario with sales coming in well under expectation, and a good scenario with projected sales well over expectation.

Financial scenarios should be based on likely sales, weak sales, and strong sales figures.

Pro forma income statements should show sales, cost of operation, and profits on both a monthly and annual basis for each plan year. For all but the largest businesses, annual pro forma balance sheets are all that are necessary. Cash-flow pro formas should be presented in both monthly and annual form. If your business is already established, past annual balance sheets and income statements should also be included.

Include information that will assist potential lenders in understanding your projections. Lenders will give as much credence to the assumptions your projections are based on as they do to the numbers themselves.

A SAMPLE BUSINESS PLAN

Business Plan for Internet Consultants, Inc.

Summary

Internet Consultants, Inc. (IC) has been formed to provide expert advice and technical and creative assistance for companies interested in creating a presence on the Internet. The market for Internet consulting services is growing rapidly. IC will assist companies with all phases of creating an Internet presence, including development, Home Page design, and maintenance.

IC plans to position itself as a provider of "cutting edge" technology to businesses, offering both systems and design help. IC will use a low-key approach to gaining new business, relying on referrals from satisfied customers. To date, the company has worked on projects for eight clients.

At this time, John Smith, President, is the lone member of management. Mr. Smith has previously worked as a Senior Internet Developer at Web World, Inc., and has more than ten years of experience in the computer industry.

Internet Consultants, Inc. was formed ten months ago as a Massachusetts corporation.

At this time, the corporation seeks $100,000 to lease new equipment and supplies and to hire additional employees.

The Concept

Internet Consultants, Inc. will focus on providing leading-edge Internet services. These services are targeted at companies ranging in size from small businesses to large corporations. IC will continually work to stay abreast of the latest technology in order to better service its market.

Internet Consultants, Inc. provides support for all aspects of establishing a presence on the Internet, from assisting with hardware needs to designing Home Pages. IC believes its related services, such as Intranet development, will set it apart from the competition. IC will also rely on its ability to access cutting-edge technology to distinguish itself from the competition.

The company will, in part, rely on networking and client referrals to gain new business, but it will also target prospective clients through an aggressive marketing and promotion campaign using direct mail and advertising in select trade magazines.

Current Situation

IC has successfully furnished Internet services for eight clients, which has already led to five referrals. Research indicates a strong demand for these services among small- and medium-sized businesses, as well as large corporations.

A SAMPLE BUSINESS PLAN

Initial capitalization was provided solely by John Smith, President. At this time, IC seeks $100,000 in financing to expand its services. This money would be used to lease new computer and office equipment, buy supplies, and hire two employees–an additional consultant and an administrative worker to handle office support.

The Market

Over thirty million people are currently using the Internet, including thousands of businesses. Internet users are expected to grow in number by at least twenty-five percent each year for the next five years. Recent trends indicate that the number of businesses seeking an Internet presence will continue to grow at a similar rate.

Market Segmentation

The market is divided into two relatively distinct segments. They are the corporate segment and the small business segment.

Corporate Segment

This market includes large corporations, institutions, and government agencies. This market requires more complex and elaborate Internet systems. Obviously, these organizations typically have a generous budget allocated for Internet expenses.

Small Business Segment

This market includes all businesses–from start-ups to corporations with up to $50 million in annual revenue. In general, small businesses need more basic systems with fewer features, and they typically have less money budgeted for Internet development.

IC is positioning its services for both the corporate and small business segments.

Customer/Consumer Analysis

The target group of consumers is both large corporations and institutions, and small businesses. Large corporations generally have their own information systems departments in place, but prefer to use a specialist to handle their Internet needs. Typically, small businesses do not have a separate information systems department, and want information and advice regarding more than just their Internet needs.

The decision makers in the target group most often choose outside consultants based upon the recommendations of colleagues or word-of-mouth. At the same time, targeted advertising and promotions have also proved to be effective in reaching the target group.

A SAMPLE BUSINESS PLAN

Companies in the target group have annual revenue ranging from $1 million to more than several hundred million, and have an equally wide range of available funds to spend on creating an Internet presence. These companies may not yet have a presence on the Internet, or they would like to redesign their current one.

Competition

While dozens of Internet consultants advertise on the Web, with more and more emerging every day, only a handful of these are marketed towards businesses, and only two appear to be real competition for Internet Consultants, Inc.

Web Designer, Inc. is currently the market leader. They were one of the first computer firms to specialize in providing Internet services, and they soon abandoned all additional services in favor of Internet services. With ten consultants and two full-time salespeople, Web Designer boasts an impressive client list. They also advertise heavily in trade publications and direct mail. While they produce consistently high-quality work, their designs have a tendency to look alike and lack real imagination, often failing to take advantage of new technology. They also seem ready to eliminate their systems services.

Eastern Internet, Inc. has been in business for six months and is steadily building its client base. Eastern Internet is staffed by three consultants, and two additional employees provide office support. Eastern does not provide supporting systems for their clients, only Web page design. They tend to take more chances in their designs, but are often too cavalier. They rely heavily on graphics, but their designs are often short on substance. Eastern does not appear to engage in much advertising or promotion.

Service's Features and Benefits

There are already several businesses in this field that offer similar services. Most of these firms offer either Internet system development or Web page design, although some do offer both.

Internet Consultants' main distinctive feature is that it will offer both Internet system development and design. The benefit to clients is that the company can fill all their Internet needs, from systems start-up to designing a new company Home Page. Web Designer, Inc. seems to be slowly phasing out the systems aspects of its business and devoting itself to design, thus making Internet Consultants, Inc. the only full service Internet consulting firm in this region.

A SAMPLE BUSINESS PLAN

Competitive Analysis

Strengths

Services Offered: Internet Consultants, Inc. offers both Internet systems development and Home Page design. Only one other firm in the region offers both services, and that company appears to be phasing out the systems development aspect. This strength should help Internet Consultants, Inc. stay ahead of its competition.

Personnel: John Smith maintains dozens of close contacts at this country's most noted Internet development companies, such as Net Tools, Inc., ensuring that the company will stay abreast of all the latest developments in this area, and subsequently, will be able to use this cutting-edge technology in its applications.

Weaknesses

Financial: Currently, the company is low on working capital. The small amount of capital limits the level of advertising and promotions that can be done, and also limits the number of new staff that can be hired.

Small Staff: With a staff of only two consultants, and only one office support person, it will be difficult to take on a large number of clients, which in turn limits the earning potential of the company.

Positioning

This company will position itself as the premier provider of Internet systems. It will emphasize the dual functions the service provides: system implementation and Home Page design, as well as the technological edge the company has.

Internet Consultants will not embark on costly advertising and promotion campaigns to gain new clients. Research indicates that these methods are rarely effective with the company's professional target group. Since the target group is more likely to use services based on reputation and referrals from colleagues, the company will focus on solidifying its reputation among existing clients by completing excellent work and providing superior service after a project is complete.

Advertising and Promotion

With a limited advertising budget, Internet Consultants, Inc. will use minimal advertising to attract new clients. Instead, IC will employ direct mail, along with carefully targeted advertisements in trade publications, to attract clients. The company will not engage in direct public-

A SAMPLE BUSINESS PLAN

ity (i.e., mailing out press releases), but John Smith will organize seminars and write articles for trade magazines in order to enhance name recognition for the company.

Sales

Currently, the company does not require a sales staff, John Smith takes all query calls.

Research and Development

Currently, research and development do not play a role in Internet Consultants, Inc.'s future business plans. At this point, the company will rely on technology and products already available.

Operations

Internet Consultants will buy all necessary systems equipment from a computer goods wholesaler, thus avoiding all retail mark-ups. The company will also design its own advertisements and other marketing materials. Printing of such materials will be contracted out.

People

President: John Smith

Mr. Smith has worked as a Senior Internet Developer at Web World, Inc. Mr. Smith has a strong technical background and a long history of pioneering work on the Internet. Mr. Smith is highly recognized in the industry as a noted expert and has been profiled in several leading magazines.

Other Key People:

The company is ready to hire another consultant who has worked with John Smith in the past. The company is also ready to hire an assistant for office support.

Payback and Exit Plan

Because the market for Internet services is expected to continue its rapid growth for many years, IC anticipates strong revenue growth. The company believes it can have all debts paid within five years.

Financials

See spreadsheets.

BUSINESS PLAN TEMPLATE FOR CONSULTING

[TITLE PAGE]

BUSINESS PLAN

for

_______________ CONSULTING, INC.

Date ____________________

Prepared by:______________

Copy Number ____________

- CONFIDENTIAL -

BUSINESS PLAN TEMPLATE FOR CONSULTING

TABLE OF CONTENTS

BUSINESS PLAN TEMPLATE FOR CONSULTING

1. **Summary**
   [Write a brief overview of what your consulting business will be, making sure to include powerfully written statements of your business strategy, your target customers, and the logic supporting your belief in this business. If you have already been in business for some time, be sure to include an explanation of your past track record, your vision for the future, and the anticipated growth and profits. If possible, make this a one-page section, for many people will scan this first before making a decision to read the rest of the plan.]
2. **Concept**
   [Include a clear explanation of your business strategy. Make sure to stress the key reasons why your business or service is distinctive from your competition. These points should also be the key reasons why you will have a unique competitive advantage over them. In consulting, this likely will center on some unique capabilities, knowledge, and experience you bring to your potential customers.]
3. **Current Situation**
   [While you should focus on financial need in this section, use it to describe the exact situation and stage of your business. This can be anything from a raw start-up to an ongoing business seeking growth capital. Be sure to explain what capital has already been invested in the business (especially by you), and exactly what will be the use of funds from the new financing. If you are not seeking funding with this plan, this is still a good time to review your current and anticipated financial situation.]
4. **Market**
   [Describe the market or markets in which you will be selling your services. Avoid being too general in your description, and put as much specific detail in as you can to accurately quantify the market size and potential customers. Include an overview of the markets and explain if they are healthy and growing, or whatever else may be pertinent to their understanding.
5. **Market Segmentation**
   [As a small firm, you will likely want to focus on a small market niche where you can have some distinct advantages. You will need to discuss what segment of the market you have chosen and how this segment is unique and identifiable. Focus on type of ser-

BUSINESS PLAN TEMPLATE FOR CONSULTING

vice or product, not on pricing or quality, as this will give your business a greater identity and value.]

6. **Customer/Consumer Analysis**
   [Describe who your typical customer will be. Focus on explaining the link between what they will purchase from your business and what the key features and services are that you offer. Explain why the customer will buy your service over that of your competition. Be sure to include an explanation of your customer's ability to afford your services or products.]
7. **Competition**
   [Give a complete overview of your competition and what services, and strengths and weaknesses they have with respect to your business. Emphasize how you will be able to compete and on what grounds. Your competition may not be another firm, but perhaps other uses of the same funds your customers might use for your services.]
8. **Service/Product Features and Benefits**
   [This section should detail a fuller description of your consultancy's main features and benefits as mentioned earlier in the concept section. Again, be sure to stress in what ways they are superior and different from those of your competitors and what ways they can bring superior benefits.]
9. **Competitive Analysis**
   [Use this section to give a detailed analysis of your business's strengths and weaknesses with respect to the competition. Make sure you address how you anticipate compensating for the weaknesses, and try to allay concerns regarding their impact on your business. It shows confidence and thoroughness in your plan if you make a point of addressing particular threats that you anticipate will come from your competition, but make sure to give solid reasons why you will be able to overcome them.]
10. **Positioning**
    [After you have defined what specific services or products you will be offering, it is imperative that you also define how you are going to portray these to your target market. Positioning your business means strongly defining the message you will be sending out into the marketplace to attract the customers best suited to purchase your services. As a small firm, you will likely be focusing on a narrow target market where you can offer a product or service advantage over much larger firms.]

BUSINESS PLAN TEMPLATE FOR CONSULTING

11. **Advertising and Promotion**
    [Explain in detail how you will be promoting your consultancy, including use of advertising media, publicity, industry speeches and publications, and other programs that will give you visibility with potential customers. Show the logic to the various marketing vehicles you have chosen and why they will be effective. Be as specific as you can in identifying how you will go about reaching and developing prospective accounts. Your message should be simple and direct, and strongly reinforce the key strengths of your business.]
12. **Sales**
    [If applicable, describe the organization of your sales program and strategy, and how it will be implemented. You may choose to omit this section if you have no sales department and your sales efforts usually consists of one-on-one presentations of consulting proposals.]
13. **Research and Development**
    [If this section applies, make sure you include the basis of the technology that your business will be relying upon. You may, for instance, be basing your consulting practice on the application of a software program that you have purchased and are budgeting monies that allow you to purchase ongoing revision updates.]
14. **Operations**
    [Describe how your business will be functioning on a day-to-day basis. Briefly describe how you have organized your business and how your facilities will adequately meet the business's needs. Give more details and justification if the funding you seek is for facilities expansion. This is an area where your costs should be very much under control, only allowing for some expenditures after you have had first successes with the business plan.]
15. **People**
    [This should be one of the strongest sections in your business plan as consulting is a people business, and you will likely be selling personal skills, knowledge, and experience. Make sure to highlight your background and those of key associates, being sure to include not only prior employers, but also strong industry affiliations and overall knowledge as indicated by your publications and seminars. Explain how your experience and that of your staff supports the unique services and products that you offer.]

BUSINESS PLAN TEMPLATE FOR CONSULTING

16. **Payback and Exit Plan**
    [If this plan is written to seek investment, make a specific point of explaining how the investors will be repaid and defining the timetable for this repayment. If this plan is solely a management plan for yourself, make an effort to develop a strategy that will build some long-term value and that can be cashed in, perhaps through the sale of your business, at some time in the future.]
17. **Financials**
    [This section should show your "pro forma" income statements, balance sheets, and cash flow. It is best to have some flexibility in the financial numbers that demonstrates the business's ability to survive even with weaker sales numbers than projected.]

BUSINESS PLAN TEMPLATE FOR CONSULTING

Pro Forma Income Statement Template

	Year 1	Year 2	Year 3
SALES			
Consulting sales	______	______	______
Speaking engagements	______	______	______
Publications, royalty income	______	______	______
Other	______	______	______
Total Income	______	______	______
DIRECT COSTS (if applicable)			
Consulting salary	______	______	______
Related expenses	______	______	______
MARKETING			
Direct mail	______	______	______
Advertising	______	______	______
Press packages, literature	______	______	______
Publicity	______	______	______
Travel, entertainment	______	______	______
Sales rep salary (if applicable)	______	______	______
GENERAL & ADMINISTRATIVE			
Facilities and equipment	______	______	______
Salaries (if applicable)	______	______	______
Phone, mailings (incl. postage)	______	______	______
Auto/truck	______	______	______
Insurance	______	______	______
Professional fees	______	______	______
Interest on loans	______	______	______
Other	______	______	______
TOTAL COSTS	______	______	______
PROFIT BEFORE TAXES	______	______	______
TAXES (estimated)	______	______	______
NET INCOME	______	______	______

BUSINESS PLAN TEMPLATE FOR CONSULTING

Pro Forma Balance Sheet Template

	End of Year 1	End of Year 2	End of Year 3
ASSETS			
Current assets			
Cash	______	______	______
Receivables	______	______	______
Total current assets	______	______	______
Fixed assets			
Equipment	______	______	______
Less accumulated depreciation	______	______	______
Total fixed assets	______	______	______
Total Assets	______	______	______
LIABILITIES & OWNERS' EQUITY:			
Current liabilities	______	______	______
Accounts payable	______	______	______
Taxes payable	______	______	______
Total current liabilities	______	______	______
Owners' equity			
Common stock	______	______	______
Retained earnings	______	______	______
Total owners' equity	______	______	______
Total Liabilities and Owners' Equity	______	______	______

BUSINESS PLAN TEMPLATE FOR CONSULTING

Pro Forma Cash Flow Template, Monthly for Year 1

	Jan.	Feb.	...Dec.
STARTING CASH	____	____	____
CASH SOURCES			
Consulting Services	____	____	____
Speaking Engagements	____	____	____
Publications	____	____	____
Other	____	____	____
Total Cash from Sales	____	____	____
Total Cash	____	____	____
CASH USES			
MARKETING			
Direct mail	____	____	____
Advertising	____	____	____
Press packages, literature	____	____	____
Publicity	____	____	____
Travel, entertainment	____	____	____
Sales rep salary (if applicable)	____	____	____
CONSULTING SERVICES			
Direct payroll	____	____	____
Other expenses	____	____	____
GENERAL & ADMINISTRATIVE			
Facilities and equipment	____	____	____
Salaries (if applicable)	____	____	____
Phone, mailings (incl. postage)	____	____	____
Auto/truck	____	____	____
Insurance	____	____	____
Professional fees	____	____	____
Interest on loans	____	____	____
Other	____	____	____
Taxes (estimated)	____	____	____
Total Uses	____	____	____
NET CHANGE IN CASH	____	____	____
ENDING CASH	____	____	____

BUSINESS PLANS

QUESTIONS & ANSWERS ABOUT SPECIALIZING VS. STAYING GENERAL

How do you decide on a specialty?

Your specialty is selected from your career experience–those things you have done well that have market value, and are professionally rewarding to you.

Should you base your decision on your expertise or on what will make you money?

I believe it is difficult in the consulting field to make money in a field in which you have no expertise.

Is it better to specialize or remain general?

Specialize–with the options of expanding your horizons. If you chase after a variety of general assignments, it's difficult to be known (and valued) as an expert in your field.

Do you recommend functional consulting (i.e., sales/HR) or specializing in one industry (i.e., being a consultant for all functions within the computer industry)?

I definitely recommend functional consulting because it draws from a proven area of expertise. For example, I grew up with the computer industry, specializing in sales, marketing, and executive management in these areas. Although I could consult with credibility about organizational issues to this industry or related industries based on my experience, it would be difficult for me to consult on manufacturing techniques in the same business.

Usually you'll want to define your expertise by function, not by industry.

If you are a functional consultant, what should you do if you win a proposal, but it's in an industry where you haven't worked before? Or isn't that important?

It is pretty difficult to win proposals in an industry that's far afield from your area of expertise. Even though my area of functional expertise is sales and marketing for computer companies, I can easily move to telecommunications, software, and peripherals because these are related industries. Going after an assignment in the retail business most likely wouldn't work. If I did win the proposal, I'd either have to spend a good bit of time learning the indus-

BUSINESS PLANS

try, or I would have to hire someone to work with me who is already up-to-speed.

Should you take any job just to keep money coming in, or is it better to be more selective about which jobs you agree to take on?

Try to remain selective about jobs, even when trying to boost sales.

The few times I've strayed from my consulting mission to bring in some dollars, I've regretted it. First, a consulting assignment can be all-consuming, and doing a good job may mean that you are taking time away from something else–your main mission. I once got involved with an executive "temp" situation. The assignment was expected to be three months, but it ran about eight. In the meantime, I lost a lot of momentum that was building for my core business.

Is it better to use highly customized strategies or to use the same basic approach with all your customers?

The answer to this question is yes. Every client assignment is highly customized because corporations culturally operate differently from one another. I have a standard survey that I use to obtain the information necessary to design a highly custom approach. In the consulting business, one size doesn't fit all. I work with a client to improve his or her current situation–not to force them into my standard model.

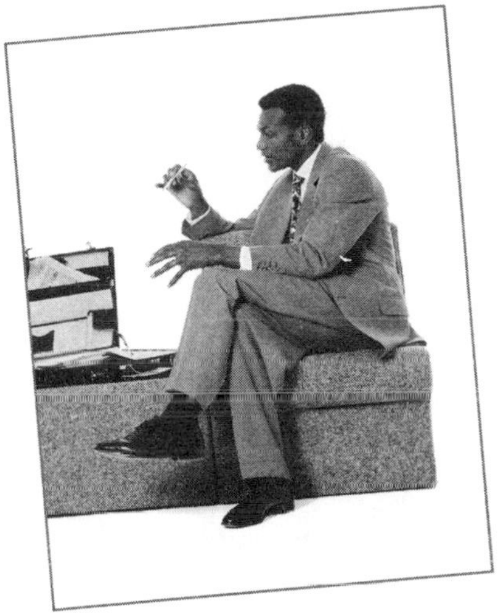

CHAPTER 3
PROSPECTING FOR CLIENTS

Just selling hard and making lots of phone calls is not a good plan for landing clients. *What* you say, *how* you say it, and *how* you interact with potential clients is going to make all of the difference in your ability to develop new business. This section includes selling scenarios that show exactly how to conduct yourself when you make presentations to potential clients so that you'll go home with their business.

INGREDIENTS FOR SUCCESS

Here are five ingredients for success in the consulting business:

- Continually hustle for business
- Pursue business that matches your mission
- Forecast business realistically
- Flow with the client's timing
- Persist, persist, persist

Three Dimensions of Hustling for Business

When you have a consulting practice, selling your services is a number one priority. Here are three tips:

- Promote your services continually and relentlessly
- Take daily actions to contact, write, and sell
- Use your time effectively

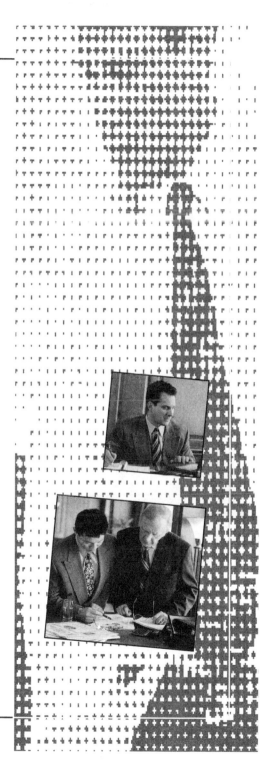

Continually sell your service? Yes. Those who have successful consulting practices hustle virtually all the time. They spend their time with people who are either potential clients or those who will pass on good words about their services. Those who succeed are subtly (or perhaps not-so-subtly) ferocious.

Taking daily actions to grow your business produces results and avoids the income gaps. Every day, do five things that will directly help you grow your consulting practice. That means letters, phone calls, personal contacts, or whatever it takes.

You have two personal resources–your capabilities and your time. Use your time effectively. Use your time on things that count. Certainly, this means dedicating your time to your current clients. This also means setting aside time on a regular basis to sell your services. If you're on a current consulting assignment, this means using weekends or breaks during the day to review your mission and take the steps required to grow your business.

PROSPECTING FOR CLIENTS

Being focused on a particular market will help you refine and hone your expertise on that market.

PURSUE THE RIGHT KIND OF BUSINESS

Be very particular about the business you pursue for your consulting practice. There are three keys:

- Serve the people you've selected in your target market
- Choose challenging assignments
- Walk away from the wrong kind of business

1. **Serving you target market**
   When you dedicate your efforts to serving a defined market niche, you will achieve a consistency in your effort and both your skill set and your reputation will be refined. Focus creates a powerful sales message, because you know exactly who you are, what you're doing, and the type of clients that you serve.
2. **Choosing challenging assignments**
   Stretching your capabilities builds your skill set. When you accept challenging assignments, you provide more value to the customer because new ideas will be brought to bear on the client's issues. New perspectives can provide solutions to problems that have no apparent resolution. When you succeed at challenging assignments, you enhance your reputation in the industry you've chosen to serve.
3. **Walk away from the wrong kind of business**
   Isn't all business good business? Absolutely not. For example, what if you continually accept consulting assignment that are priced below the goal you have set for yourself? You are spending time making less money than you need–time that could be used to pursue clients that are more lucrative.

Don't compromise your business goals in order to gain more clients.

In my consulting business, I make it a practice not to accept assignments unless I can earn my target fee. I may get fewer assignments this way. So what? By sticking to the financial model I've designed for my business, I've achieved the long-term success I wanted.

Be particular. Pick and choose those assignments which provide the most value to the customer and provide you with your target income. There is an exception to this rule. From time-to-time you'll come in contact with opportunities that are not directly aligned with your mission but have two other important features:

- The learning experience will provide you with skills you can use in growing your consulting practice
- The assignment is short-term—one month or less

One mistake I made in my consulting practice was to get caught up in a temporary position as a Vice President of Sales and Marketing for a small systems company. I did not develop any new skills—I just replayed the skills that I used in corporate life. I also made less than my target income. And most importantly, I lost a great deal of momentum in building my business. As a result of that experience, I never accept long-term assignments that don't match my mission.

Forecast Realistically

Is reality the dark side of optimism? Reality is what it is and you need to have a healthy dose of reality when you're forecasting bookings for your consulting practice. Optimism is a characteristic of most successful consultants. However, in your contact with potential clients and within your network, don't become over-optimistic about business that may be coming in.

Business optimism has to be tempered with the reality of the market.

What if you have a great sales call and the potential client is interested in your services? This does not mean that you're going to get the business. A successful sales call just means that you've made one in a series of sales calls that will be required to close the sale. That sales call may have been with someone who doesn't have the authority to sign for the business. Or it could be someone who's just collecting information, has no intent of using your services, but just happened to be interested in what you had to say.

To forecast realistically—and channel that good optimism you have—think of selling your services as a process of moving the prospect through a series of phases in the sales cycle. The six sales cycle phases I use in running my business are:

PROSPECTING FOR CLIENTS

The sales pipeline looks like this:

Phases of a Sales Cycle

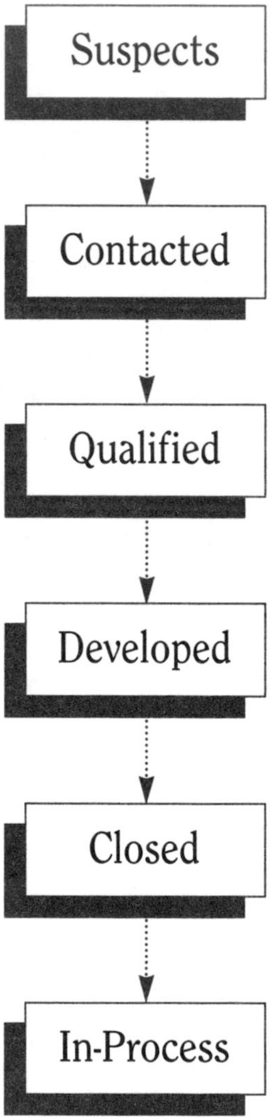

1. **Suspects**
   Suspects are those people you have selected to contact. These are the companies–the people, by title–that you will target with phone calls, sales calls, and direct mail campaigns.
2. **Contacted**
   A contacted suspect is one you've contacted by phone or met with face-to-face. Established contact means that you've talked with the prospective client, and he or she is potentially interested in your services.
3. **Qualified**
   A qualified prospect means that you've identified the results that the client needs and you understand:
   - The budget available
   - Project timing
   - The decision-making process
   - The decision-makers
   - Your capabilities match the project needs
   - The client will make a decision in ninety days or less
4. **Developed**
   Developed is the next phase in the sales cycle and it means:
   - You've identified and quantified the specific results the client needs
   - You can complete the project to meet the client's schedule
   - A proposal has been submitted and a presentation made
   - You fit within the budget
   - You're on the short list (top three)
   - The client will make a decision in thirty days or less
5. **Closed**
   Closed means you've won the business.
   - You have a Purchase Order
   - A start date is committed
   - A consulting agreement has been executed

   With an existing client, Purchase Orders can be either verbal or written. Much of my consulting business has actually been done with a verbal agreement based on a proposal letter.

6. **In Process**
   In process means that you're on your way. You actually may have received the up-front payment as part of the contract signing, and you've begun billable services against the consulting contract.
   Look at forecasting as a series of phases in the sales cycle. This makes it easier for you to determine whether you're going to get the business or not. Using sales cycle phases tells you what you need to accomplish to move to the next phase. This approach avoids the pitfalls and inaccuracies inherent in "gut feel" or mathematical probabilities. When I was in corporate life, I used this method to improve our forecasting from +/- 20 percent to +/- 8 percent in a given quarter. In my consulting practice, it means the difference between making my numbers and not.

> Sales cycle phases help you formulate a concrete plan to forecast a successful project.

Flow with the Client's Timing

Timing is everything. Remember how relatively simple things used to be with regard to timing in corporate life? As a manager, director, or vice-president, you could make things happen by issuing a directive, a memo, or an order. Things got done. Perhaps they didn't get done on time every time, but they usually were accomplished. Back then, you were working within a system that you understood and you had authority. You were in control of time.

What about a consulting practice? Do you control the timing of your client? Are you in a position of authority? Not anymore. The control that you have as a consultant in selling your services is the control that's available through your ability to influence.

> The control you wield as a consultant is that of influence.

RESOURCES FOR LEADS

Leads are the raw material for the Suspect Phase of your forecasting process. This work in process comes from six major sources:

- Current industry contacts
- Professional associations
- Directories (the raw material for direct mail and other marketing campaigns)

PROSPECTING FOR CLIENTS

- Networking
- Chambers of Commerce
- Internet Home Pages

Let's discuss each one of these lead sources and the potential benefit to your consulting practice.

Current Industry Contacts

Your current industry contacts are potentially the richest source of leads for your consulting practice. These are the people who already know you and what you can accomplish. The business associates you've come to know over the years could be potential clients for your services, or they may be able to effectively refer you to someone else.

Maintaining relationships with current industry contacts helps to maintain a positive level of business.

Keeping in regular touch with your contacts is essential. You want your name to be the first on their mind if they either have a consulting opportunity directly or can refer one to you. If anyone has given me business in the past, they can count on regular calls from me–and can look forward to receiving articles in the mail from me that I believe will be of interest to them.

My Contact Manager database has 393 names in it at the present time. Use Contact Manager software on your personal computer to keep track of and maintain regular contact with your friends in industry. It's like mining for gold.

Pros

- You have an existing relationship–it's not a cold call
- They are aware of your capabilities and accomplishments
- These business associates may have high visibility in the industry you serve

Cons

- They may not be in a position to help
- They may not be associated with your target market

Professional Associations

Your membership and participation in professional associations can be an excellent lead source if handled correctly. Join those associations that have participation by decisionmakers in your target

PROSPECTING FOR CLIENTS

market. Consulting associations, such as the Society for Professional Consultants can also be beneficial because they have a proactive lead referral service. I recommend getting involved with committee efforts in the associations you join. The give and take can result in more referral business than if you occasionally attend a meeting.

Beware of participating in association activities where there is no lead-generating benefit. There's a trap in the consulting industry where meetings may consist of consultants selling to consultants. I'd rather belong to "Time-Wasters Anonymous."

Current contacts are good sources for referrals.

Pros

- Professional association can be a rich referral source
- Association participation increases the circle of influence in your target market
- Consulting associations provide lead-generating seminars

Cons

- You could be spending a lot of time talking to your peers
- Associations can be time-consuming, especially with volunteer committee work

Directories and Lists

Directories and lists in your target market area are essential in identifying the names and titles of people you intend to contact in your target market. Some directory sources are:

CorpTech® (Corporate Information Technologies, Inc.) *Directories*
Directory of Corporate Affiliations
Dun and Bradstreet–Million Dollar Directory
Hoover's Handbook of American Business/World Business
Massachusetts High Tech Directory and Newsletters
Moody's (Banks and Finance, Industrials, Public Utilities, Transportation)
Standard and Poors Reports
State Manufacturers Directories
Thomas Register (product information)
Various association membership directories

PROSPECTING FOR CLIENTS

Networking helps to establish new contacts to encourage your business to grow.

Many directory services offer data on CD-ROM as well as the books they publish. Computer-compatible media can save a great deal of time in preparing direct mail campaigns by using the mail merge capability on your word processing software. The quality of the list has a multiplier effect on your success hit rate with a direct-mail campaign. Check the publications serving the industry or industries you've targeted and look for classified ads for prospect lists. Qualify any list source extensively. Some are excellent–some are a waste of time and money.

Pros

- Great raw material–company information and management names and titles
- Readily available–at the library or through standard industry sources and list brokers
- Material in CD-ROM format saves time in conducting a direct-mail campaign

Cons

- Lists are inaccurate–ninety percent accuracy is about the best you can expect
- Additional effort is required to find the specific people you want to contact (That means telemarketing by you or a service. This will cost you time or money.)

NETWORKING

Networking is a powerful way to grow your consulting practice. It increases the number of your relevant business contacts that may lead to consulting assignment leads and referrals. Networking among my industry contacts, through professional associations and with my peers in consulting, complements my direct mail efforts in building my practice.

After a period of time in your consulting business, the number of current industry contacts may not provide sufficient raw material for growth. That is why networking is so important. A major test of a consultant's ability to "hang in there" is the ability to establish and nurture new connections. Use the networking opportunities available within your current industry and professional associations mentioned above. Networking associated with the professional societies I am involved with has resulted in several major consulting and training assignments for my business.

In some situations, you and one of your peers have consulting services that complement one another. When you run across a situation like this, make it beneficial to both parties. For example, I offer five percent of the first year's revenue as a finder's fee for a new prospect that is referred to me (where I can use the other consultant's name in the referral). That number goes to ten percent if they actively sponsor me into a new account.

Pros

- An effective method for growing your base of contacts
- Your name and capabilities are known by a wider audience
- You always learn something talking with your peers
- Strategic alliance potential exists

Cons

- If not selective in your efforts, it can be a real time-waster
- Networking dinners can be an unwarranted expense

Chambers of Commerce

Whether you elect to join your local Chamber of Commerce depends upon whether your business is local, and if so, do the people in your target market participate in Chamber activities. If the answer to both of these questions is yes, go for it. If not, avoid the time and expense.

Pros

- Can be effective if your business is local and you'll meet decision makers in your target market

Cons

- Can be a time- and money-waster

> Chambers of Commerce are good ways to meet contacts in your market when you work locally.

Internet Home Pages

The question to ask yourself here is, "Do the people responsible for selecting the types of consulting services I offer browse the

PROSPECTING FOR CLIENTS

Web?" If so, consider using the Internet as a lead generator. If not, you may want to wait until the Web becomes more commercially useful for you. Your peers at network and association meetings can provide you with useful feedback on their experiences. Model what works. Do not adopt technology for technology's sake.

Pros

- A visit to your Home Page provides a useful return call option "See our Web Page"
- It has the capability of providing "tips" for use by your clients

Cons

- Much time and effort is involved with creating and updating a Home Page
- An expense you may not want to have when starting your practice

> Consulting uses the same skills needed in the corporate world, but use those skills to influence that corporate world to utilize your services.

SELLING YOURSELF

Your success depends on your ability to effectively sell your consulting services. So you're not a natural born salesperson, and you don't like being in sales. Wait a minute! What did you do in corporate life? You had to sell your ideas. That skill enabled you to accomplish results and get the promotions along the way. You had to convince people. You had to be able to articulate your ideas in a way that persuaded other people. What we're doing is taking the skills you used in corporate life (assuming that you were not in sales), and transposing them to selling your consulting services.

I'm not saying it's not different. It's one thing to be on the inside, sharing ideas in a closed, comfortable environment. It's another thing to be on the outside, attempting to persuade and influence those who are inside a closed and comfortable environment. Are you pushing your services onto others? No, you're not pushing your services. People are buying them because they need them.

Both consumers and those in the corporate world today are very sophisticated. They buy what they want and what they need. If you have value to offer a corporation, your selling job consists of two things. First, make them aware of your services. Second, make it easy for them to do business with you.

What about rejection? Rejection is a fact of life. You experienced it in corporate life. Remember when you didn't get that promotion, or that great idea you had was squelched? Well, you can expect the same treatment in selling your services. Remember that the rejection is not directed at you personally. It's a rejection of what you have to offer at this time. REJECT is too strong a word. It's more like, "We can't really do this now, we're comfortable doing some other things." They are not rejecting you. It's what you have to offer versus their requirements at that time.

Detach yourself from the many "no's" that you're going to collect as part of your selling activities. Play–in a creative learning sense–with your selling activities. This approach will enable you to move past the obstacle of rejection and earn the business and income that you need. Here's a six step process to help you sell yourself:

1. Develop your personal presence
2. Write effectively
3. Create the right telephone presence
4. Qualify for personal issues
5. Structure your sales calls
6. Persuade naturally

Let's look at each of these in turn, with some tips on what you can do to grow your consulting practice by selling yourself more effectively.

As consulting relies on the need of the client, rejection is just a show of the client's lack of need at the time.

Develop Your Personal Presence

Your personal presence consists of how you dress, how you conduct yourself, how you use your voice, and how other people experience your persona when you are with them. Because people are more comfortable with people that are like them, you should dress and conduct yourself accordingly.

PROSPECTING FOR CLIENTS

Appearance is important to portray a professional image to clients.

How you look

If you are a business consultant, then dress as a business executive in the industry you serve. Invest in your wardrobe. You want to convey, with the clothes and accessories you wear, that you are successful at your consulting practice. Dress to be accepted by the people you are calling on and consulting with.

Avoid those things that detract from your personal presence. Don't wear flashy jewelry, expensive gaudy watches, or high-fashion, severely tailored suits that are not likely to be accepted in your consulting world. Dress comparably to successful executives in your target market, and like people whom you respect as peers in the consulting world.

Take a good look at yourself in a full-length mirror. Dress as you would when meeting with a client. Does what you see match what you'd like to see? Is this the time to go on that weight-reduction program you've been putting off? Does your wardrobe need some updating? Suggestions for a business wardrobe can be found in books, such as John Molloy's *Dress for Success* and *Live for Success*.

How you sound

Tape record your voice. Do you like what you hear? You don't want a voice like a radio announcer (unless that's the field you're consulting to). Does your voice have the qualities of resonance, vitality, clarity, and support that you'd like? If you don't like what you hear, head to the nearest Toastmasters Club or to your local voice/speech instructor.

WRITE EFFECTIVELY

How well do you write? What is your style? How are your letters and promotional materials perceived by your potential clients? As you move from the corporate world into consulting, you will find that the things you used in corporate life for letters and memos are not useful in your consulting practice.

Traditionally, people have been trained to write in a very stiff, formal, politically correct style. That's exactly the image you don't want to convey in your consulting practice. Consulting is a people

PROSPECTING FOR CLIENTS

business–your letters and promotional materials must reflect a people orientation. Write person-to-person. Share information–don't tell 'em. Put the prospect first, and discuss the ways that you can help them. Write with the intent to communicate your sincere desire to create value for the clients you serve, and use an informal, personal style to convey your message.

As a consultant, you need to write in a very personal way in order to demonstrate your concern for your client's success.

Don't be an *"I"* sore. As the principal of your consulting practice, eliminate references to what *you* have done, what *you* think or what *you* believe. What's important is what *they* will find out about improving *their* operations, what *they* will experience as a result of using your consulting services, what *they* will know are the reasons for choosing you.

When I started my consulting practice, my first letter was a dud. I wrote a four-page letter to introduce myself and my new company. I counted twenty "I's" in that first letter. When I showed the letter to a consulting firm, they said, "David, you talk as if you are very formal and that you're totally concentrating on yourself as opposed to the other person. They're not interested in you, they're interested in themselves."

Promotional materials are also a challenge. I've made every mistake that can be made in generating promotional materials. The five biggest mistakes in promotional materials and how to avoid them are:

Spending a lot on promotion does not guarantee a positive image for your company.

1. Using an advertising agency to design your marketing message. Most likely, it will sound "artsy" and it won't be from you. It will be from them and their interpretation of what you do. Write the copy yourself and have them help you fine-tune the wording. Don't let them write the copy, because your message will get lost in translation.
2. Don't spend a lot of money. My first major promotional piece cost me $18,000, and it chewed up a good part of 1992s profits. I could have created a piece for $1,000 (like the one completed recently), which had far more return in terms of direct mail response and buyer interest.
3. Lack of direction. Some promotional pieces wander, and they don't catch the attention of the buyer in terms of the mes-

PROSPECTING FOR CLIENTS

Develop a consistent logo and color scheme and stick to it.

sage until too late. Some people say that you have six seconds to catch the buyer's attention with a letter or promotional material. Unless your message pops right out in those first few seconds, the message is wasted, and your promotional material ends up in the round file. The way to avoid this is to clearly articulate the benefits arrived at from your unique selling proposition up front, and use the rest of the piece—whether it be a one-page piece or an eight-page flyer—to support the benefits you provide for your clients.

4. Everything looks different. Make certain that the literature you provide, the letters you write, and the promotional items that you put together all have the same image, the same feel, and the same perception by your prospective clients. That means keeping the colors and the fonts the same. That means keeping the style of the literature, the brochures, and the letters identical. As David Ogilvy strongly emphasized in *Confessions of an Advertising Man,* project a consistent corporate image. As you create literature, lay it beside other items that you created and make sure they have a family resemblance rather than looking like orphans. Make the changes necessary so the family plays together.

Create the Right Telephone Presence

A telephone call may be the first contact you're going to have with a potential client. How you conduct yourself in that phone conversation, especially the first few seconds of the call, can make a major difference in the future direction of the relationship. People find out several things about you in the first five seconds of a call. They can tell:

Your telephone presence accounts for many of the "first impressions" a prospective client receives.

- Your gender
- Your educational background
- Your regional dialect
- Your mood
- Your confidence and competence

PROSPECTING FOR CLIENTS

Therefore, think through and design the openings that you use with prospects on the phone. Don't read from a script! Have your opening internally wired in a way that conveys what you want in terms of your confidence, your mood, and your intent to serve the person you're calling.

In your opening, use your name, the name of your consulting practice, and the reason for your call. Work to create a partnering type of environment. One of the questions that I have found useful to ask is "Is this a good time to talk?" That simple question offers a courtesy and respect not found in many phone calls. Your opening should also give the reason for your call–and the potential benefit to the prospect. For example, "Bob Harvey suggested that I call you because of the results that we were able to attain in his manufacturing operation. He felt that we could do the same for you. I'm wondering if you have a minute to answer a few quick questions?"

Respond to your prospective client; don't just transmit information. When you're on the phone, create the same type of environment that you might have in a face-to-face meeting. You wouldn't dream of walking up to someone and dumping everything you know about your consulting practice on them and hoping to interest them. They would be bored to tears in seconds. That's doubly true on the phone, and they can get away a lot easier on the phone than when you're face to face. So, as the call progresses, really respond to what the prospect says. Listen to what they say–and *how* they say things. Notice the nuances in their tonality and inflection that convey meanings far beyond the words that they use.

QUALIFY FOR PERSONAL ISSUES

Discovering your clients' needs is a vitally important foundation for the consulting process. Your clients' issues drive the requirement for your capabilities and services, and the more you can learn about those issues, the better your chances of landing the business.

Discover more than just what they would like to accomplish. Find out why certain issues are important to them. Use questions like, "What's important to you about this consulting effort?" Or,

PROSPECTING FOR CLIENTS

It's essential to discover the needs and goals of the client in order to serve them better.

Be flexible enough with the client in order to build a positive relationship with them.

"How would you know at the end of this assignment, that it's been truly successful?" Questions like this uncover the prospective client's personal criteria for selecting your services–information that won't be spelled out in a Request for Proposal.

STRUCTURE YOUR SALES CALLS

Develop a structure and flow for your sales calls. Use a planned structure for both your face-to-face meeting as well as your telephone calls. Better structure leads to better results, and you accomplish your call objectives. You provide the interpersonal framework for understanding your prospective client's needs and for sharing how your skills can help your prospect to meet those needs. The structure begins with the opening comments and continues, though the process of discovering your prospect's needs, to the closing part of a call. Here are four steps to structuring sales calls that work:

1. Set objectives for each and every call, whether it is a telephone call or a face-to-face call. Have secondary objectives in mind if the first objective is not achievable.
2. Structure the flow of the call. Have an agenda in mind, or better yet, written down. Arrange the call flow so that it is comfortable for the client and it facilitates achievement of your call objectives.
3. Be prepared to answer questions. This doesn't mean objections–it means questions that the prospect is likely to have as you go through the sales call. Have these answers in mind so that you're not stopped dead in your tracks by a question that you're not prepared for.
4. Go with the flow. Sales calls have a natural rhythm or flow, and sometimes the flow can't be predicted. Because your responsibility is to respond to your potential client, go with the flow. Within the call structure you set up, have the flexibility to do what you have to do to be able to build a relationship with your prospect. The quality of your relationship with your prospective client will be the driving factor in whether

or not you do business together. Going with the prospect's flow helps to forge that relationship.

PERSUADE NATURALLY

We're in the 90s. Techniques that worked years ago, don't work anymore. Buyers are more sophisticated. They are increasingly focused on their needs, especially in the intense corporate environments that we find these days. Prospective clients want to make sure that their needs are satisfied so that they can both survive and grow in corporate life.

Perhaps one of the reasons that you became a consultant was because of your dissatisfaction with the corporate environment. Consider that your prospective clients have much the same pressures you had when you were in their position. The old methods of manipulation and sales pressure to close a prospect don't work anymore. In fact, this type of "traditional" approach can be downright irritating! Your prospects want you to understand their problems and share how you and your consulting practice can solve those problems. With this approach, the time and effort spent closing the sale is minimal. Professional salespeople, even in earlier years, didn't spend their time in the close. They expended most of their effort in needs discovery and only then would they outline how their product or service could meet the prospect's needs. Using that method, closing is natural, not forced.

Try to envision consulting as a team effort, rather than a service that you supply to the client.

In order to persuade, create an atmosphere of working together. You can't hide your intent. If your intent is to manipulate, it will come across to the prospect. If your intent is to create value for the client's company and for your prospect, that intent will also come across. The prospect will hear it in your voice and language, and they'll notice it in your non-verbal communications.

Approach each client's situation as a "working-together opportunity." In many cases, you'll be working with a person who would have been a peer in corporate life. Team with the prospect so that you can take a load off his or her shoulders and add value to the operation.

PROSPECTING FOR CLIENTS

Presentations, reports, and a professional image all help in selling your consulting service to potential clients.

SELLING SCENARIOS

These selling scenarios demonstrate the importance of the material covered earlier in Selling Yourself and add the elements of stand-up presentations, presentation flow, and audio-visual materials. The first scenario compares effective and ineffective personal presentation styles.

FTL Industries is not getting the results it wants from its marketing and promotion efforts. A recently conducted direct-mail campaign yielded a dismal 0.3 percent response rate. The sales force has been complaining about the quality of the promotional materials—prospects have asked them if their literature comes from the same company—everything looks different. The last straw is that the President, Mr. Goodnow is upset with the Marketing Department because stockholders have complained about the poor quality of the last annual report.

The Director of Marketing, Jim Johnson, has recently joined FTL Industries and needs to fix these issues fast or his career is in jeopardy. Johnson also realizes that his internal resources are insufficient and incapable of doing the job. Johnson has decided to go outside for consulting assistance. There is budget money available, but he has not disclosed the amount to the consultants. What he will pay depends on the perceived value of the proposals, and the consultants are aware of this. The two consultants he is considering are SWI Marketing Concepts and Roger Q. Morris III and Associates. Both of the scenarios below assume an initial meeting for each with Jim Johnson. Each of the consultants was provided identical information.

Scenario No. 1: Effective Presentation: SWI Marketing Concepts

Consultant: Joe Kazinsky

Kazinsky, dressed well–no distracting accessories–good voice–confident, poised, is ushered into Jim Johnson's office

PROSPECTING FOR CLIENTS

Joe: Good morning, Jim. Isn't it a beautiful day out there? You mentioned you were going to the Cape last weekend. How'd that go?

Jim: OK, the family and I really enjoyed ourselves. It got my mind off of those issues we discussed last week.

Joe: Jim, that's exactly why I wanted to see you today. I've been thinking about your issues this weekend, and I'd like to run an approach by you for solving those issues to see if it makes sense to you.

Jim: OK, go ahead, but I have another meeting in about one hour.

Joe: We can cover what we need to in an hour with no problem. When we met last week you mentioned three issues you'd like to get resolved–and quickly!

1. FTL's direct mail efforts are not providing the results desired
2. Your promotional material projects different images–the product bulletins don't match the look of the product family brochure and technical bulletins
3. FTL's annual report needs work to gain the support and approval of your CEO

Jim: Yes, you're right those are the issues.

Joe: You also mentioned that the direct mail campaign was your biggest business headache at the present time.

Jim: Oh–is it ever. The Sales VP is complaining loudly that his sales force needs leads, and he is blaming my department!

Joe: Thanks for confirming those issues and priorities with me. The approach I'm going to share with you addresses each of these issues and is implemented to match your priorities.

We'll have your new direct mail campaign in place by October 1. Then we'll revise your technical and

> Good consultants work with clients on a personal level, making the clients' needs their top priority.

> Address the concerns of the client, and determine a logical and equitable solution to the problem.

PROSPECTING FOR CLIENTS

Show the benefits that your company has to offer the client and the innovations that you have developed.

product bulletins by December 31, and produce the next annual report by mid-February of next year.

Jim: Well, the completion dates you are giving me look fine, especially with the pressures I am getting from both the CEO and the VP of Sales. But how are you going to have results from a direct-mail campaign for me by the first of October?

Joe: Good question. The time frame is tight. To make the schedule committed, we'll have the letters ready for your approval for mailing by August 18. We'll make any final revisions and have them out by August 26. Results will be ready for you to present to the VP of Sales by October 1.

Jim: What kind of results can we expect?

Joe: I'm glad you asked. The last client we worked with was able to increase their direct mail response from 0.8 percent to 5.5 percent. We have a letter methodology that makes the difference. I wish I could patent it!

Jim: The direct mail campaign you described works for me. What about the image of our promotional pieces?

Joe: We've been thinking about how we could provide you with the most cost-effective solution. As I understand it, your sales force likes the look of the Product Family Brochure, but is upset with the appearance and inconsistent look of the Product and Technical Bulletins.

Jim: Yes, that's right.

Joe: The approach we suggest is to make the modifications required to the Product and Technical Bulletins to give them the same image as the Family Brochure. This keeps your costs down, and we finish the job by the new year.

Jim: Well Jim, it looks as if you've thought through our issues and have come up with an implementation plan and ideas I could live with. I have two questions.

PROSPECTING FOR CLIENTS

What about the Annual Report, and how much is this going to cost me?

Joe: Let's hold off on the annual report until we've earned our spurs on the first two projects. I want to make sure that you and your VP of Sales–and the CEO are totally satisfied with the results of our first two projects together.

With regard to pricing, I've brought a letter proposal that includes pricing, a list of references, and some additional background on our consulting firm. Our total price for the direct mail campaign is $9,500.00. That includes everything, including mailing the 2,000 pieces you wanted. The new promotional image for the nine bulletins you have is $22,500.00, including the development work, photography, and printing

Jim: Based on my past experience, those prices are in the ballpark. How can we get started?

Joe: In order to make that first deadline, I'm going to need your go-ahead this week.

Jim: Let's do it. I'll review your proposal, check your references, and fax you a commitment by Friday.

Joe: I am looking forward to working with you on this project–and to the successes we'll both have. As soon as we get your fax, we're off to work.

{End of sales call and presentation}

The consultant works within the guidelines of the client and is up-front with projected costs.

Good consultants are both professional and personable.

COMMENTARY:

This call will be evaluated based on the tips contained in the Selling Yourself section.

1. *Develop your personal presence*
2. *Write effectively*
3. *Create the right telephone presence*

PROSPECTING FOR CLIENTS

4. Qualify for personal issues
5. Structure your sales calls
6. Persuade naturally

We don't have information on items (2) and (3) on this sales call. Let's review the interview based on the other items.

Develop your personal presence

Joe did an excellent job in this area. He looked and talked as a professional, conveyed a knowledge of the customer's issues, and provided approaches without giving away his trade secrets.

Qualify for personal issues

Joe found out that Jim Johnson is getting a lot of heat in his new position–especially from the VP of Sales. Joe took this factor into account and responded in ways that reflected his awareness of Jim's situation.

Structure your sales calls

The structure of the call made the results happen. Notice the flow that Joe used:

The consultant has to have the best interests of the client's company in mind.

1. *Salutation and rapport*
2. *Stated the purpose of the meeting*
3. *Recapped the observations from the previous meeting*
4. *Checked the validity of his approach*
5. *Outlined the proposed solutions with timelines*
6. *Handled questions effectively as they came up*
7. *Minimized risks*
8. *Closed without being pushy*

Persuade more easily

Joe used language that reflected they were working together and that he was committed to Jim's success. He used Jim's direct mail deadline pressure as a reason to go ahead with SWI Marketing Concepts now.

PROSPECTING FOR CLIENTS

SCENARIO NO. 2: INEFFECTIVE PRESENTATION: ROGER Q. MORRIS III AND ASSOCIATES

Consultant: Roger Q. Morris

Morris, dressed extremely casually-flashy, gold accessories-good voice, but sounds somewhat arrogant, is ushered into Jim Johnson's office

Roger: Good morning, Jim. How's it going today?

Jim: Fine thanks, except for those issues we discussed last week.

Roger: Yes, those are tough issues. But because of my experience with situations like this in the past, I should be able to fix thing up in short order.

Jim: OK, go ahead. Tell me about what you have in mind, but I have another meeting in about one hour.

Roger: We can cover what we need to in an hour with no problem. Here's what I have in mind.

First of all, I want to get your Annual Report in shape–no need to have your CEO all upset about this.

Jim: Wait a minute. We won't be issuing another annual report until the first quarter of next year.

Roger: I know, but there is no time like the present to get started. That's the highest visibility issue you have. It's also the most expensive, but that's how those things are.

Next, I'd like to tackle your promotional pieces. We'd take the best ideas from the new annual report format and re-do your Product Family Brochure. It's time for a whole new look, in my opinion.

After that, we could re-create the Product and Technical Bulletins. I'd probably want to completely restructure these to go along with the new look.

> Ineffective consultants fail to connect on a personal level with clients.

> Consultants are hired to suggest improvements, and not to reconstruct the client's business.

PROSPECTING FOR CLIENTS

Jim: Seems like a lot of effort and money!

Roger: You're right. It will be lot of effort–and, as you know, you get what you pay for.

Anyway, after the new look is complete, we'd handle your direct mail campaign, although from my experience, you should ask your Sales VP to get his people out of their offices to cold call and prospect.

That's our approach . . . I think it will really work well for you. When do think we could get started?

Jim: Sounds interesting. There is an attraction to creating a whole new look. How do you know that it will be the right look for FTL Industries?

Roger: It's simple–we're the experts. And because we charge for our consulting efforts at a daily rate, we'll continue making the modifications you need until you are totally satisfied.

Jim: Sounds a bit open-ended. How much do you think this is going to cost?

Roger: Oh, I'd guess about $100K. That's what it cost the last time we did one of these.

Jim: Do you have a proposal for me?

Roger: No, but I'll be glad to send a letter proposal confirming my approach and our daily rate–along with our latest brochure.

Jim: It's time for my meeting. Thanks for dropping by today.

Roger: I appreciate your time and look forward to doing business with you.

{End of sales call}

COMMENTARY:

As with Scenario No. 1, this call will be evaluated based on the tips contained in the Selling Yourself section.

Develop your personal presence

Roger needs to read John Molloy's Dress for Success, *and get his attitude straightened out. Calls like this give the consulting profession a bad name.*

PROSPECTING FOR CLIENTS

Qualify for personal issues

Roger didn't bother to do this. He also didn't pick up on the priorities that Jim had mentioned in their previous meeting

Structure your sales calls

Roger's call gave a new meaning to free-form. The lack of structure provided no benefit to Jim Johnson, and it severely damaged Roger's position. The approach Roger mentioned of starting with a new look top-down, beginning with the Annual Report works for some companies, but that wasn't the prioritization desired by Jim Johnson for FTL Industries.

Persuade more easily

Roger made it tough on himself. He went for the close ("When do think we could get started?") before he had addressed the issues faced by his prospect.

All in all, not the way to make a sales call. Typically, no sales call will go quite as poorly as this one, but many of us from time-to-time can get a mild case of "Roger-itis."

Lack of structure and unclear goals do not effectively sell consulting services.

TELEPHONE SCENARIOS

Sandy Miller has just started her own financial consulting firm–called Financial Consulting Associates. She has a BA in Accounting and an MBA in Finance. She is also a certified CPA. In her work in the corporate world, she was the CFO of a $20 million computer systems value-added reseller. Her old company, LumberSystems, Inc. sold UNIX-based systems to independent lumberyards in the U.S.

Sandy is extremely familiar with this industry and has selected her target market–her old firm's competitors and the major independent lumber dealers. She has an in-depth knowledge of financial issues because of her familiarity with both her old company's financial operations and situations faced by her old customers.

The CEO of LumberSystems, Tex Hanson, has offered to be a strong reference for Sandy. Her position was eliminated because of

PROSPECTING FOR CLIENTS

> The savvy consultant is confident without sounding pushy.

downsizing of the company, and she elected to leave rather than take a substantial cut in pay to stay.

To introduce her services, Sandy has decided to telemarket to find interested prospects. The telephone audio scenarios below have examples of Sandy making two types of calls to typical prospects. Listen to the following and notice the differences in:

- Sandy's voice–does it sound confident?
- The first five seconds
- How she handles the gatekeeper
- The telephone call from the prospect's point of view–would you be interested?

The prospect is Cyberlumber Systems in Denver. Sandy is calling on the VP of Finance, John Hollister, to offer her services in tax preparation. She's calling just after the first of the year–tax season is just around the corner. This is an initial cold call. If the prospect is interested, Sandy will follow up with a letter proposal for her services.

Scenario No. 1: Effective Telephone Presentation

Call is placed, and

Cyber: Good Morning, Cyberlumber, how may I direct your call?

Sandy: John Hollister, please.

Cyber: Certainly. One moment, please.

Admin: Good morning, Mr. Hollister's office. How may I help you?

Sandy: Hello. This is Sandy Miller, Principal of Financial Consulting Associates. We specialize in helping companies find tax benefits. Tex Hanson at LumberSystems suggested I give Mr. Hollister a call (strong, confident, friendly voice–downward inflection at the end of sentences).

Admin: Thank you Sandy. Let me see if I can get Mr. Hollister on the line.

John H: Good morning, John Hollister.

PROSPECTING FOR CLIENTS

Sandy: Good morning, Mr. Hollister. I'm Sandy Miller, and Tex Hanson suggested I call you. I was able to save his company a good deal of money by finding some tax benefits he was unaware of, and he thought my company, Financial Consultants Associates, might be able to do the same for you.

Is this a good time to talk?

John H: I've got just a couple of minutes before I go into a staff meeting.

Sandy: Great–I have just a few quick questions to see if I might be able to save you some tax dollars.

John H: Fine, go ahead.

[The call progresses]

COMMENTARY:

How did Sandy do against our list of telephone effectiveness criteria? Let's evaluate her telephone presence:

1. *Sandy's voice–did it sound confident?*
   Yes, confident and friendly. Confidence comes across when the pitch of your voice is appropriate for your age and gender, and you use a downward inflection at the end of a declarative sentence.
2. *The first five seconds*
   Sandy's opening was businesslike. She provided her name, the name of her company, and the reason for her call.
3. *How she handles the gatekeeper*
   The gatekeeper in this example was John Hollister's Administrator. Sandy provided her with enough information to be put through to her prospect.
4. *The telephone call from the prospect's point of view–would you be interested?*
   Put yourself in Hollister's shoes–you know what Sandy does, and what she's done for someone you respect in the industry. Wouldn't you answer a few quick questions? (It might save your company some money.)

PROSPECTING FOR CLIENTS

A confident voice can make or break a business deal.

SCENARIO NO. 2: INEFFECTIVE TELEPHONE PRESENTATION

Call is placed, and

Cyber: Good Morning, Cyberlumber, how may I direct your call?

Sandy: John Hollister, please.

Cyber: Certainly. One moment, please.

Admin: Good morning, Mr. Hollister's office. How may I help you?

Sandy: Hello. This is Sandy Miller? Could I speak with Mr. Hollister please? (voice–tentative, unsure, with upward inflection at the end of sentences)

Admin: Yes, Sandy, and what is the purpose of your call?

Sandy: Well, it's personal–I'd like to talk with Mr. Hollister directly.

Admin: Mr. Hollister is going to want to know why you're calling him, Sandy.

Sandy: Well–I've got my own consulting firm, and I was referred to Mr. Hollister by Tex Hanson at LumberSystems.

Admin: I know Tex Hanson. He's one of the most respected CEO's in our industry. Let me put you through to Mr. Hollister.

John H: Good morning, John Hollister.

Sandy: Good morning, Mr. Hollister? I'm Sandy Miller? Tex Hanson suggested I call you?

John H: Could I ask why you are calling?

Sandy: I was able to help Mr. Hanson with some tax benefit issues?

John H: Sandy, thanks for your call. I have to run to a meeting. If you'll put something in the mail to me, I'll look it over.

Sandy: I'll get something to you by the end of the week. Thank you for your time.

John H: Good-bye, Sandy.
[end of conversation]

COMMENTARY:

How did Sandy do against our list of telephone effectiveness criteria in this second example? Let's evaluate her telephone presence

1. *Sandy's tone–did it sound confident?*
   Absolutely not. No confidence–tentative attitude. The tone of her voice was OK, but every sentence ended in a question mark–like she was totally unsure of herself.
2. *The first five seconds*
   Sandy's opening sounded like she needed work. The first five seconds on the line with Hollister and his Administrator did not help her case.
3. *How she handles the gatekeeper*
   She didn't. If it were not for the Administrator's knowledge of Tex Hanson's reputation, she would have never have been put through.
4. *The telephone call from the prospect's point of view–would you be interested?*
   If I were John Hollister, I would not be sure what Sandy could do for me, and by the tone of her call, I'm not confident that she could do a good job, I'd ask her to send me some information and get her off the line.

Presentations should be informative without being flashy.

QUESTIONS & ANSWERS ABOUT PRESENTATION

How should you present your proposal during a client presentation?

If possible standing up, with visual aids.

What are some general suggestions you would give a new (or even experienced) consultant that could help him or her during a presentation?

First, use the presentation flow recommended in the sections on developing a proposal and presentation. The flow is key to winning the business. Second, use visual aids that convey that you are a

PROSPECTING FOR CLIENTS

value organization (without being too flashy). This means color transparencies and a simple but effective presentation that focuses on the client's issues without whiz-bang distractions.

Is it really necessary to make a verbal presentation of the proposal or is it better to simply let the proposal speak for itself?

Proposals do not speak for themselves. Consulting is a people business. I have never won an assignment from a new prospect where I have not been able to present the proposal, either in a stand-up presentation, one-on-one with the prospect, or both.

What should you be sure to mention?

Follow the eight-step proposal outline suggested, and focus on the client's current condition and what you–and uniquely you–can do to make it better.

Don't leave a meeting with a potential client until all relevant issues are resolved.

What are the biggest mistakes a consultant (experienced and inexperienced) can make?

Here are some major ones I've made:

- Not understanding the decision criteria and buying cycle
- Not sufficiently understanding the prospect's needs
- Not differentiating myself
- Underestimating the scope of effort on a fixed price contract
- Proposing too soon in the sales cycle

Is it better to get a signed agreement at the meeting, or should you give the potential client time to digest the information, then send a signed contract at a later date?

Yes to the first part of the question–if possible. If the prospect needs to run the agreement through their legal department, you can still gain agreement that he or she will go ahead with you–and I would not leave the meeting until all issues are resolved (who knows how the client may digest the information on their own).

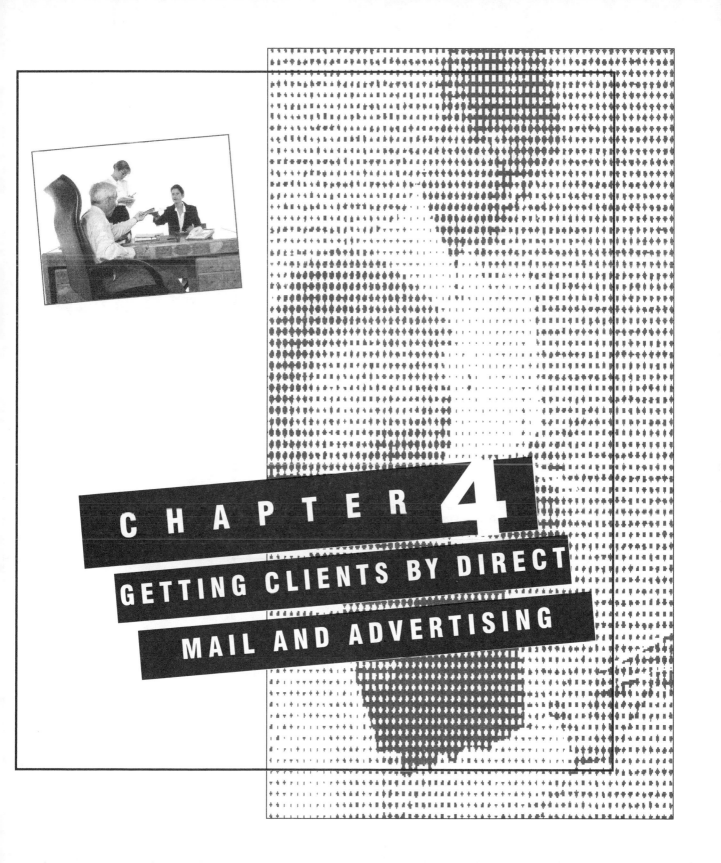

CHAPTER 4

GETTING CLIENTS BY DIRECT MAIL AND ADVERTISING

Don't let the words "direct mail advertising" scare you. A lot of people get a lot of consulting work by simple sales letters—and they'll work for you too! You'll learn how easy it is to put together an impressive direct mail package—but you'll also learn how to write powerful sales letters that can get prospects knocking on your door. Always test direct mail in small batches first.

DIRECT MAIL

Direct mail allows you to target a specific market better than any other advertising medium. You decide who gets your message, when they get it, and where they get it.

A direct-mail piece can be as simple as a postcard or as elaborate as a catalog. Direct mail is a terrific medium for creating action. Sending a direct-mail piece is much more likely to elicit an immediate response than television, radio, or newspaper advertising.

Direct mail usually costs more per person reached than any other advertising medium. The advantage of direct mail lies in its ability to target a specific consumer group. It allows you to concentrate your advertising budget on those people most likely to purchase your product or service.

You can budget as little or as much as you like to launch a direct mail campaign. How much you spend will be affected by decisions such as two- versus four-color printing, how many pages will be in your brochure or catalog, how many pieces will be in your direct mail package, paper size, and, most importantly, the number of pieces you want to mail.

HOW IT WORKS

WHY

Direct mail campaigns are good for targeting specific markets. They allow you to mail promotional material, special offers, or other advertising messages to specific groups of prospects.

WHO

Direct mail should be targeted to those segments of your market that would most likely be interested in the consulting services you have to offer. If you are marketing financial consulting services, you should target the CEOs in small firms and the CFOs in larger operations. If your consulting practice focuses on graphic design services, you may want to

GETTING CLIENTS BY DIRECT MAIL AND ADVERTISING

target Vice Presidents of Marketing and Directors of Marketing Communications in your target market.

If you don't have a list of people or businesses in your targeted market group, contact a mailing list broker. The broker will be able to compile a list according to your demographic needs and supply mailing labels for your direct mail materials.

Direct mail should be timed appropriately to catch a client's attention early.

When

Send your direct mail to your targeted customers when it would be most likely to catch their attention and fulfill an upcoming need. For example, in the case of financial services, special tax consultation services might be promoted just before tax season. Mail early enough so that you will catch their attention before they choose a direction for handling tax issues. That will give you enough time to follow-through and do a top-notch job for them.

Where

You should send your direct mail to the attention of the decision maker responsible for selecting your consulting services–to their business address, or to their home address if you are involved in consumer consulting activities.

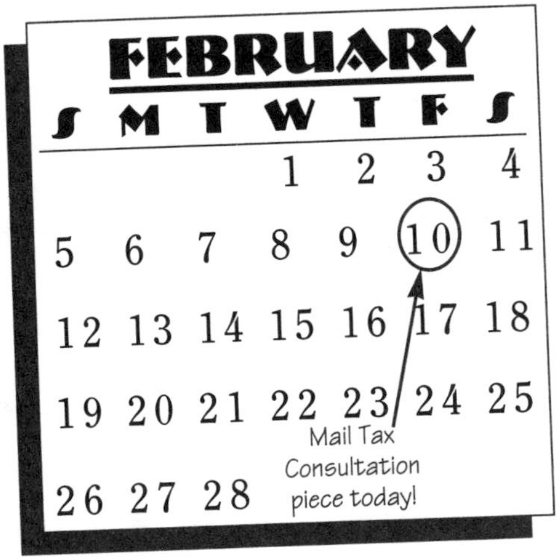

FEBRUARY
S M T W T F S
1 2 3 4
5 6 7 8 9 10 11
12 13 14 15 16 17 18
19 20 21 22 23 24 25
26 27 28
Mail Tax Consultation piece today!

How

You can collate, stuff, and label your direct-mail materials yourself. If your mailing is large, mailing list houses usually offer a full range of mailing services.

What

Direct-mail materials should include all of the information potential customers need in order to understand what you can do for them, be interested in the benefits you have to offer, and act on a decision to follow-up with you.

DIRECT-MAIL PIECE

Direct-mail packages vary from simple postcards to fat envelopes stuffed with full-color flyers and, typically, consist of the following:

GETTING CLIENTS BY DIRECT MAIL AND ADVERTISING

SALES LETTER

The sales letter is usually the first thing you see when you open a direct mail package. This is an important piece, because the letter must quickly grab the prospect's attention or the rest of the package will be trashed. The letter is often printed in black ink on standard letter-size paper. It might be personalized with your prospect's name, or it could be a form letter addressed Dear Sir or Madam.

MAIL PIECE

A brochure or flyer is the next piece one typically sees. This piece is designed to reinforce the sales letter and to set an image for the company and product. It is typically 11" x 17", folded to letter size. This brochure might be printed in one or two colors or feature four-color printing.

BUSINESS REPLY CARD

A postage-paid business reply card allows the customer to reply to the mailing easily. Or a postage-paid business reply envelope may be used so that the customer is able to mail a check back.

NO. 10 BUSINESS ENVELOPE

Direct mail is usually sent in a standard business size (No. 10) envelope. Sometimes a "teaser" is printed on the envelope to entice a prospect to open it. The post office has kits that provide setup information for designing envelope "teasers" and placing important mailing information to ensure fast delivery.

DOT560 FINANCIAL SERVICES
157 Elm Street · Manchester, NH 03103 · 603-555-5678
Results-Based Financial Consulting

September 1, 1997

Mr. Alan Kolman
Chief Financial Officer
Von Weinstein Products, Inc.
657 Eastern Avenue
Manchester, NH 03104

Dear Mr. Kolman:

Your company has been mentioned in the press as one of the fastest growing companies in New Hampshire. Achieving the good financial results that you have means that you're doing things right.

The reason we're writing is to suggest methods that you can use to reduce the tax bite on the results you've been able to obtain. Our consulting services are specifically designed for companies like yours, so that you can save tax dollars and increase the return to your shareholders.

How do we know how much we'll be able to help you? We don't yet. That why we're offering you a free tax consultation. It will only take 90 minutes of your time—and it could prove to be extremely profitable for you. Naturally, we're hoping you notice how our expertise will benefit you so that you'll consider us as the outside source for financial consultation services—and to help with some of your overload this tax season.

I'll call you next Friday to follow up. Please call me before then if you have any questions.

Sincerely,

Ross Pinkerton

Ross Pinkerton
Principal

NO POSTAGE
NECESSARY
IF MAILED
IN THE
UNITED STATES

BUSINESS REPLY MAIL
First Class Permit No. 4 Manchester, NH

DOT560 FINANCIAL SERVICES
157 Elm Street
Manchester, NH 03103

Take a Bite
Out of
Your Taxes

Dot560
Financial
Services

Free Consultation

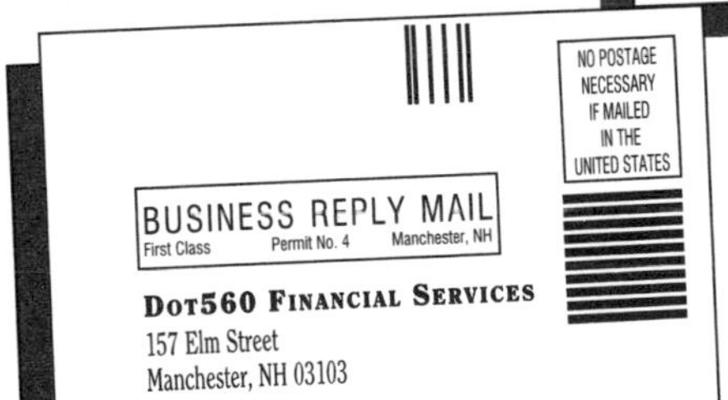

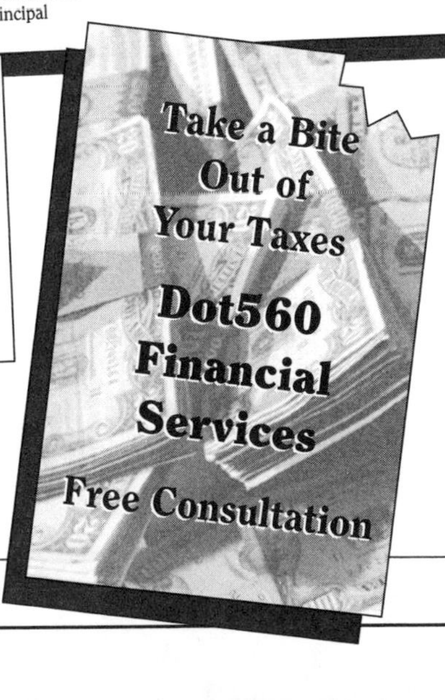

GETTING CLIENTS BY DIRECT MAIL AND ADVERTISING

TexTech Graphic Design
775 Ranchero Parkway ■ Texastown ■ TX 76010 **1.**
(800) 555-5555

September 1, 1996

Mr. Martin Johnson
Vice President of Marketing **2.**
Widget Enterprises
12600 Commercial Blvd.
Texasville, TX 75237

Dear Mr. Johnson:

How would you like to get a 20 percent increase in your response rate for your company's direct-mail campaigns? **3.**

TexTech Graphic Design specializes in measurably increasing the effectiveness of your direct-mail efforts. **4.**

"Because of TexTech's efforts, **I was able to improve my direct mail response rate by 22.3%**. This can be directly attributed to TexTech's response to my needs and their expertise in designing high impact graphics direct mail pieces."–*Dave Malloy–Vice President Marketing, Malloy Computer Services, Bartow, Texas* **5.** **6.**

The difference in results is the difference that TexTech Graphics provides–high resolution digital imagery that brings a direct-mail piece to life, makes it interesting to the user, and gets you the response you want.

For further information, send the enclosed postage-paid business reply card to receive your free Direct Mail Survey Report along with our information package. Or, call me directly at (800) 555-5555 so we can discuss your graphic design requirements. **7.**

Sincerely,
A. L. Huffman
A. L. Huffman
President

P.S. If you contact us before September 20, we'll conduct a free graphics effectiveness survey for your company. **8.**

GETTING CLIENTS BY DIRECT MAIL AND ADVERTISING

WRITING A DIRECT-MAIL LETTER

1. **Letterhead**
   A sales letter should include your company logo, name, and address. You can have a printer print your letter on your existing letterhead stock, print the letter in combination with your standard letterhead design, or print a letterhead that has been specifically designed for your direct mail piece.
2. **Addressee**
   Many direct mail pieces, particularly those mailed by local businesses, do not personalize each letter. Instead, the letter begins with a generic introduction, such as Dear Sir or Dear Madam. If you are using a generic introduction, do try to personalize as much as possible with greetings, such as Dear Sales Professional or Dear Computer User. Addressing the letter to a specific person is preferable, but it will add to the cost and the complexity of the mailing. If you are buying your mailing list from a large mailing list company, they can provide you with names and addresses on a computer disk. Most mailing houses will be able to print personalized letters using this disk for an additional charge.
3. **Attention-grabber**
   Grab the reader's attention in the first sentence. This is the most important part of the letter. Unless your first sentence is highly compelling, most readers will not continue reading the letter.
4. **Focus on benefits**
   You want to focus on the benefits of the services your consulting practice offers in the body of the letter. Your services have many characteristics that your prospects will ask about, but it is the benefits that will sell them. A benefit is what your customers derive from your consulting services.
5. **Testimonial**
   A testimonial can be used to add credibility to you and your consulting practice. The most important aspect of the testi-

Try to address direct mailings to a specific person.

GETTING CLIENTS BY DIRECT MAIL AND ADVERTISING

Keep the reader's attention by highlighting important phrases and stressing the timeliness of their response.

monial is the person who offers it. Make sure the person is someone the reader will respect.

6. **Highlight key phrases**
   Keep the reader's attention. Some readers will skim through your letter and could miss the most important points. Highlight key phrases that stress benefits to keep the reader interested in your services.
7. **Call to action**
   Call your readers to action. They need to feel like they should act quickly or they will lose the offer. Make it easy for the readers to act by listing a toll-free order number or including a postage-paid reply card.
8. **Add a postscript**
   Add a postscript at the end of the letter. Many readers skip to the end of the letter for the "bottom line." A grabber "P.S." statement will ensure that your message isn't lost.

PRODUCING A DIRECT-MAIL PIECE

A direct-mail piece should be carefully planned and executed. If you don't have advertising or marketing experience, enlist a creative service to assist you in strategizing your unique selling proposition–your unbeatable selling point. Once you have developed your "message strategy," contract for various execution and distribution services.

MAILING LIST BROKER

If you don't have a mailing list, contact a mailing list broker. Ask the mailing list broker where their lists are sourced from–specialized industrial or membership directories, telephone books, and/or magazine subscription lists. Inquire about the availability of lists that have been used to sell products similar to yours. Narrow your list focus to match the demographics of your potential customers.

COPYWRITER

A professional copywriter will know how to phrase your unique selling point(s) to create a pitch that will grab the attention of your

GETTING CLIENTS BY DIRECT MAIL AND ADVERTISING

prospective customers. I recommend that you first try developing the copy yourself.

Graphic Designer

For a "professional look," hire a graphic designer to create your direct mailer. He or she will know how to present the elements of your piece–type, photographs, illustrations–to command attention. The designer will also provide you with the camera-ready art.

A professional-looking mailing can catch the attention of potential clients.

Illustrator

If you need eye-catching illustrations of the results produced by your consulting practice or of the methods you use, hire an illustrator.

Photographer

A photograph is the best way to depict and sell your services. If your can, hire a photographer to take pictures of you and your team in action. If you want to "dress up" your piece with photo illustrations, you can purchase the rights to use stock photographs available through stock photo houses. For royalty-free photographs, check with your suppliers or end users.

Printer

Choose a printer that specializes in printing pieces similar in quantity, size, and configuration to yours. Don't pay a four-color printer to print a one-color job or expect a quick printer to do professional four-color printing. Request samples and get quotes. Once you have chosen your printer, find out what its press and camera-ready art requirements are. Relay that information to your designer.

Mail House

For large mailings, contract the services of a mail house to fold, collate, stuff, label, and/or prepare your mailing according to postal regulations.

Post Office

The post office publishes guides that outline formats and rules for designing and organizing advertising mail that will flow through the postal system quickly and efficiently. Ask!

GETTING CLIENTS BY DIRECT MAIL AND ADVERTISING

Direct mail is viewed as one of the most effective marketing techniques.

DIRECT MAIL SUCCESS STORY

SalesWinners provides sales training and consulting services to high-tech industries. David Kintler, President, is a strong believer in direct mail. Using this medium for reaching his potential customers was critically important when SalesWinners opened a New England Regional Office this past year. Here's how David chose direct mail as his chief advertising medium and how he made it work for SalesWinners.

A Cost-Effective Method

"I've always been a believer in Direct Mail as one of the best direct response mediums there is. That was true for me when I headed corporate sales and marketing organizations–and is even more important to me now. It's the most cost-effective way of getting your marketing message across that I know of."

Test Until You Get it Right

"When we first started using direct mail, results were not encouraging. The first time, we were able to get only one response out of 600 mailings. We could have done two things–drop the idea and try something else–or test various letters and enclosures to build our response rate up to an acceptable level. We decided to test various letters. With our latest mailing, our response rate is one out of every thirty-five pieces mailed. This is a phenomenal improvement, and we wouldn't have achieved this without perseverance and continually testing our mailings."

STREETWISE ADVICE ON DIRECT MAIL

Don't Expect to Make Money on Your First Mailing

Direct mail marketing is effective for many small and large businesses, but it can be hard to find the direct-mail package that works best for you. Don't get discouraged if your first mailing doesn't increase sales. Keep trying!

GETTING CLIENTS BY DIRECT MAIL AND ADVERTISING

KNOW YOUR BREAK-EVEN POINT

Successful direct mail campaigns typically get a response rate of one to three percent. Figure out how many responses you need to break even.

TEST SMALL MAILINGS

Test small, inexpensive mailings until you find the formula that works. Let's say you need two responses per hundred to break even on your mailing costs. If you do a two hundred-piece mailing, you need four responses to break even. If you get one response or no responses on your two hundred-piece mailing, it is not working. Chances are, it won't work no matter how many pieces you mail.

CHOOSING THE RIGHT LIST IS CRITICAL

Choosing the right mailing list will make a much faster improvement in your response rate than changing the direct-mail piece. Choose your list very carefully.

YOUR BEST LIST IS USUALLY YOUR CUSTOMER LIST

Your best list is a list of people who have previously bought a service from you. Keep a good list of current and past clients.

WORK YOUR BEST LISTS HARD

Use your best mailings lists frequently. Mail to these lists again and again, until response dwindles off. Focus on using your best lists repeatedly, as opposed to testing a wide variety of new lists.

FOCUS YOUR MESSAGE

Be specific. Direct mail is good at targeting a specific audience. Be sure to develop copy and a layout that are appropriate to your audience.

CALL THEM TO ACTION

Direct mail is great for calling clients to action. Don't forget to put a call to action in your piece.

USE COUPONS AND REDEMPTION OFFERS

Give prospects a reason to act soon. Coupons with redemption dates give the offer urgency.

Before attempting a huge mailing, test small mailings until you receive adequate responses.

GETTING CLIENTS BY DIRECT MAIL AND ADVERTISING

MAKE IT EASY TO RESPOND

Always think ahead to what you want the recipients to do. Make it easy for them to take action. If you want them to return a reply card, make it postage-paid. If you want them to call you, include a toll-free number.

TEST AND REFINE

Don't give up after one shot. You could have a wonderful design, great copy, and a solid offer, but be mailing at the wrong time. In the end, you have to test it until you see what works for your situation. Test variations on design and timing to find out what works.

Making it easy for the client to respond to your mailing with postage-free cards can better guarantee a response.

QUESTIONS & ANSWERS ABOUT DIRECT MAIL

Should I send my mailing first class or bulk rate?

Generally, you should use bulk rate. But personalize your mailing as much as postal regulations permit. Your envelope doesn't have to have "bulk rate mail" stamped across it, nor do you have to use a preprinted block in the top corner that says bulk rate. Instead, you may want to consider having the mail stamped in a meter with the abbreviation "blk. rate" in small type running vertically beside the correct rate. Ask the mail house about this option.

Bulk mail moves slower and less predictably than first-class mail since it is not given priority. But only a very small percentage of bulk mail is actually lost, and using it can save you a lot of money.

Is a phone response or a mail back response better?

Both response mechanisms are effective. Some people prefer to phone in their response to direct mail offers, others prefer to respond by mail. So offer both options if possible.

Do I need a toll-free number for phone responses?

If you are doing local mailings and your number is a local call for prospects, you don't need a toll-free number. Otherwise, you do, especially for national mailings. Because of the high costs generally associated with using consultants, prospective clients will expect you to offer a toll-free number. However, not having one will likely not stop business people from calling you.

GETTING CLIENTS BY DIRECT MAIL AND ADVERTISING

Why do many direct-mail pieces include dated offers?

Dated offers generate more sales by pushing people to respond by a certain deadline. If you are using bulk mail, be sure to give people plenty of time to respond. If you really aren't confident about when your mailing will arrive, you may want to make a special offer contingent upon "responding within ten days of receipt" for example, as opposed to a specific date. I recommend that you give people between ten and twenty-one days from the time they receive the offer to respond to a direct mail solicitation.

Dated offers push people to respond and take action.

MEDIA ADVERTISING

Consultants use a wide variety of advertising, mainly depending on the size of the firm, availability of resources, and specialization of products and services to reach their target markets.

Examples of the forms of media advertising are:

- Trade journals and periodicals
- Magazines, both professional and trade
- Direct mail
- Radio and television
- Newspapers
- Yellow pages listings

Typically, consultants will use one of the first two sources of advertising to inform both current clients and new prospects of their areas of specialty (e.g., sales trainers, multimedia advisors and developers, Internet service providers, financial services, human resources, and any other specific field that will gain recognition). Should you consider media advertising? One way to decide is to find out what has worked successfully for other consultants, and follow their success strategies. Here are a few of the steps necessary to implement a successful media strategy:

Media advertising can be effective, depending on the size of your firm.

1. Determine what the decision makers in your target market read in terms of national or regional publications. This can be done via surveys–phone calls to selected target market

GETTING CLIENTS BY DIRECT MAIL AND ADVERTISING

companies. You should use your own background as a decision maker as a prime source for this information.

2. Review trade journals, magazines, and other publications to determine any sources that your competitors are using for their advertising campaigns. A good way to start is by going to either local libraries or colleges and universities to review their periodicals.
3. Request a media kit from publishers of the selected periodical or magazine base. This source will provide you with rates, circulation, and readership profiles.
4. Call your competitors to get their impressions of advertising in various publications.
5. Run small ads in a few media sources and monitor their effectiveness.

Choice Ad Mediums

While business-to-business marketing efforts should be centered on sales or telemarketing programs, advertising can play an important role in your effort to get your name recognized and obtain clients. It can help you develop leads that you can follow up by a phone call or by setting up a personal meeting with a key decision maker. Following are two of the more prominent forms of advertising used by successful consultants.

Test small ads first.

GETTING CLIENTS BY DIRECT MAIL AND ADVERTISING

Magazines

One of the most effective methods of advertising is taking advantage of trade-specific publications that cater to your industry. Using this method means you have a reasonable degree of assurance that the decision makers of your target market most likely subscribe to the periodical. However, don't rush out and buy a full page ad in a general national publication (e.g., *Time, Newsweek, Business Week, Fortune,* etc.). The results will most likely be negligible. There are hundreds of trade publications that will allow you to target your customer base more narrowly and at a much lower cost.

Costs for advertising vary greatly from publication to publication as well as for certain special issues. Positioning is the key when starting out as you want to gain some prominence and credibility by maximizing the likelihood that your ad will be seen.

Trade journals are one of the most targeted, cost-effective advertising alternatives.

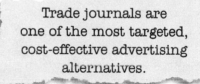

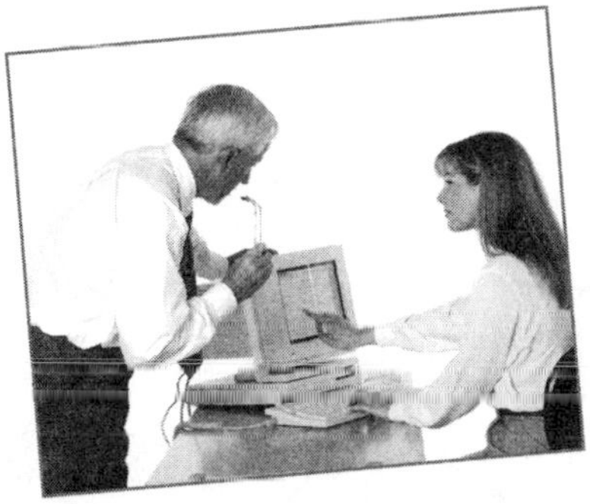

CHAPTER 5

ATTRACTING CLIENTS WITH FREE PUBLICITY

The consulting business is a natural for free publicity, something often overlooked when considering marketing. A small article or even mention in the right publication can attract a lot of interest in your consulting practice—and best of all it's free! You'll learn how to find the publicity hook for your business, how to create a mini-press kit, how to follow up with phone calls, and what to say when you meet the press!

Publicity is often overlooked as a primary marketing tool to gain attention and interest in a consulting service. Using publicity as a sales tool can be a more cost-effective method for generating sales than buying advertising.

No matter what type of consulting practice you are operating, you can be your own publicist! If you want to act as your own PR firm, you can produce a simple press kit. This kit should include a "pitch" letter and press release regarding your company, the results you've produced for clients (with their permission), or the services you offer. Once you have targeted and established appointments with print and broadcast media contacts, you can act as your own spokesperson to pitch your image, capabilities, or services. You will become the focus, the center of attention, as you create an awareness of your business that will turn into sales leads.

Publicity can take a variety of formats. You or someone connected with your business could appear on a local radio or TV talk show with your business being the topic of a particular segment. You could be the subject of an article in a local or national newspaper or magazine. You might become part of a broadcast business panel discussing issues that are pertinent to your product or service, or you could speak at trade association meetings, trade show seminars, or Chamber of Commerce gatherings. The creative publicist can find thousands of publicity opportunities that allow for increasing image or product awareness.

The best part of publicity is that, for the most part, it is free! This is especially true if you manage your own publicity campaigns. However, if you do choose to hire an outside PR firm, the costs can still be a lot less than building the same amount of awareness via paid advertising.

ATTRACTING CLIENTS WITH FREE PUBLICITY

You don't necessarily need to hire a publicist in order to get the best publicity possible.

Drafting a list of media contacts who might be interested in your firm will help to narrow your focus.

HOW PUBLICITY WORKS

1. **Decide whether or not you want to do your own publicity**
   One advantage of being your own publicist is that you know your consulting services better than anyone else. A great amount of time and effort can be expended apprising a PR firm or freelance publicist about your company and your consulting services. Additionally, no one will have the same enthusiasm for your company that you do. This sense of excitement will serve you well as you spread the word about your services. It's a lot easier than you might think to create a "pitch" letter, develop a press release, find and approach media contacts, and make follow-up phone calls.
2. **Create the hook**
   To create your own publicity, you need to communicate your story to those who access the public through the media—television, radio, newspapers, and/or magazines. You need to develop a "hook," or a compelling reason why someone should listen to your story. Media contacts must feel strongly that knowledge of your consulting service would be of some value to their audience. Take time to build a cohesive "pitch" that really conveys the unique qualities and benefits of your consulting practice.
3. **Make a list**
   Make a list of media contacts who you think would be interested in your consulting services. Prioritize the list and decide what you want to tell each contact. This will give you a good idea of how much time you will need to spend compiling and sending press materials, as well as placing follow-up telephone calls.
4. **Create a "mini" press kit**
   It isn't necessary to send an elaborate press kit to get a newspaper, magazine, or broadcast outlet to tell your story. If you are doing your own publicity, it is often just as effective to send a personalized "pitch" letter and a press release in a standard-size business envelope to your media contacts.

ATTRACTING CLIENTS WITH FREE PUBLICITY

5. **Follow up with a phone call**
   Follow up your mailings with a phone call to each media contact. If you fail to get through the first time or if your media contact is too busy to talk to you, be persistent. When you do manage to get through, make an appointment to visit your contact.
6. **Take extensive notes to the interview**
   If you sent your media contact a simple "pitch" letter and press release, you need to take additional material relating to your practice to the media contact meeting. Testimonials, brochures, and a list of current or previous customers (with their permission) that have successfully used your service will assist you in conveying an interesting and powerful story about your practice.
7. **Make a list of potential questions and prepare answers**
   Prepare yourself for your meeting by creating a list of the possible questions the media contact might ask you. Be ready with answers!

Prepare a list of questions to answer for the media.

HIRING A PR FIRM

You should consider doing your own publicity first. You will make the best spokesperson for your consulting services. However, if you are extremely busy or uneasy about certain aspects of handling your own PR, you can hire a freelance PR specialist or a PR firm.

PR firms typically charge either an hourly or monthly rate. And they won't guarantee success no matter how many hours they bill you for! Some PR firms have extensive client lists, and if you aren't a top account, you won't be a priority account. Try to find out how important a client you will be. It could make or break the success of your publicity efforts.

Before you set up meetings to interview potential PR representatives, do a reference check. Ask individuals in your business community whom they recommend. Once you have compiled a list of firms you are interested in, set up meetings so that the firm can "pitch your account."

ATTRACTING CLIENTS WITH FREE PUBLICITY

You must stay in contact with your PR firm in order to fulfill your needs effectively.

Remember that you have control over the meeting because the PR firm is bidding for *your* business. It is up to the firm to try to sell you on its ability to effectively deliver your message to the right people. During the meeting, you need to articulate your objectives in an up-front manner. Have a list of issues and questions prepared that focus on your agenda. Listen carefully to their "pitch" and the answers they give to your questions. Include the following in your query:

- Who will be working on your account–a senior account executive, a junior account executive, or an entry-level trainee?
- How will you and the PR firm work together as a team?
- Who will be responsible for copy?
- Who is on the firm's media contact list?
- What have been their most effective recent media placements?
- What success have they had in creating publicity campaigns for businesses such as yours?

Don't leave the meeting until you feel that all of your questions and concerns have been answered.

If you do decide to hire a PR firm, you must stay on top of it and keep a proactive relationship in motion. This will ensure that your PR needs are fulfilled to your satisfaction.

ELEMENTS OF A STANDARD PRESS KIT

1. **The "pitch" letter**
   The first piece of information that an editor should see in your press kit is your "pitch" letter. This letter needs to immediately grab the editor's attention. It should be typed or printed on a letter-quality computer printer in black ink and on standard-sized 8.5" x 11" stationery. Ideally, it will be printed on your company letterhead. It should be personalized, because editors typically disregard "blind" or "cold" letters.

A "pitch" letter tries to grab the editor's attention.

ATTRACTING CLIENTS WITH FREE PUBLICITY

2. **Press release**
   The next piece an editor will look for is your press release. This piece should describe your consulting practice in detail and should provide the editor with enough newsworthy material to enable him or her to write a story about your consulting services directly from the release. The press release should also be typed or printed on a letter-quality computer printer in black ink on your letterhead stationery.
3. **Business card**
   Include your business card. Your business card should contain your name and title, company name, address, phone, fax, and/or any other communication avenue open to you, such as e-mail. You should staple the card to the top left-hand corner of the "pitch" letter or to the top left-hand corner of the press release, if you have decided against enclosing a "pitch" letter.
4. **Company background**
   A company background gives a short history of your company. It often includes profiles of key players within your organization. Again, it should be printed on your letterhead in the same manner as the "pitch" letter and the press release. Include the name of your company as a header or title in larger type at the top of the page. Indicate that this is the company background.
5. **Photos**
   Photos or slides of your services can support the press release and create a more compelling story for your business. Use color photos if possible.
6. **Testimonials**
   The testimonial sheet should be a one-page collection of quotes from anyone who has used your services and is willing to publicly support you. Again, use your letterhead for the testimonials.

Testimonial sheets are good ways to bolster the image of your company.

ATTRACTING CLIENTS WITH FREE PUBLICITY

Concordia 2000 Consulting Services
1566 Main Street ▲ Concord, NH 03220 ▲ Phone (603) 555-8765 ▲ Fax (603) 555-8766

PRESS RELEASE
For Immediate Publication

2.

Concordia 2000 Consulting Services
1566 Main Street ▲ Concord, NH 03220 ▲ Phone (603) 555-8765 ▲ Fax (603) 555-8766

September 6, 1997

1.

Mr. James Clark
Executive Editor
Mass High Tech
200 High Street
Boston, MA 02110

Dear Mr. Clark:

With the changes taking place in New England's economy—and specifically in high-technology companies—I'd like to share with your readers an approach that has helped make a major difference in the organizational effectiveness of the high-technology companies we've served.

Specifically, tha... ...ompany's organizational effectiveness. Here's ...with the key functional managers at the clie... ...ugh operational data to perform an on-line ...ding firms in the industry. It's a process we ca... ...clients.

Photo **5.**

...napshot of ...ly for the

...hods
...ational
...the
...like

Concordia 2000 Consulting Services

Roscoe Williams
President

3.

1566 Main Street ▲ Concord, NH 03220
Phone (603) 555-8765 ▲ Fax (603) 555-8766

8.

Concordia 2000 Consulting Services
1566 Main Street ▲ Concord, NH 03220 ▲ Phone (603) 555-8765 ▲ Fax (603) 555-8766

7.

DATA SHEET

Concordia 2000 Consulting Services
1566 Main Street ▲ Concord, NH 03220 ▲ Phone (603) 555-8765 ▲ Fax (603) 555-8766

6.

TESTIMONIALS

Concordia 2000 Consulting Services
1566 Main Street ▲ Concord, NH 03220 ▲ Phone (603) 555-8765 ▲ Fax (603) 555-8766

4.

COMPANY BACKGROUND

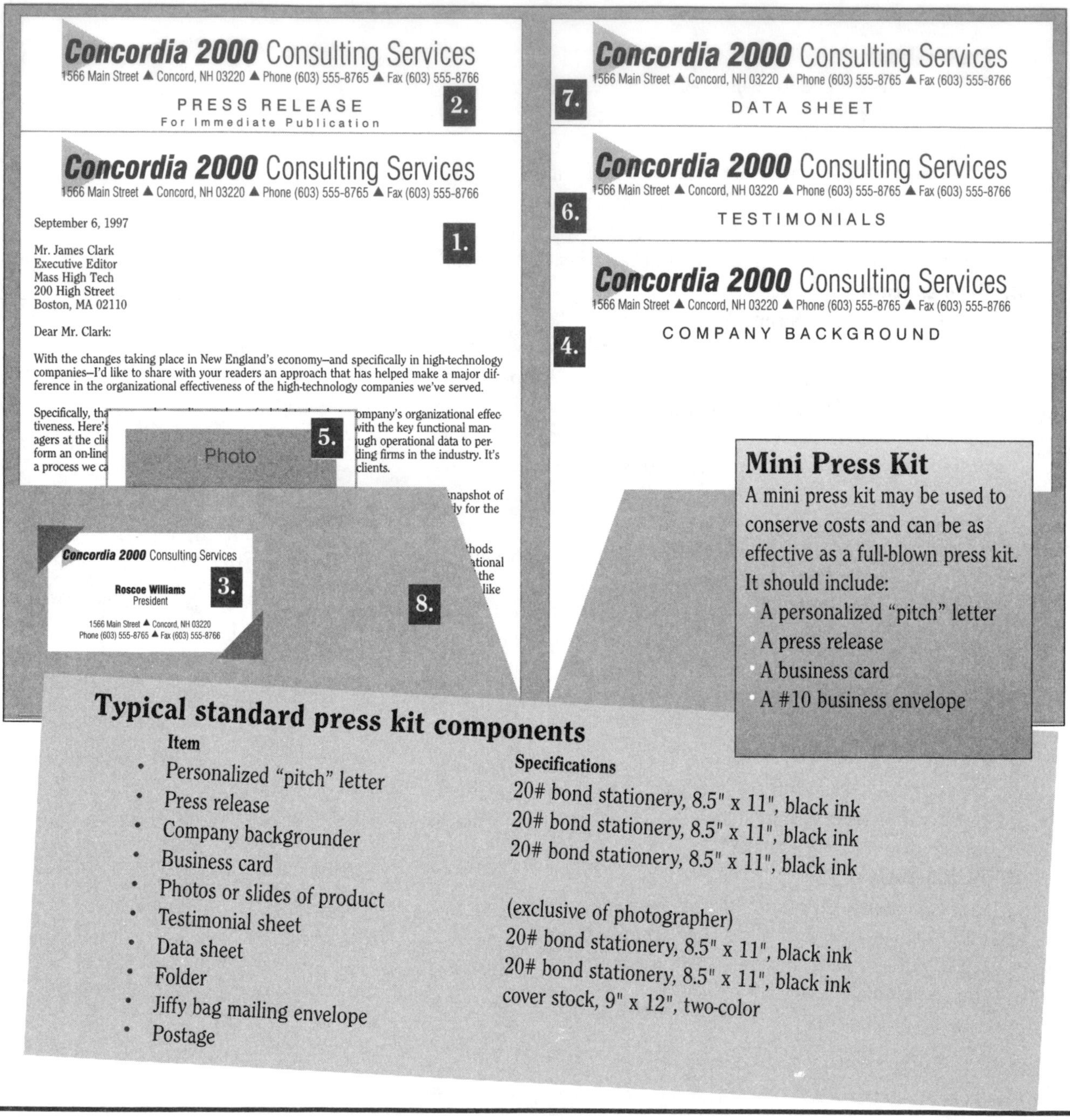

Mini Press Kit

A mini press kit may be used to conserve costs and can be as effective as a full-blown press kit. It should include:

* A personalized "pitch" letter
* A press release
* A business card
* A #10 business envelope

Typical standard press kit components

Item	Specifications
Personalized "pitch" letter	20# bond stationery, 8.5" x 11", black ink
Press release	20# bond stationery, 8.5" x 11", black ink
Company backgrounder	20# bond stationery, 8.5" x 11", black ink
Business card	
Photos or slides of product	(exclusive of photographer)
Testimonial sheet	20# bond stationery, 8.5" x 11", black ink
Data sheet	20# bond stationery, 8.5" x 11", black ink
Folder	cover stock, 9" x 12", two-color
Jiffy bag mailing envelope	
Postage

ATTRACTING CLIENTS WITH FREE PUBLICITY

7. **Data Sheet**
   If your consulting practice uses analysis, process, or productivity tools in providing results for your customers, outline the capabilities of these tools in a Data Sheet. Give some information about the benefits provided by the tools, but don't give away proprietary data your competitors may want to copy and use.
8. **Folder**
   The folder that will hold all your press materials should be simple in design, perhaps including your logo in two colors. The folder size should be 9" x 12" with an insert on the right- or left-hand side for your business card. If you are reluctant to spend the money to have a custom folder designed and printed, many office supply stores carry folders in a variety of styles and colors.

ATTRACTING CLIENTS WITH FREE PUBLICITY

Press releases should be informative without being too flashy.

CREATING A PRESS RELEASE

1. **Letterhead**
   The letterhead should include the company name, address, phone number, and fax number on a standard 8.5" x 11" piece of stationery and be printed in black or two-color ink.
2. **Press release**
   Indicate "Press Release" in the top left-hand corner in black ink with a bold typeface.
3. **Contact names**
   Indicate contact names and phone numbers in the top left-hand corner under "Press Release."
4. **Headline**
   The headline should be in bold type and should articulate your story angle.
5. **First paragraph**
   The first paragraph should tell a brief story so that if nothing else is published, it will highlight your main reason for sending the release. Include who, what, where, why, and when as may be applicable for the news you are conveying.
6. **Body**
   The body of the press release should give the editor or producer exhaustive details on your consulting practice. You want to be able to answer all questions about how the consulting service was developed, who the market is for the consulting service, how the market will benefit from using the consulting service, and where the consulting service is located.
7. **Testimonials**
   Include quotes from influential individuals who have used your consulting service and who are people that readers will respect.
8. **Concluding paragraph**
   This paragraph should describe how to get literature or more information about your consulting practice.
9. **Notation**
   The number "-30-" is used to signal the conclusion of the story. Any information following this notation are notes to either the editor or typesetter and are not intended for printing.

ATTRACTING CLIENTS WITH FREE PUBLICITY

1. **Concordia 2000** Consulting Services

1566 Main Street ▲ Concord, NH 03220 ▲ Phone (603) 555-8765 ▲ Fax (603) 555-8766

2. **PRESS RELEASE**

3. For additional information, please contact:
Roscoe Williams
Concordia 2000 Consulting Services
1566 Main Street
Concord, NH 03220
603-555-8765

4. **On-Line Modeling Provides Instant Snapshot of Organizational Effectiveness**

5. Concord, New Hampshire, September 6, 1997–Concordia 2000 Consulting Services has developed a unique on-line analysis tool to analyze organizational effectiveness. In just 90 minutes–with the basic facts about an organization at hand–a company's organizational effectiveness in all functional areas can be compared with leaders in their industry. Problem areas can be pinpointed and directions set to improve company performance.

6. Here's how it works. Members of Concordia's consulting team sit with the key functional managers at the client company. Within 90 minutes, sufficient operational data is gathered to input key organizational parameters into a computer system brought on-site by the team. Files are safeguarded, and no information leaves the premises without permission from the client. These key organizational parameters are then compared with published data from similar industries and from competitors.

Within seconds after data entry, the initial analysis report begins printing. This report provides a useful snapshot of how well a company is performing. It suggests areas for additional study for the purpose of recommending changes–changes that can make an immediate difference.

7. "Concordia 2000 Consulting Services provided timely, key information regarding our company's performance." Jonathan Burke, Star Investment Services.

8. To receive more information regarding this unique service, call (603) 555-8765 today.

9. -30-

ATTRACTING CLIENTS WITH FREE PUBLICITY

PITCH LETTER

Concordia 2000 Consulting Services
1566 Main Street ▲ Concord, NH 03220 ▲ Phone (603) 555-8765 ▲ Fax (603) 555-8766

September 6, 1997

Mr. James Clark
Executive Editor
Mass High Tech
200 High Street
Boston, MA 02110

Dear Mr. Clark:

With the changes taking place in New England's economy–and specifically in high-technology companies–I'd like to share with your readers an approach that has helped make a major difference in the organizational effectiveness of the high-technology companies we've served.

Specifically, that approach is on-line analysis of a high-technology company's organizational effectiveness. Here's how it works. Members of our consulting team sit with the key functional managers at the client company. Within 90 minutes we've gathered enough operational data to perform an on-line analysis of the company's operations versus the leading firms in the industry. It's a process we call *On-Line Modeling,* and it works wonders for our clients.

Naturally, the initial analysis does not tell the whole story, but it provides a useful snapshot of how well a company is performing. It pinpoints those areas that need additional study for the purpose of recommending changes–changes that can make an immediate difference.

Your readers will also learn three new methods they can employ for increasing the organizational effectiveness of their company as a result of the article we'd like to write for you. It would be like a mini-version of our on-site consulting efforts.

I'll give you call on Thursday, September 19 to follow up. Should you have any questions before then, please call me at 603-555-8765.

Sincerely,

Roscoe Williams
President

ATTRACTING CLIENTS WITH FREE PUBLICITY

PUBLICITY SUCCESS STORY

Ewa Erdman, Vice President and Marketing Director, is one of the founders of Take Two Photocraft, a business that specializes in digital photo retouching. Most of their work is restorative, but they can also remove undesirable backgrounds (or people) from prints. Ewa has had great success with publicity by playing off some of the more interesting "retouching" the firm is capable of–like removing ex-spouses from photographs!

SERENDIPITY

"I sent out a sample of our work and a short press release, and it appeared just three months after we opened. It was a huge boost to our business. But what made it even better was that they wrote copy to go with the example I sent. The first line of the story was 'Take out the no-good bum you divorced.' Monday morning we had a line of divorced people at our door waiting for us to get 'the jerk' out of their photos."

FOLLOW UP

"In that particular case I did not have to follow up. But in every subsequent case, I've had to be a bulldog about it."

Publicity tends to be more effective than advertising.

STREETWISE ADVICE ON PUBLICITY

BEFORE ADVERTISING

If you can get publicity for your business, do it! It can be much less expensive than advertising and much more powerful. With a good press release and a couple of days of follow-up phone calls, you may be able to generate significant media coverage for your consulting practice.

BETTER THAN ADVERTISING

Clients tend to pay a lot more attention to feature coverage in newspapers, television, and radio than they do to advertising. A full-page feature article on your business in your local newspaper may generate several times the amount of inquiries or sales as a full-page advertisement.

ATTRACTING CLIENTS WITH FREE PUBLICITY

In Advertising

Publicity can also be used to make your advertising copy more effective. For example, movie reviews almost always contain quotes from reviewers. Even if you are not selling movies, you can use favorable quotes from print, radio, and/or television interviews in your advertising copy. You may even want to reproduce the entire interview, frame it, and place it in your place of business. And definitely consider sending copies to your clients.

Keep in mind, though, if you are reproducing all or part of an interview, you should contact the publication or media outlet where the story appeared to get "reprint" permission. Even though the interview is about your business, the publication or media outlet has copyrighted the material and effectively owns it. Very few publications or media outlets refuse "reprint" permission or levy a charge for reprinting. There are exceptions, however. *Consumer Reports,* for instance, is concerned about maintaining the fairness of its image and completely prohibits the reprinting of any information from that publication.

Clients tend to pay a lot more attention to feature coverage in newspapers, television, and radio than they do to advertising.

Like Selling

Getting publicity is like selling in many ways. You usually need to make a lot of phone calls to get publicity. You need to make a presentation, overcome any objections, and close the sale. In making publicity calls, you will get a lot of voice mail or be stalled at the receptionist's or assistant's desk. You will certainly experience a lot of rejection. But if you can succeed in getting publicity for your company, it can go a long way toward making your business succeed.

QUESTIONS & ANSWERS ABOUT PUBLICITY

Which media should I target?

Unlike advertising space, you are not directly paying for publicity coverage. So target every media vehicle imaginable! But give primary focus to the media avenues most relevant to your customers and those that you are most likely to get a story aired on or published in.

ATTRACTING CLIENTS WITH FREE PUBLICITY

If you have a small local business and an equal number of people in your town read either the local newspaper, the nearest metropolitan newspaper, or view broadcasting from a particular television station, then it would be wisest to concentrate on the local newspaper as a suitable venue for disseminating your story. Even though each vehicle reaches an equal number of readers or viewers, realistically, your chances of being published by the local newspaper are far greater.

However, once you scope out the local media and either succeed or fail in your attempt to receive publicity, begin calling on the less obvious media choices. You never know! The more stories you can get published, the more company awareness you create, and the more sales potential you build.

Does publicity work consistently?

Not at all. The results of publicity are highly erratic and depend upon many factors. The reach of the medium is very important. So, of course, is the viewpoint of the media. Did the media like your product or hate it? Did your service receive enough attention to actually motivate people to purchase it?

Many other factors affect the results of publicity. These factors can range from "Was it a sunny or rainy day when the publicity ran?" to "What other products were being featured by the same paper?" Often even the most experienced public relations professionals can't figure out why a particular publicity piece worked or didn't work. Because media results are difficult to predict, get as much different media coverage as you possibly can.

Should I plug my services aggressively?

The ideal situation in a radio or television interview, naturally, is for the host to recommend your services–not you. A radio or television host who sees that you are blatantly plugging your own services isn't going to do it for you. Wait a moment at the beginning of the interview to see if the host is going to recommend your services to the audience. If the host doesn't do this, you need to kick into gear. But do it with finesse. Don't sound like an advertising pitchman, but work your service in with subtlety. For example, "Any good

Small businesses in a local area can publicize effectively in a local newspaper.

ATTRACTING CLIENTS WITH FREE PUBLICITY

consultant typically spends more time in analyzing the problem than in proposing the solution. At XYZ Consulting, we've determined that we spend an average of four man-days of preparation and analysis, for every two days spent on solutions proposals." You've mentioned your company's name and service without being overbearing, and you've even given the impression that you have significant experience in and knowledge of your field.

What's the big difference between radio and television interviews?

Generally, it is a lot easier to obtain radio features for your consulting practice than television features. In either case, you need to find an appropriate feature show. For example, if you are in the home repair business, try a handyman show, if you are a nutritionist, find a cooking show, if you are software developer, find a computer show. Maybe you can come up with a good reason why you should be interviewed on a public service show. Or you can try to tie your story in to a recent news event. Just remember, television, except for local cable stations, generally offers fewer opportunities for local guests, the competition for interviews is high, and your likelihood of obtaining publicity through this venue isn't as high as it will be through radio.

Radio interviews are easier to obtain than television interviews.

During a radio interview, you need to focus on repeating the name of your consulting practice and services more often than you would on television. People who listen to radio are typically in their cars channel surfing or listening with only half an ear while negotiating traffic. Television viewers, on the other hand, are generally captive to the programs they are watching.

Radio hosts, on the whole, tend to choose interview topics that are of personal interest to them or are, in their opinion, of value to their listeners. Prepare carefully for a radio interview so that you can maintain the attention of your host. Television hosts, however, are driven by audience ratings–how they are perceived as personalities–and their chances of moving up in the world of television hosting. They will not be as concerned with the intricacies of your particular consulting practice. But it is always wise to be well prepared.

How should I handle newspaper interviews?

ATTRACTING CLIENTS WITH FREE PUBLICITY

Newspaper writers like to feel that they are making a discovery for their readers, not promoting your business. Most newspaper writers hate to write puff pieces on business services. Some, but by no means all, think of themselves as soon-to-be-discovered Pulitzer Prize winners.

Don't plug your services or engage in any hyperbole with a newspaper journalist. Stick to the facts and let them "discover" and develop the story. Let them ask their questions first. After they are done, try to add a summation. Mention a few important points about your business or product that they may have overlooked.

Do I have to sound like a polished pro on radio or TV?

Not at all. I've done numerous radio and TV shows, and I don't have a perfect broadcast voice or smooth intonations. You don't have to be an actor or a radio announcer—just being an expert in *your* business is what is important.

I'm nervous about being on the radio or on TV. What can I do?

Do lots of shows and any nervousness will fade away. I was especially nervous when I did my first television show locally, and when I first went on national television. But after you've done a bunch of shows they become old hat. I actually began to really enjoy interacting with media people.

Public seminars are other effective venues for publicity.

OTHER PUBLICITY OPTIONS

There are other options open to a consultant which are relatively low cost, yet are extremely effective in getting you and your consulting practice before the public. You may want to offer some of these options free of charge, depending on the publicity benefit to you.

Seminars and Workshops

Seminars and workshops can be extremely effective publicity generators either through a corporate meeting or by means of public seminars. Many financial consultants conduct public seminars (at attractive prices) or get themselves aligned with the adult educational services of colleges and universities in their areas. These educational institutions are looking for additional sources of revenues and

ATTRACTING CLIENTS WITH FREE PUBLICITY

Seminars increase the public awareness of your services, while helping you to hone your services.

have facilities readily available in the evening hours. Typically, these seminars and workshops are offered on a revenue-sharing basis.

Many professional organizations also sponsor workshop-related revenue-sharing opportunities for consultants. For example, those involved with sales and marketing consulting in New England may want to consider working with Sales and Marketing Executives of Greater Boston to conduct half-day seminars in their area of expertise. Your name and expertise becomes known to the SME membership through the mailings they send out, and your reputation in the corporate world is enhanced by the successes you achieve.

A third possibility to consider is to offer a brief seminar or workshop to corporations in your target market at a reduced fee. You'll want to do this locally or coordinate multiple seminars in a given geographical area to keep your costs down.

Seminars increase the awareness of your capabilities to the people in your target market. Your credibility as described in the biographical information you may be asked to submit is enhanced. These seminars and workshops also allow you to hone the presentation of the capabilities you offer, making you more effective in selling situations.

E-MAIL

More of a communications option than a publicity-enhancer, e-mail is becoming increasingly important as a means of getting through to decision makers in your target market area. The newness of fax marketing has worn off, and this medium has been so abused that many people believe that faxes fall into the category of junk mail.

Many companies have their own interface to the World Wide Web—and their own Web site address. Some companies will provide the e-mail addresses for names you request—or you can attempt a first initial and last name combination to attempt to get through (jwillaims@encore.com). Experiment with the e-mail option if you've been unsuccessful in getting phone calls returned, and use it regularly to keep in touch with your existing clients and support resources.

ATTRACTING CLIENTS WITH FREE PUBLICITY

INTERNET MARKETING

The Internet, commonly referred to as the Information Superhighway, is an interconnected group of computers linking businesses, government, and academia. Although a precise count of subscribers to the Internet is impossible to calculate, a good guess would place the number at approximately thirty million and growing daily.

MARKETING THROUGH A HOME PAGE

Marketing your services on the "Net" is relatively easy and inexpensive. A graphical user interface, such as Mosaic, allows potential customers to access the World Wide Web. The Web is a part of the Internet. One click can take a potential customer to a screen that has been created by your business. This type of screen is called a Home Page.

A Home Page resides at a particular place on the Internet that has a specific address. You can use a Home Page to promote your business with text, graphics, sound, and video. You can provide pointers as well. Pointers highlight text and act as navigational tools. Clicking on a pointer will take your potential client to additional information within your Web site that might provide important product and ordering details, for instance.

To set up a Home Page for your business, you can hire an outside consultant who specializes in assisting small businesses in creating Home Pages for the World Wide Web. Contact your local computer user group or local Internet service provider for the names and numbers of qualified consultants.

The Internet and the World Wide Web are growing advertising media.

DESIGNING YOUR HOME PAGE

Your Home Page should provide specific information about your consulting practice and the services you offer. It should be fun for your potential clients to view and use. Include interesting photos and/or entertaining videos that will gain and hold a potential client's attention. Try to create a Home Page that creates interest about your services so that the prospect will want to learn more.

ATTRACTING CLIENTS WITH FREE PUBLICITY

If you anticipate that the typical prospect will have questions or would like to receive information about your consulting practice through the mail, you can provide a pointer that takes them to your electronic mailbox. Through the mailbox, an interested prospect can leave a message for your response. Your prospects should also be able to come away from your Home Page with an understanding of the capabilities you offer and a sense of your Unique Selling Proposition.

WALK BEFORE YOU RUN

A lot of companies have invested huge amounts of money into building elaborate Web sites and have been nevertheless disappointed with the resulting sales. Other firms have spent little money, built simple sites, and generated strong sales. Be sure to test a simple Web site before you "bet your business" on this tricky area.

Test simple web sites before you plunge headlong into this tricky media.

SPEECHES

If your public speaking skills are adequate, get sponsored and featured at professional society meetings. If you're not a reasonably good public speaker, drop this idea. The reason is that if people are not interested in something you've written, they quit reading it—no harm done. But if you bore an audience of your potential customers, you may have hurt your chances of doing business.

If you're a star—join the National Speakers Bureau. If not, here are some suggestions:

- Join a professional speaking organization, such as Toastmasters. They provide an excellent forum for developing your speaking skills.

ATTRACTING CLIENTS WITH FREE PUBLICITY

- Get speaking engagements at groups in your area to test a full-blown speech in a public situation. These groups do not have to be in your target market (Rotary Clubs and Kiwanis are usually looking for speakers).
- Record your speeches. With the permission of the groups you address, audio and video tape these speeches. This will provide you with feedback for improvement, as well as some tapes that are suitable to send to the professional societies where you really want your speaking engagements.

Authoring articles in areas of your expertise is the best way to get known and provide valuable reprints for potential clients to see.

Writing Articles

Having articles authored by you published is one of the best ways to get known. It's cost-effective, requires a minimum of time, and gets your name before the readership of the publications they appear in. The major benefit of having articles published is you can often use reprints in your marketing and sales collateral. Your prospects may not have read the article when it came out, but he or she will notice it when you include it as part of your sales information package.

Let's face it, *Business Week* is not going to publish your article if you have not established a reputation as a writer. Start with smaller local and regional publications. This will enable you to become better known in your local area, will help you develop your writing skills as a result of the feedback you get, and will give you the raw material for article reprints. Typically, publishers will either give you permission to reprint or they will provide you with the reprints at a modest fee.

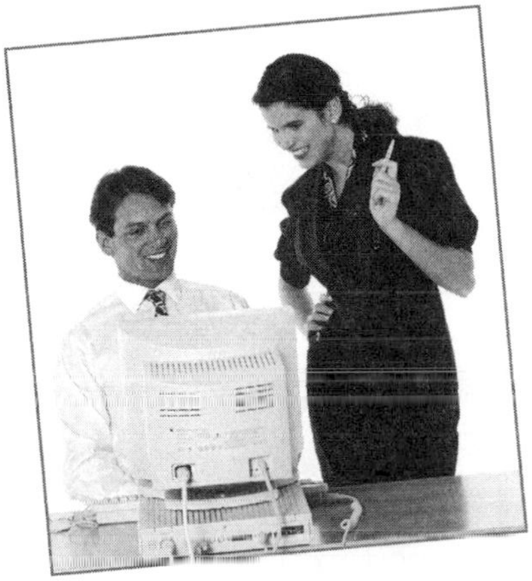

CHAPTER 6

PRICING YOUR SERVICES

Prices in the consulting world are wide-ranged and all too often determined without any sense or sensibility. Here you'll learn different criteria for determining your pricing structure and the pro's and con's of different pricing strategies. A few minutes spent on pricing can make a huge difference in your income.

In the consulting world, one of the greatest variations is in pricing. None of the market niches you serve have any set norms. I've walked away from assignments because I couldn't live with the price the client would pay, and consultants with similar capabilities were glad to get the assignment at the lower price. The prices you charge depend on three factors:

- Your perceived capability to deliver results
- The lifestyle you want
- What the market will bear

These three factors determine what you're going to earn from your consulting practice. How you set your prices is the foundation for your financial success. You level-set the expectations of your clients and potential clients. As you grow the number of assignments you are handling, your income benefits in proportion. If you begin working for peanuts and don't put the value on your work that it deserves, you'll have a hard time significantly increasing your prices in the future. Let's examine the three pricing factors.

Ability to Deliver Results

Perception is everything. Your perceived value depends on how your prospects evaluate:

- The industry reputation that you developed when you were in corporate life
- The reputation of your consulting practice
- Testimonials and referrals

PRICING YOUR SERVICES

Your reputation travels quickly, whether it be good or bad, through the industry network.

One of the benefits of a successful consulting practice is the money you can make.

1. **Industry reputation**
   While you were in corporate life, you developed a reputation for the results you produced. Any resumes you wrote in your career probably mentioned the specific results you were responsible for–such as cutting costs by twenty percent, increasing net income by fifteen percent, or increasing sales by thirty-eight percent. What you accomplished in corporate life created your industry reputation. You are remembered not only by the firms that you worked for, but also by the people that worked as competitors and associates in the industry that you served.
2. **Reputation from your consulting practice**
   News travels fast–and bad news travels faster in the consulting world. When you've done an exceptionally good job for a client, word gets around. People in the same industry talk to each other and have a good word-of-mouth network that operates among the participants. It doesn't matter if it's the paper industry, the simulation industry, or the health care industry. The reputation of the consultant is informally broadcast throughout the network over time.
3. **Testimonials and referrals**
   Get your clients to refer your services to others. Have them do this with a letter or through a referral they'll provide you over the phone. When they communicate to others the results you've accomplished for them and how satisfied they are, you have the best advertising around.

THE LIFESTYLE YOU WANT

You may have started your consulting business to provide a lifestyle for yourself and your family. The money you make is one of the benefits of operating a successful consulting practice. Here is a short list of items to consider:

- The salary or income that you can take from your consulting practice
- The operating expenses of your business
- Gaps between assignments

PRICING YOUR SERVICES

1. **Salary/income**
   Do you have a lifestyle built upon what you earned in corporate life? Let's suppose that income was around $80,000 per year. What wasn't shown on your W-2 were the expenses paid by your employer. These included holidays, days off, medical leave, medical plans, and the employer portion of the FICA tax. In order to duplicate a salary of $80,000, recognize that any benefits provided by the company were somewhere between twenty and thirty percent of your gross salary. Your consulting income should be about $100,000 to cover the salary plus the benefits that used to be paid by your employer.
2. **Operating expenses**
   In corporate life, your employer took care of your operating expenses–office space, furniture, computer equipment, telephone, travel, and entertainment. Now, you're paying for these items. These are the expenses of running your business. Many consultants don't realistically consider operating expenses, and this leads to financial difficulties. Adding marketing to the list could increase your operating expenses to $30,000 per year.

   In order to attain the lifestyle that you had in corporate life, your gross income would have to be around $130,000. Dividing $130,000 by 220 working days per year gives a minimum consulting rate of roughly $590 per day.
3. **Gaps between assignments**
   Let's face it. You're not going to work all of those 220 available working days per year. The vast majority of consultants experience gaps in their income. Assignments dry up, and it takes time to close some new ones that are in the pipeline. Many consultants try to hedge on this bet by keeping multiple clients active at one time. This is an excellent idea, but when one of the clients falls by the wayside, your income can be adversely affected.

   Plan for the gaps. Include in estimating the price for your services provision for the gaps. Many consultants

Though your practice may gross high fees, you must take into consideration expenses and benefits that lower your net income.

PRICING YOUR SERVICES

spend as much as twenty-five percent of their time on marketing (when you are first starting out it could be as much as 50 to 100 percent, but using this in your price model may price you out of the market). In the example we are using, let's assume the income gap at $20,000 per year. Your salary, benefits, operating expenses, and provision for gaps brings the total income to $150,000. Your pricing is now in the area of $750/day to maintain the lifestyle you had as an employee.

WHAT THE MARKET WILL BEAR

What your consulting clients will pay for your services depends on four factors.

Your prices should reflect the industry served, as well as the perceived value of your services.

- The industry served
- The perceived value of your services
- Competitors' consulting fees
- The position of the decision maker for your services

1. **The industry**

   The compensation for consultants in different industries varies widely by a factor of at least five. At the low end of this scale are consultants to secondary education and outplacement services. Rates there can be as low as $400–500 per day. At the high end of the scale are technical, management, and marketing consulting for major corporations. In these examples, the perceived value of the consultant's capabilities are higher. Fees could range from $750 per day up to $2,500 per day and beyond, depending on the company, the task that needs to be performed, and the industry.
2. **The perceived value of your services**

   People pay for perceived value, and the perceived value of your services directly impacts your fee schedule. If it's for a mundane task, or if you don't have the requisite skills or industry reputation, then your fee schedule will be somewhat less. You may be asked to accept assignments where you have no prior experience for a bit less in order to gain the experience and reputation in that type of work.

3. **Competition**
   In the consulting world as in any other business, people look at what the competition charges. If your rates are wildly out of line–and that can be either too low or too high–they'll be suspect, and you'll be far less likely to win the business.
4. **Position of the decision-maker**
   A Director of Education for a secondary school system has less economic clout than a CEO of a billion dollar corporation. This relates to the fees that can be paid to consultants. Two things come into play, the amount of budget available and the income level of the key decision-maker.

   If the amount you want the decision maker to pay you is considerably higher than his or her salary, your ability to get the fee that you would like is limited. There's a leveling effect in the consulting business that says that the consultant's fees are limited by the salary of the person deciding to use their services.

Your rates should be comparable with those of your competition.

TYPES OF FEES

There are various ways that you can charge for services:

- Hourly
- Daily
- Weekly or longer term commitments
- Project fees
- Payment for results

Hourly and daily fees may make a client more reluctant to use your services.

Hourly and Daily Fees

We've talked about the calculation of daily fees and how that relates to the income that you'd like to achieve and the ability of your clients to pay for your lifestyle. Hourly and daily fees in some industries can be self-limiting. They're viewed by the user as a time for money exchange, and many users are reluctant to call their consultants because the money clock starts ticking and they have to start paying.

PRICING YOUR SERVICES

I have daily rates in my fee schedule because it's expected in my business–a potential client wants to make sure my published prices are not out of line. However, I much prefer a partnership with the client that allows me to quote on a project or a results fee basis.

WEEKLY OR LONGER TERM COMMITMENTS

Weekly rates are charged for projects that last from a week to a month or longer.

Some consultants charge by the week instead of by the day. The projects they typically work on may require that their services be available for a week or for a month–perhaps even longer if the consultant is serving as a temporary executive for example. Again, your fees are dependent upon the perceived value of the services rendered and the income level of the decision-maker. I once consulted to a company where my fee schedule was somewhat higher than the salaries of the CEO and the corporate officers. I filled in for three months as a "temp" VP of Sales and Marketing. In almost every staff meeting, the expense associated with my fee was brought into question. It goes back to the company's unwillingness to pay you more than they're paying their own top people.

PROJECT FEES

I recommend that you price your services as project fees, whenever possible. Do this when the client's issues are well-defined and you can correspondingly propose a well-defined set of services for the consulting assignment. The client then understands exactly what they are getting for the project fee quoted.

By charging project fees, you are able to give the client a well-defined service schedule.

If you are efficient in your efforts, you can price project consulting that provides you with an income higher than your quoted fee schedule. That's a "maybe" because of some surprises you may encounter in accomplishing the tasks you proposed as part of the client's Statement of Work.

PAYMENT FOR RESULTS

Sometimes, a consulting opportunity will allow you to directly impact the bottom line of your client. In other words, what you accomplish means more profit to them or less cost. In these cases

PRICING YOUR SERVICES

you may be able to price your services based on the results that you obtain. When the price of your services is relatively small compared to the financial benefits, you have the possibility of charging a fee substantially higher than your daily or weekly rate.

> Despite the risk of non-payment, charging fees on results can gain significantly more revenue than project fees.

Four conditions must be in place:

1. You understand in depth the prospect's needs and the effect your services have on heir bottom line.
2. You possess the capability to deliver those services in a cost-effective manner.
3. The prospect has the confidence in your ability to deliver on the results desired.
4. You can live with non-payment if you don't achieve the desired results.

Non-payment? Yes. Because if you are charging a premium for your services on a money-back guarantee basis, the prospect has no risk in the transaction other than the time that they have spent with you. That removal of risk from the equation allows you to charge a premium for your services. It also opens the door for guarantees and the possibility that you may not be successful. Therefore, only take results-guaranteed projects when you are totally confident you can make results happen.

SETTING YOUR FEES

Relative Income Levels

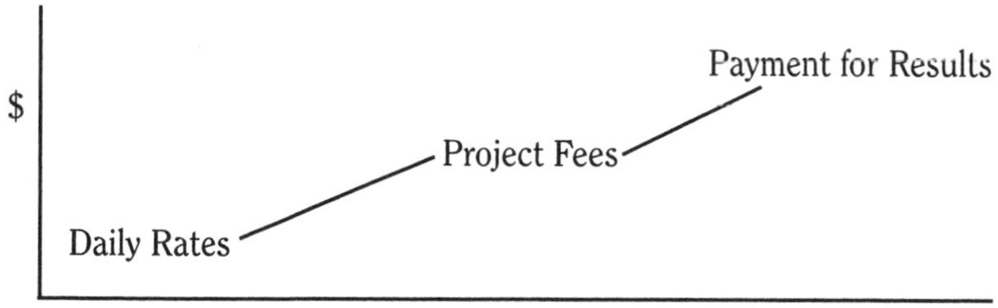

PRICING YOUR SERVICES

Here's a quick way to project your net income.

1. Multiply hourly rate × maximum possible billable hours	$125,000
2. Subtract time between assignments × billable rate	$ 12,500
3. Subtract operating expenses	$ 12,500
4. Subtract benefits	$ 30,250
Projected net income (before taxes)	$ 69,750

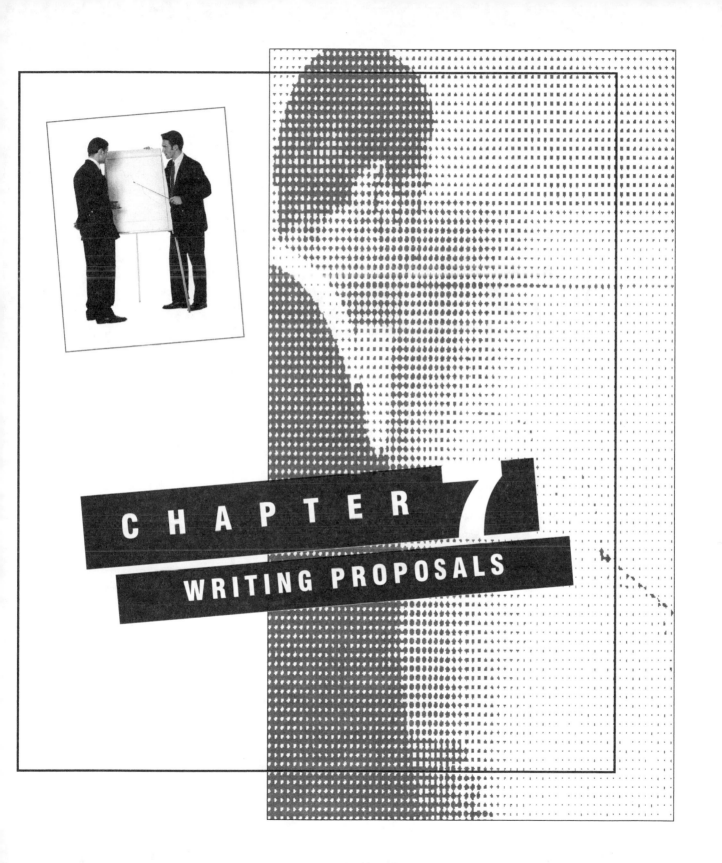

CHAPTER 7

WRITING PROPOSALS

The growth and develop
ment of the modern econom
c world h n identifie
most with high
volu roduced
stand ducts an
servi aditiona
conce ction wa
carrie nagemer
and characterized by aut
cratic management practic

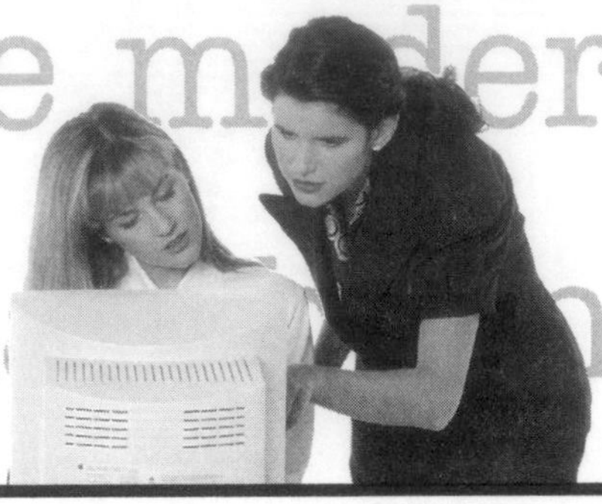

Proposals take all kinds of different forms and to really succeed at consulting you should be versatile at writing a number of different types of proposals. This chapter shows you how to write different types of proposals by taking you step-by-step through the process and includes templates and examples of successful proposals.

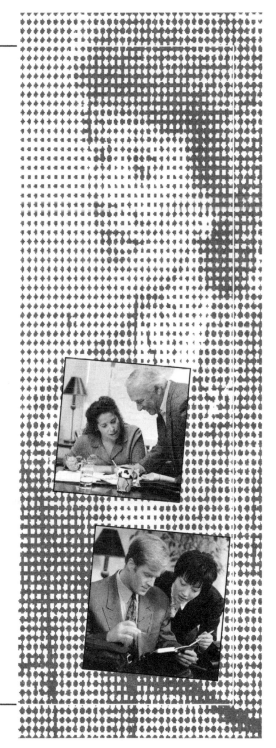

Proposals are an essential part of your job as a consultant. The quality of your proposals directly affects the success of your consulting practice. Proposals provide your prospective clients with a document that enables them to evaluate you, your competence, and your capabilities for successfully accomplishing a consulting assignment. Designed properly, proposals can be a powerful and effective sales tool.

Proposals are time-intensive, and they can consume a major part of a consultant's marketing effort. Shortcuts don't work. Stating your daily fee in a cover letter and including some of your promotional material does not constitute a selling document. A proposal must show your prospects that you understand their issues and showcase your capabilities to handle each and every one of their requirements. Your proposal should provide enough information–and only enough information–so that the client understands that you can effectively handle the assignment. Instead of providing detailed solutions, outline your approach to their issues and describe the unique capabilities you will bring to the project.

Don't give away the store in your proposal. Because of your past experience in corporate life, a complete solution to a client's issues may come to mind. Be careful not to share too many of the details of your solution in the proposal. You would be giving away for free the value that you bring to that potential client. If you disclose all of your approaches, information, and solutions in the proposal, the client may well decide to solve his or her own problems.

WRITING PROPOSALS

Proposals are an important way to prove to a client that you can effectively handle the assignment.

Many times the best proposal is no proposal at all. These situations can arise when you are working with an existing client and you have established a good consultant-client relationship over a period of time. The client may verbally ask you to continue working on a project or to extend an existing consulting agreement already in place.

In some cases your proposal may consist of a letter confirming your agreement to provide services that you have verbally agreed to with a client. This situation also presupposes that a trusting relationship exists and that the letter provides enough information for the client to proceed.

DEVELOPING A PROPOSAL

LETTER PROPOSALS

Letter proposals are the easiest way to gain more business through past clients.

Simple letter proposals are appropriate for many opportunities. These could be smaller consulting assignments for $10,000 or less. A letter proposal may suffice when the client is an existing customer and is already familiar with your work or when you've met with a new potential client and have come to agreement on the scope of your services required to satisfy the client's issues. Typically, all that may be required is a letter of transmittal and a brief one- or two-page description of the services you will provide. The letter is usually to confirm agreements and provide documentation for his or her records.

This is by far the easiest approach to booking additional business. The letter simply states what the client has agreed to as a result of your discussion with him or her. I use this confirmation letter most often in my consulting practice. In addition to confirming the client's decision to go ahead with your services, it also sets their expectations and provides a basis for your invoices.

The following example is for a training assignment for one of my clients. The name of the client has been changed to respect their privacy, but the approach is otherwise verbatim.

WRITING PROPOSALS

SalesWinners
INCORPORATED

June 7, 1997

Mr. Fred Johnson
Vice President - Development
Accolade Systems, Inc.
5400 Lyndon Lane
Sarasota, FL 34243

Dear Fred:

It was good meeting with you this past Friday. On the basis of your inputs, I have made revisions to the agenda for the customer support. These reflect eliciting from the participants 'Five things they need to have to get their jobs done more effectively' as part of the Accolade Systems environment in the Relationship Building module, as well as customer feedback on requested enhancements–plus some tuning to the words to reflect customer support instead of sales.

The date we agreed upon for the meeting is Saturday, July 16. The price for conducting the meeting is $3,000 plus expenses. This includes the services of Bob Smith and myself. Expenses should be minimal because we will be driving over from Ft. Lauderdale on Friday evening. The estimated mileage, food and lodging costs are $350. Payment is net 10 days after invoice.

We are looking forward to our session for your people in July. Should you have any additional inputs or suggestions, please call me at 555-752-7878, and I'll make sure we incorporate them.

Sincerely,

F. David Kintler

F. David Kintler
President

▪ 2139 University Drive ▪ Suite 425 ▪ Coral Springs, FL 33071 ▪ 555.752.7878 ▪

WRITING PROPOSALS

Unsolicited and informal proposals are good ways to outline your services to clients.

UNSOLICITED PROPOSALS/VERBAL REQUESTS FOR A PROPOSAL

Developing unsolicited proposals and responding to informal verbal requests for proposals can be invaluable in helping you accelerate the growth of your consulting practice. Most of the business projects that I have closed over the past six years have resulted from these types of proposals. This approach works to your advantage with existing clients or with potential clients where you have an existing contact because of a prior business relationship.

A major benefit of proposals is that clients may let a sole source contract to you for your services. In other words, you will be the only one they talk to and contract with for the services outlined in your unsolicited proposal. If a formal Request for a Proposal (RFP) is issued–and they liked your unsolicited proposal–chances are that many of the items that you mentioned in your unsolicited proposal will be contained in the RFP. This could well provide you with a much better chance of winning the assignment when the decision is made.

Factors to consider in creating an unsolicited proposal or responding to an informal request for a proposal are:

1. A relationship exists between you and the client.
2. You truly understand the issues that client is facing.
3. You have an approach or a solution in mind that will resolve the client's issues in a cost-effective manner.
4. The client will seriously consider your unsolicited proposal.

Existing relationship

Trust is an invaluable commodity. When you have an existing, trusting relationship with your client, that relationship can help set the stage for the acceptance of an unsolicited proposal.

Understanding the issues

You should understand all of the important issues impacting the client. Additionally, you should be aware of peripheral issues. For example, if the issue is sales productivity, you may want to consider the competitive pressures the client is facing, changes taking place in the business climate, and the client's organizational dynamics.

Have an approach in mind

Possessing specific knowledge and knowing how to apply your skill provides the basis for your approach. For example, you may become involved with a project involving competitive positioning. Your understanding of technology and the competitive products in an industry served by your client can be invaluable in helping them to better position their products and train their sales force.

Your knowledge of the issues at hand and your ability to apply that knowledge form the basis of your approach.

Willingness to consider your proposal

When considering whether to develop an unsolicited proposal, make sure your contact (or contacts) have a sincere interest and can gain the approval from their organization to proceed.

Structuring Your Proposal

How you approach writing your proposal can make a major difference in the percentage of proposals you generate that result in business for your consulting practice. In other words, your hit rate goes up when you do it right. Doing it right means that your proposal directly addresses the business issues of the client—the bottom line. Because people buy from people, you may also want to consider the aspect of personal gain.

Personal gain

Personal gain is the benefit that people who use your services will realize as a result of the successful conclusion of your consulting assignment. While personal gain or benefit has many dimensions and directions, here are four possibilities:

- Being a hero for getting the job done
- Receiving accolades for selecting the right consulting firm
- Making a politically correct decision
- Keeping his or her job

Your success as a consultant gives the client a sense of personal achievement.

As you develop your proposal, make sure you have fully considered and addressed both personal benefits and company results. This

WRITING PROPOSALS

> To get good results, you have to thoroughly analyze the client's issues and suggest feasible solutions.

combination of corporate results and personal gain is an unbeatable one in the consulting world as well as in other areas.

Getting results

Since starting my consulting practice six years ago, I have been using a simple model to quickly analyze a potential client's issues and to effectively suggest approaches that result in business success. Businesses place a high value upon a consultant's understanding of the issues associated with their current situation. You must understand where they want to go–their desired results–so that you can propose useful approaches to help them achieve those results.

That means really analyzing the facts associated with their current condition and designing actions for each one of those facts. This analysis provides the basis for formulating a combination of action plans, approaches, and plans to help them meet their objectives.

Here are the five steps to follow to get results:

1. Determine the client's current situation (A).
2. Determine their objectives or goals–their future desired outcome (B)
3. Determine how you (or your consulting practice) get them from (A) to (B)
4. Determine the personal factors for those responsible for the decision.
5. Write the proposal focusing on results and appeal to the personal factors of the decision makers.

> The proposal should focus on the anticipated results of your services and appeal to the client's personal needs.

Guidelines for Winning Proposals

You can use several approaches and methods to increase the number of assignments you close. How you structure your approach with the client and package your proposal are prime factors in the client selecting you rather than someone else. Here are some factors to consider:

1. Have an inside sponsor. Develop an ally within the client organization who will sponsor you as the consultant of choice for the assignment being considered.

WRITING PROPOSALS

2. Meet with the client before you submit any proposal. This will enable you to develop greater insight into the client's situation. You will also be building a relationship based on trust.
3. Participate in shaping the client's requirements. The approach and methods you introduce may influence the client to request skills, abilities, and knowledge that only you can bring to the situation.
4. Provide specific deliverables and schedules for those deliverables. This level of detail shows that you have thought through the proposal request in depth. As a by-product, you help shape their expectations and build their confidence in your ability to deliver on schedule.
5. Quote the project cost–not the daily rate–unless the client prefers otherwise. Clients are interested in the bottom line–what will it cost him or her to resolve a current business challenge. Estimates using daily rates do not provide bottom line costs–estimates also introduce uncertainty.
6. Present the proposal. Your chances of winning increase considerably if you can present the proposal to the client. The presentation interaction allows you to present your approach in the most favorable light. During the presentation, you have the invaluable opportunity to interact with the client, and uncover and resolve any open issues.

Presenting a written proposal directly to the client significantly increases your chance for their business.

REAL-WORLD EXAMPLE

Let's take as an example my first consulting assignment. I knew the Vice President of Sales for a competing computer systems company, and we had become good friends over the years.

As a result of competing with him and understanding the industry, I was familiar with his company and the issues they were facing. I also knew that I had knowledge, experience, and capabilities that could help him resolve some of the issues that were troubling him in his current situation. Although I will not mention the name of the company, I will describe the issues they faced, and how I designed an approach that was accepted by them.

WRITING PROPOSALS

A successful consultant takes the situation and finds a feasible solution within the desired guidelines of the client.

The Current Situation (A)

The following factors were present in the current situation:

1. There was a lack of product positioning for a new product that they had announced six months earlier.
2. His sales force had limited knowledge of the competitive strengths and weaknesses of the new product versus other offerings on the market.
3. He needed to hire some additional people to help grow the business.

With these factors in mind, I talked to the client about what he would like to achieve. Primarily, he needed to make his orders, revenues, and targets and relieve some of the pressures that were being brought upon him by the CEO of the company.

Desired Results (B)

The desired results he needed to obtain in order of priority were to:

1. Arm the sales force with the information they needed to better position the new product against their cheap competitors in this market.
2. Improve the orders and revenue flow for the new product.
3. Hire two new people.

Getting from (A) to (B)

As a result of knowing the current condition and knowing what the client wanted to accomplish, I wrote an unsolicited proposal for the following:

1. Create new product positioning tools for the field sales force.
2. Conduct competitive analysis against major competitors.
3. Help him recruit additional personnel.

WRITING PROPOSALS

PERSONAL FACTORS

As mentioned previously, the prime personal factor was to improve sales results in competitive situations and to relieve some top-down pressure.

DEVELOP THE PROPOSAL

I provided an unsolicited proposal to the Vice President of Sales and the CEO resulting in my first consulting contract for $25,000. This was for the competitive analysis effort which was the toughest issue of the three for the VP of Sales, and it could not be easily accomplished with the client's internal resources. Following is the sheet I used as a basis for my unsolicited proposal.

WRITING PROPOSALS

XYZ CORPORATION: OCTOBER 23, 1997

SalesWinners Solutions to Increase XYZ Orders and Revenues

1. **Product Sales Positioning**
   Develop sales tools to assist the XYZ Sales Force to position the D-2000 computer systems to protect and grow revenues in the XYZ installed base:
   - Sales Tools promoting protection of software investment
   - Trade-in sales programs
   - Maintenance revenue sales programs (hardware and software)
2. **Competitive Analysis**
   Design sales tools that the XYZ Sales Force can effectively use to win new program business from competitors
   - Provide an in-depth comparison of the XYZ D-2000 product line against the four top competitors in its market.
   - Develop a competitive sales review of factors other than product issues which relate to prospective customers buying decisions (e.g., management, financial data, organization, and support). This sales review will be designed to effectively position XYZ against competitors.
   - Develop overhead sales presentations designed to show XYZ to advantage over their traditional competitors.
   - Provide Life Cycle cost sales positioning against board set vendors (including a white paper and presentation for use by the XYZ sales force).
3. **Recruiting and Training**
   - Bring for XYZ Sales Management's review, qualified sales and analyst candidates who can help build XYZ's orders and revenues. In addition, help sell desired candidates on the benefits of joining XYZ.
   - Design and tailor a sales training seminar for the XYZ sales force. Sales training modules will be designed to position XYZ sales personnel to achieve wins at the expense of their competitors.

HANDLING A FORMAL REQUEST FOR PROPOSAL

RFPs AND RESPONSES

I believe that letter proposals, unsolicited proposals, and responses to verbal requests for proposals are most likely to be your main area for consulting practice business growth. From time-to-time you may receive a formal RFP. Request for Proposals (RFPs) are typically highly detailed, formal documents that contains the following items:

1. Cover letter
2. Background information on the client company
3. A description of the client's issues and why consulting services are required
4. A detailed statement of work that describes the scope of work requested
5. The client's terms and conditions

Formal requests for proposals are highly detailed and require more effort than a simple letter proposal.

The extent of your proposal effort depends on the magnitude of the scope of work described by the RFP.

A challenging (and most likely, not winnable) proposal situation is when you receive a request for a proposal five days before the bid is due. You have had no face-to-face contact with the potential client, nor do you know anyone in that organization who may be able to provide you insight into the issues. To make matters worse, you cannot schedule an appointment with the client before the proposal is due.

WRITING PROPOSALS

Since your audience can vary greatly, it's important to customize your proposal to the client's specific needs.

Formal RFP Responses

For larger projects, proposal generation requires more effort than a simple letter proposal. Clients typically expect:

1. A letter of transmittal
2. A proposal overview
3. A detailed response to the client's statement of work
4. Schedule and pricing

Bidding Major Opportunities

Major bids, those for $100,000 or more, will require additional research and coordination on your part. Large consulting contracts usually call for services beyond the capabilities of an individual consultant. These large RFPs may require you to team with other consultants to provide the resources and total capabilities required.

Major proposal efforts can cost thousands of dollars and a lot of your time. When responding to one of these, qualify the opportunity effectively to assess your chances of winning. Factors you will want to consider include: understanding the client's requirements, possessing insight into the organization, and believing in your capability to propose and perform more effectively than your competitors.

Considering Your Audience

The type of proposal that you will be putting together will also depend on the recipient of the proposal. Consider these factors when writing your proposal:

1. Are you responding to the requirements of a commercial business or a governmental agency?
2. What are the various departmental functions that are involved in deciding upon consulting services?
3. What is the organization's decision-making process, and what are the decision criteria for consulting services?

These questions illustrate why your proposal must specifically tailored for your audience. Your ability to craft a proposal that is custom-tailored to the client's needs will go a long way in helping you to win.

WRITING PROPOSALS

Major differences exist between Requests for Proposals issued by governmental agencies and those issued by companies in the commercial business world. Governmental agencies include state, local, and federal branches of government. Commercial businesses include small businesses, medium-size industrial firms, and large corporate giants. In writing your RFP response, you may want to consider some of the differences between commercial and governmental clients:

Keep in mind that requests for proposals are sometimes used for informational purposes only.

Commercial and Government RFPs

Differences	Commercial	Government
RFP response structure	Format flexible as long as requirements are addressed	Strict adherence to RFP guidelines
Consulting practice reputation	Important	Incidental if a qualified bidder
Consultant proprietary methodology	Can be stolen	Rights carefully observed
Decision criteria solution	Emphasis on results	Most cost-effective
Recover if lost	Typical turn-around sale	Can formally protest and typically won't win

Why Clients Want Proposals

Requests for Proposals stem from a variety of motivations. In your discussions with a potential client about your services, they may say, "Well, just send me a proposal, I'll look it over." That request may be only a thinly veiled way to get you off their back. They are not sincerely interested, and are using their request as a way to end the conversation.

WRITING PROPOSALS

Requests for Proposals are sometimes used to acquire information. Just because a request is made does not mean that the client will contract for the services required. A budget may not be approved or the request may be based on evaluating the potential of a consulting solution. In some rare cases, unscrupulous organizations may be looking for information that they can use to implement their own solutions to the issues described. The message here is to qualify the client's interest before investing your valuable time in writing a proposal.

The vast majority of the time, you will find that clients are serious when they issue an RFP. They need your help in resolving a current business situation, and they do not have the resources, the time, or the short-term capability to resolve their predicament. Some of the things they expect to learn from your response to their proposal request are:

1. Your capabilities–they want to know that you are somebody who can help them
2. The deliverables–they want to know the specific services that you will provide
3. Sufficient information–enough to determine if the approach you are suggesting will help them resolve their current business issues

Most of the time, clients who request a formal proposal are in definite need of a consultant's help.

A proposal can be likened to a written test. You are graded on your ability to understand the current condition described by the proposal and to suggest approaches that will achieve the results desired by the client. You are also graded on how well you express your capability and background and the unique advantages of the approach that you propose to use to help the client.

WHEN TO WALK AWAY

If you responded to every request for proposal that crossed your desk, you could spend most of your time responding to RFPs. You can, by diligently searching documents such as the Commerce Business Daily or your local trade publications, find numerous projects that you can bid upon. I do not recommend this approach. It has been my experience that by the time a formal RFP is issued, it has been written with a specific vendor in mind.

Intuitively, you know that bidding does not mean winning. Most consultants find that building a relationship before providing the proposal dramatically increases their odds of winning. Consider walking away if:

- You have had no prior contact with the firm requesting the proposal
- You lack in-depth knowledge of the issues involved
- There is no way you can differentiate your approach
- The time frame for response is unrealistically short
- The RFP verbiage reflects another consultant's offerings

Avoid your opinions about the situation in your proposal—the facts of the client's situation should be your focus.

When you run across situations like this, you may be better served by pursuing another client. You are committing a lot of time and energy when you say, "I can turn this situation around, even if it's the eleventh hour. I can do a good enough job so that my proposal will win the day." Most likely that's not the case. If they are unwilling to meet with you, if they are unwilling to have you present your proposal, you will probably want to walk away. Only in bids to the government, which require the consultant to remain distanced from the people writing the RFP, would you want to reconsider this guideline.

WRITING WINNING PROPOSALS: A SEVEN-STEP PROCESS

This section is designed to provide you with the tools you need to analyze a client's situation and to write a winning proposal. The available information from a real-world situation will be examined, along with personal and organizational dynamics issues.

The proposal example that follows is derived from my consulting practice. The name of the company, their products, and the names of the individuals involved have been changed to protect their confidentiality. Their requirements also have been reworded slightly for the same reason.

WRITING PROPOSALS

> After analyzing the current situation, develop a solution for the issues at hand.

Before beginning to write your proposal, make sure that you are aware of all of the factors that relate to the client's situation. These include the client's organization, people, and the specifics of the client's requirements. The emphasis is on dealing with facts–not opinions. Facts include what you know and don't know about the situation. Templates are provided for your use, and a completed sample is included.

As background for this consulting assignment, this approach was used with the Industry Marketing Director. We worked with the fourteen specific performance objectives they gave me. We also learned a great deal of information about the client's current situation that is not outlined in those objectives. We agreed upon issues where change was desired and issues where change was essential, and we set actions in place to achieve objectives for each of the important issues, and many of the not-so-important issues.

The first step in the proposal preparation process is to gather essential information to be used as the foundation for building your winning proposal. Two types of situation analyses are conducted. The first deals with the client's specific requirements. The second relates to organizational and personal issues.

After analyzing the client's current situation, you can develop an approach to provide the client with a solution to the issues at hand–meeting the client's performance objectives requirements–and satisfying organizational and personal issues. Next, develop the approach that will produce the desired results. Provide enough information to the client so that they understand how your approach will meet their needs. As you develop your approach, be sure to emphasize areas where you can uniquely provide added value to the client's defined requirements. You do not need to disclose all of the details of your proposed solution.

Next, develop the proposal flow to convey your recommended solution to the client. Use the flow to position your services and win the business. Before you actually put pen to paper (or use your word processor), review a proposal checklist to make sure you have all of the bases covered.

WRITING PROPOSALS

After this preparatory work is complete, write the proposal and, if at all possible, arrange to present it to your client.

Following is a summary of the eight steps to preparing a winning proposal.

Step One: Situation Analysis 1
- Review the client's requirements

Step Two: Situation Analysis 2
- Organization
- Decision criteria
- Personal gain

Step Three: Summarize the Results
- State the major purpose
- Meet the stated requirements
- Satisfy organization/personal issues

Step Four: Develop the Approach
- Outline how requirements will be met
- Describe your added value

Step Five: Develop the Proposal Flow
- Showcase your solution
- Position yourself to win

Step Six: Review the Checklist
- Ensure all of the bases are covered

Step Seven: Write the Proposal
- Review the example
- Use the interactive template

Let's begin the Seven-Step Process by reviewing the client's stated requirements. In this real-world example, eleven other consultants and I were given the list of training objectives shown on the next page. We were verbally requested to develop an approach and pricing to accomplish the stated objectives. My job was to do this and win the business–which I did.

WRITING PROPOSALS

DCDA PERIPHERALS, INC.

1658 McNab Road–Fort Lauderdale, FL 33309–954.555.6600

SPECIFIC NEW HIRE TRAINING COURSE OBJECTIVES APRIL 5, 1997

There are 14 specific performance objectives for the New Hire Sales Training Program. Upon the completion of the New Hire Sales Training Program, the participants will be able to:

1. Use DCDA's corporate capabilities presentation to effectively present DCDA's success story, from both a financial and technology leadership point of view.
2. Translate the features of DCDA's products into benefits for the customer.
3. Competitively position DCDA's products against the competition.
4. Analyze and understand customer requirements and recommend appropriate DCDA solutions.
5. Tell the DCDA quality story and the steps DCDA uses to provide a quality product.
6. Demonstrate an understanding of configuring DCDA's peripheral products for various computer systems manufacturers.
7. Explain DCDA's customer support policies and the training program options available to DCDA customers.
8. Present DCDA's pre-sales technical support capabilities and on-line analysis tools.
9. Describe the key features and clauses in DCDA's contracts.
10. Demonstrate an awareness of the key marketing programs currently available to potential customers.
11. Demonstrate an understanding of computer systems peripherals technology.
12. Correctly configure and price configurations for proposal purposes.
13. Sell effectively to decision makers in DCDA's target markets.
14. Demonstrate an understanding of how to access home office support resources.

WRITING PROPOSALS

In addition to this list of objectives, we were also told that:

1. Currently no new hire sales training course exists.
2. The overall objective is to develop a New Hire Sales Training Program. This will be conducted for the thirty-two sales people and eleven sales support people who have been brought on board in the past year. This course will subsequently be conducted for additional new hires in the sales and support staff and for international distributors.
3. The key deliverables in developing the course are writing a course workbook for the participants and creating an instructor's guide for subsequent training beyond the pilot effort.
4. A key objective is achieving a high rating–a superior evaluation–for the pilot course.
5. The first step (a major factor in selecting a consultant) is to develop a course flow and agenda to maximize the learning experience for the participants.
6. The consultant will work closely with DCDA's Product Marketing staff who will be responsible for providing the raw material for the product portion of the training.
7. Each of the training modules will be designed to be interactive, with time for questions and answers.
8. Evaluation of training effectiveness must be included as part of the course design.
9. The training methodology and course agenda must address DCDA's fourteen Performance Objectives.
10. The new hire training course will be conducted over a three-day period.
11. The deadline for proposal submittal is April 26, 1997. The consulting contract will be in place by May 3, and the first pilot course is scheduled for July 10, 1997.

WRITING PROPOSALS

Step One: Situation Analysis and Actions 1: Client Requirements

Describe the facts that you are able to ascertain about the client's current condition that results from your analysis. Number each fact that you list to ensure that the actions you later plan will help to move the client from their current situation to the desired result. For the factors you don't know, take action now to obtain the information.

For each fact that you list, assign a priority–A, B, C, or U, for:

A = critically important
B = important
C = of low importance
U = uncertain of importance

The Situation Analysis and Action Table (Table 1) provides the foundation data you will need to develop your approach for solving the client's issues. Some of the facts you list may not be relevant. That's OK–you are listing as many as possible to make sure that nothing essential is overlooked. By prioritizing the relative importance of the facts in your analysis, you are ensuring the important ones are addressed.

Table 1: DCDA Peripherals Situation Analysis/Action

No.	Priority	Situation
1	A	The course length is limited to three days.
2	A	There are fourteen different performance objectives.
3	A	Nine weeks are allocated to complete the project.
4	A	Key objectives are: • course book and instructor's guide • high evaluation of initial pilot program
5	A	Product marketing resources will be available for product information.
6	A	The course flow must be optimal for the participants to learn.
7	C	The pilot program takes place after the 4th of July weekend.
8	A	I don't know the DCDA decision process or who my competitors are.
9	A	I don't know the budget available.
10	A	I don't know the organizational requirements or the personalities involved in the decision.

Comments

Considering the information that you had, would you be willing to spend your time and effort to generate a proposal? Probably not–you do not currently understand the process that DCDA will use to make their decision. You also have no knowledge of the players involved and their influence. Before proceeding further, you may want to schedule a sales call to determine their organizational requirements, their decision criteria, and the personal benefits involved.

Step Two: Situation Analysis and Actions 2: Organization, Criteria, and People

Organizational requirements

Organizational requirements include the client's motivation for going outside for consulting services. Do you know the motivation behind the requirements that were given to you? Understanding these motivational factors is essential.

Decision criteria

Decision criteria are how the client evaluates your capabilities. What capabilities do you need to have–or emphasize–to meet those criteria? Another decision criteria is budget–can you afford to do the project for the funding available? List these facts in Table 2.

Personal benefit

Here we list the "gain and pain" issues of those individuals responsible for selecting consulting services on a specific assignment. List in Table 2 those issues that you believe are most important to the consulting assignment.

List in Table 2 the facts that you are able to learn about the client's current organizational, decision criteria, and people issues. These are facts that you obtain from face-to-face conversations or by telephone. Number each fact to ensure that the approach you later plan will help move the client from their current situation to the desired result. For the facts you do not know, take the actions now to obtain the information.

For each fact that you list, assign a priority–A, B, C, or U:

A = critically important
B = important
C = of low importance
U = uncertain of importance

WRITING PROPOSALS

Table 2: DCDA Peripherals Situation Analysis

1	B	There is no sales training manager on board at the present time.
2	A	The consultant must have a sales background.
3	A	The VP of Sales is set on the July 10 course date. The Third Quarter performance is critically important. The Sales Department is the real customer for this course!
4	B	The VP of Marketing needs a career "win." He is being pressured by the VP of Sales.
5	A	The Industry Marketing Director is the key decision maker and also needs a "win." She is new to the company and wants to make her mark.
6	A	The VP of Sales must approve the consultant chosen.
7	U	They won't reveal the budget for this project.
8	A	Marketing has sales training responsibility, but no resources available to dedicate to this program.
9	U	I was not able to get the names of my competition. I do know that eleven other consultants are bidding.

Step Three: Summarize the Purpose and Objectives

From the information gathered, you have the basis for writing a summary of the results you will provide for your client. This summary could be in narrative form or a bulleted list. Following are two topical areas to consider:

1. A summary of the major purpose of the assignment. This summary can be the major focus in the Executive Summary section of your proposal. You can enhance the persuasive power of this summary by taking into account the organizational, decision criteria, and people issues you have discovered.
2. A summary of the client's specific, detailed objectives. This summarizes the specific objectives called for in the client's Request for Proposal.

In reviewing DCDA's situation, the client's major purpose and specific objectives are listed in Table 3.

Table 3: Client's Major Purpose and Specific Objectives

No.	Major Purpose
1	Measurably improved knowledge and skills for the participants
2	High quality, on-time delivery
3	Cost-effective project implementation

No.	Specific Objectives
1	These are specifically outlined in the fourteen Performance Objectives described in DCDA's Request for Proposal

STEP FOUR: DEVELOP THE APPROACH

In designing your approach, consider all of the factors surrounding the client's current situation and the major objectives to be accomplished. You will want to be confident that your approach will be welcomed by your client. Provide the following elements in creating your approach:

1. Sufficient details about your approach so the client understands and accepts that you will meet the defined requirements
2. Information about the unique qualities that you will bring to this assignment that provide added value to the client and differentiate your offering from the competition.

In the first section of Table 4, describe the particulars of the approach you intend to take in accomplishing the client's objectives. Then list all of the things that you can do to add value in the implementation of your approach.

Fully developing this step was a major factor in my being selected by DCDA Peripherals.

WRITING PROPOSALS

Table 4: Approach Summary and Value Add Items

Approach
Consolidate the fourteen Performance Objectives into four major areas. Design the course flow to address topics so that the sales and support people will:
• learn the most information possible
• participate in interactive learning exercises to reinforce learning throughout the three-day course
Define the following deliverables to meet client requirements:
• Develop the course agenda
• Create pre- and post-testing materials
• Rework existing corporate and product presentations
• Update existing competitive presentations
• Develop new presentations
• Provide speaker notes
• Write instructor's guide
Value-Add
Video tape and audio tape all current presentations for archival back-up and potential future distribution to field personnel
Offer the optional use of an industry expert to assist in the competitive analysis section
Audio tape competitive analysis information from sales reps newly on board from the competition
Offer to conduct the pilot training program (I stand behind my work) and to optionally conduct the training for all of the newly hired sales and support people
Recommend a weekly project review with milestones to be met each week–with the objective of getting the VP of Sales to buy-in at every step in the process

Step Five: Develop the Proposal Flow

The proposal you develop is more than your written commitment to meet requirements–it's a selling document. A well-written proposal guides the client through a series of steps that lead him or her to accept your solution. Developing a good proposal flow helps you to win assignments more often and provides the basis for a formal presentation if you have the opportunity to present your proposal in person to the client.

The proposal writing section that follows uses the flow illustrated in Table 5. Feel free to modify the flow for your proposal to meet the situational needs of your clients. An explanation is provided for each proposal section element. These points are expanded upon and reinforced with the interactive templates provided in this book.

Table 5: Proposal Flow

Item No.	Proposal Section	Description
1	Cover Page	Project/assignment title–including the client's logo if possible.
2	Executive Summary	Begin with the results first. Restate the elements of the major purpose of the consulting assignment.
3	Current Situation	Review the client's current situation and touch on the driving factors for seeking the services of an outside consulting resource.
4	Specific Objectives	List the objectives that support the major objectives that the client wants to attain. This reinforces that you understand their needs and provides some insight into your approach.
5	Deliverables Overview	Tell them what you're going to give them. Describe specifically what the client can expect from you in terms of deliverables.
6	Results Enhancers	Results-enhancer is a client-oriented phrase for the added value you provide. Describe those things you will implement as part the assignment that set you apart from your competition.
7	Pricing	Provide pricing for your services and the terms and conditions for the prices quoted.
Appendix	Brochures, References, and Biography	Provide background information on your consulting practice that relates to the capabilities and experience that you have that can help them achieve the results that they want.

WRITING PROPOSALS

PROPOSAL DEVELOPMENT TEMPLATES

SITUATION ANALYSIS 1: CLIENT REQUIREMENTS

Describe the facts that you are able to ascertain about the client's current condition that results from your analysis of the RFP. Number each fact that you list to ensure that the actions you later plan will help to move the client from their current situation to the desired result.

For each fact that you list, assign a priority–A, B, C, or U:

A = critically important
B = important
C = of low importance
U = uncertain of importance

The Situation Analysis and Action Table (Table 1) provides the foundation data you will need to develop your approach for solving the client's issues. Some of the facts you list may not be relevant. That's OK–you are listing as many as possible to make sure that nothing essential is overlooked. By prioritizing the relative importance of the facts in your analysis, you are ensuring the important ones are addressed.

Table 1: Situation Analysis/Action

No.	Priority	Situation

Situation Analysis 2: Organization, Criteria, and People

List in Table 2 the facts that you are able to learn about the client's current organizational, decision criteria, and people issues. These are facts that you obtain from face-to-face conversations or over the phone. Number each fact to ensure that the actions you later plan will help move the client from their current situation to the desired result.

For each fact that you list, assign a priority–A, B, C, or U:

A = critically important
B = important
C = of low importance
U = uncertain of importance

The Situation Analysis Organization, Criteria, and People provides important data needed to develop your approach for solving the client's issues. Some of the facts you list may not be relevant. But list as many as possible to make sure that nothing essential is overlooked.

**Table 2: Situation Analysis–
Organization, Criteria, and People**

No.	Priority	Situation

WRITING PROPOSALS

SUMMARIZE THE PURPOSE AND OBJECTIVES

From the information gathered, you have the basis for writing a summary of the results you will provide for your client. This summary could be in narrative form or a bulleted list. Following are two topical areas to consider:

1. A summary of the major purpose of the assignment. This summary can be the major focus in the Executive Summary section of your proposal. You can enhance the persuasive power of this summary by taking into account the organizational, decision criteria, and people issues you have discovered.
2. A summary of the client's specific, detailed objectives. This summarizes the specific objectives called for in the client's Request for Proposal.

Table 3: Client's Major Purpose and Specific Objectives

No.	Major Purpose
1	
2	
3	
4	
5	

No.	Specific Objectives
1	
2	
3	
4	
5	
6	
7	
8	

APPROACH SUMMARY AND ADDED VALUE

In designing your approach, consider all of the factors surrounding the client's current situation and the major objectives to be accomplished. You will want to be confident that your approach will welcomed by your client. Provide the following elements in creating your approach:

1. Sufficient details about your approach so the client understands and accepts that you will meet the defined requirements.
2. Information about the unique qualities that you will bring to this assignment that provides added value to the client and differentiates your offering from the competition.

In the first section of Table 4, describe the particulars of the approach you intend to take in accomplishing the client's objectives. Then list all of the things that you can do to add value in the implementation of your approach.

Table 4: Approach Summary and Value Add Items

Approach
Value-Add

WRITING PROPOSALS

STEP SIX: REVIEW THE CHECKLIST

Before beginning to write your proposal, you will want to be certain that all of the bases are covered and that you can effectively position your proposal. The checklist below lists a number of factors for your consideration.

Table 6: Proposal Checklist

- ☐ Do you know the decision makers within the client organization and the influences that affect the decision?
- ☐ Do you adequately understand what the client's needs are and the results required and desired?
- ☐ Can you meet all of the most important objectives stated by the client and a sufficient number of the secondary items to win?
- ☐ Are you sufficiently aware of the organizational and personal factors that will affect the selection of a consultant?
- ☐ Do you know the decision criteria that will be used for selecting the winning consultant?
- ☐ Have you confirmed that you can provide the services required for the budget available?
- ☐ How many other consultants are competing for this assignment, and do you know their strengths and weaknesses?
- ☐ Have you thought through the added-value you can provide to the client with your proposed approach?
- ☐ Can you adequately differentiate your services and value-added from the competition?

STEP SEVEN: WRITE THE PROPOSAL

Writing proposals can take a great deal of time and effort–writing *winning* proposals takes the same amount of time and effort. What's the difference? How you structurally approach your proposal makes the difference between winning and losing.

From your review of the checklist, you have the information required to decide to bid or not to bid. If you have decided you are in a no-bid situation, consider meeting with the client to gather additional information to confirm your decision. The checklist is used to avoid writing proposals that have very little probability of winning and to make sure that you have enough information to win.

The proposal writing process

When you generated the material in the previous sections, you completed the preparation necessary to begin writing your proposal. You've done most of the hard work–the rest is easy. Just go with the flow you have decided upon and use the tools we have provided.

WRITING PROPOSALS

We will take you step-by-step through the interactive templates for each section of the proposal. On the following pages are examples of proposals that won the business. These proposals are typical—and have the following flow:

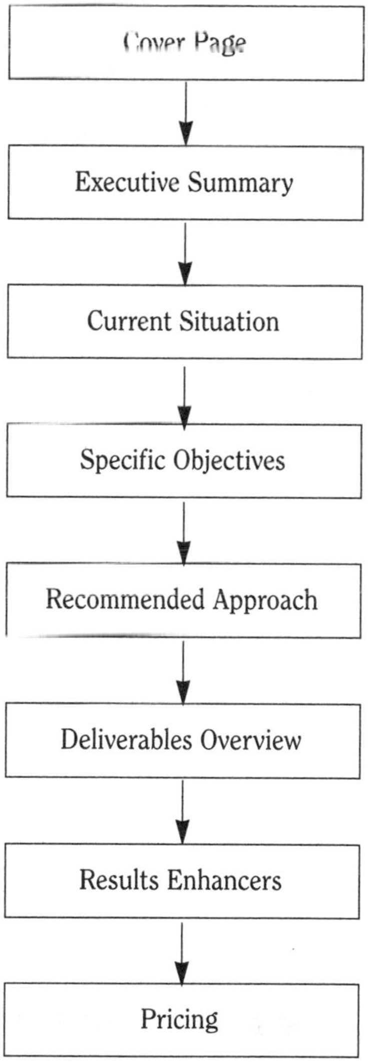

WRITING PROPOSALS

Sample Proposal
Sales Training

Proposal for:

DCDA Peripherals, Inc.

New Hire Sales Training Program

By:

SalesWinners
INCORPORATED

April 25, 1997

WRITING PROPOSALS

Contents

Section	Proposal Topic
I	Executive Summary
II	Current Situation
III	Performance Objectives
IV	The Approach–Achieving the Major Purposes and Specific Performance Objectives
V	Deliverables Overview
VI	Results Enhancers
VII	Pricing

WRITING PROPOSALS

I. EXECUTIVE SUMMARY

This proposal is designed to meet the requirements of DCDA Peripherals to develop a New Hire Sales Training Program by July 10, 1996. This course will be structured to provide a major boost to the new-hire participants, both in terms of their knowledge of DCDA's products and services, and, more importantly, to effectively position DCDA Peripherals to build orders and revenue performance.

The overall objectives of the course are:

1. Measurably improve the participants' knowledge and skills in positioning DCDA's products and services
2. Achieve high quality as determined by the participants–and by DCDA's Sales and Marketing management
3. Provide the course development in a cost-effective manner

These are the major overall objectives. A specific list of Performance Objectives will be met as outlined in the following paragraphs.

II. CURRENT SITUATION

There are four critically important factors affecting the outcome of the proposed training course. First, this project is being outsourced because a Sales Training Manager is not currently on board. Even if one could be interviewed and brought on board in the near term, it is unlikely that the course development work could be completed in the required time frame.

Second, the list of published Performance Objectives is extensive. Therefore, a significant course development is required to make sure that each of the fourteen Performance Objectives are met.

Third, the amount of effort necessary to create the desired deliverables is not trivial. Fortunately, much of the basic presentation material exists. We propose to video tape presentations to shorten the course development time.

Finally, time is short to create a set of deliverables by July 10. Direct, personal effort (no outsourcing except for optional competitive analysis) will ensure the schedule is met. In my opinion, knowledge of your products and your Company operations is a critically important ingredient in designing course curriculum and courseware. Concentrated effort will enable me to get up-to-speed quickly. We're talking about a week, not six months.

III. PERFORMANCE OBJECTIVES

DCDA Peripheral's list of Performance Objectives for the proposed sales training course development is as follows:

1. Use DCDA's corporate capabilities presentation to effectively present DCDA's success story, from both a financial and technology leadership point of view.
2. Translate the features of DCDA's products into benefits for the customer.
3. Competitively position DCDA's products against the competition.
4. Analyze and understand customer requirements and recommend appropriate DCDA solutions.
5. Tell the DCDA quality story and the steps DCDA uses to provide a quality product.
6. Demonstrate an understanding of configuring DCDA's peripheral products for various computer systems manufacturers.
7. Explain the DCDA customer support programs and training capabilities.
8. Present DCDA's pre-sales technical support capabilities and on-line analysis tools.
9. Describe the key features and clauses in DCDA's contracts.
10. Demonstrate an awareness of the key marketing programs currently available to potential customers.
11. Demonstrate an understanding of computer systems peripherals technology.
12. Correctly configure and price configurations for proposals.
13. Sell effectively to decision-makers in DCDA's target markets.
14. Demonstrate an understanding of how to access home office support resources.

WRITING PROPOSALS

IV. THE APPROACH—ACHIEVING THE MAJOR PURPOSES AND SPECIFIC PERFORMANCE OBJECTIVES

A. Organizing the Material to Enhance Learning

The sales training objectives described by DCDA can be grouped into functional areas to enhance the organization and consistency of the training. Four major areas are identified for course curriculum focus.

1. Organization and Capabilities
2. Positioning
3. Creating Solutions
4. Qualifying and Selling

A first cut at grouping the Performance Objectives into these major topic areas is as follows (the numbered items are cross-referenced to DCDA's Performance Objectives):

1. Organization and Capabilities

1 - Present DCDA corporate capabilities
5 - Tell the DCDA quality story
7 - Explain DCDA customer support programs and training options
8 - Present pre-sales technical support and on-line analysis capabilities

2. Positioning

2 - Translate product features into benefits for prospects and customers
3 - Competitively position DCDA's products against the competition
10 - Demonstrate an awareness of key marketing programs available to customers

3. Designing Solutions

4 - Analyze customer requirements and recommend appropriate DCDA solutions
6 - Demonstrate an understanding of how to configure DCDA peripheral products for customer applications

11 - Demonstrate an understanding of computer systems peripherals technology

12 - Correctly configure and price configurations for proposals

4. **Qualifying and Selling**

9 - Describe the key features and clauses in DCDA contracts

13 - Sell effectively to decision-makers in DCDA's target markets

14 - Know how to access home office resources

B. Structuring the Course Flow for Maximum Impact

The flow of the course determines how well the participants learn and their perception and evaluation of the course. It has been our experience that new hire training programs provide the opportunity for a company to re-sell its positive aspects to its employees. This is especially important for sales organizations and that's why the course flow will be structured to regenerate excitement about DCDA in the participants.

Elements to be incorporated in the course flow are:

- DCDA executive staff participation—a group dinner the first evening of the course.
- The course will be structured so that each subject builds upon the previous topic covered. The overall flow suggested is: Corporate Capabilities > Product Capabilities > Customer Applications.
- A case study will be included in the course material. This will provide a real-world customer situation to be used as a basis for product, configuration, and services training.
- A team presentation will conclude the course. This will create a competitive environment. The presentation to a simulated customer will immediately demonstrate the participant's competence in areas covered by the course.

V. DELIVERABLES OVERVIEW

The sample presentation material that was sent to me provided a useful overview of DCDA and its capabilities. Naturally, we will be working closely with you to gather the additional information required to meet the

Performance Objectives outlined in your Request for Proposal. The deliverables we propose are:

1. Create a course agenda developed to meet stated objectives
2. Provide pre- and post-testing materials
3. Rework existing overhead presentations to enhance the training process where required
4. Develop new presentations where required
5. Update existing competitive presentations using the latest data from DCDA
6. Create speaker notes to be added to overhead presentations. This will make it easier for the sales force to use the material in customer situations after the course
7. Develop an instructor's guide for all course modules

As an option, DCDA can consider using my experiences as both a Sales Manager and Sales Trainer, and I could participate in conducting the course. With regard to facilitation of the meeting, I would be glad to provide active support to a DCDA facilitator, or to handle the direct facilitation of the course.

VI. RESULTS ENHANCERS

A. Video and Audio Taping

To make best use of DCDA personnel time, I recommend that my consulting practice video tape the presentations that are currently available. These video sessions will be interactive. We will work with the presenters in a Q & A fashion to clarify any open issues and to elicit further information for the course. These videos will provide you with an archival record of all of DCDA's current corporate, product, and support capabilities. This will provide you with a resource for use downstream for marketing bulletins, additional training, etc.

In addition, the audio portions of these videos will be transcribed. You will be provided with the raw transcriptions in hard copy and audio tape form—as well as the edited version for the course material. This will provide you with resource material that can be used by DCDA (or my firm can use) to produce audio tapes about DCDA capabilities that your sales and support people could listen to in their cars.

B. Weekly Project Schedule

This proposal includes implementing the course development as a project with weekly, measurable milestones. This involves conducting regularly scheduled weekly meetings to present progress against milestones to make sure that we meet the committed deadlines. The first cut at seven weeks of development activity is outlined below. We realize that we have nine weeks from your scheduled commit date to July 10. However, I recommend using the two additional weeks for any modifications required and to provide ample rehearsal time for DCDA to conduct the pilot program.

Even though we will be implementing the majority of the course development at our Coral Springs facility, I would appreciate access to an office at DCDA. This would provide a base of operations for meetings with DCDA personnel involved in the presentations.

The seven-week project is proposed as follows:

Week 1	Obtain DCDA company and product information Develop course agenda
Week 2	Framework presentations to capture missing information Video tape presentations
Week 3	Transcribe the audio from the video taping sessions Edit transcriptions for future use Develop speaker notes
Week 4	First cut of revised and new presentations, excluding competition
Week 5	Augment existing competitive presentations
Week 6	Dry run–final presentation review and modifications
Week 7	Pilot development Write instructor guide

C. Train the Sales Team

The closer the real world can be simulated in the training seminar, the more the participants will learn. Therefore, I recommend that we train the technical support people in the same sessions as the sale reps. This would provide training for a team selling environment. The support people could help the sales reps with the configuration exercises, and the sales reps could coach the support people for the final case study presentation. These sales teams of a sales rep and a support person would jointly present the case studies on the third day of the course.

D. Options

Options that are not priced with this proposal are:

1. Conducting the pilot course and facilitating all aspects of the first sales training seminar.
2. Using the services of an industry expert in the computer peripherals area to provide any additional competitive information you may need.

VII. PRICE PROPOSAL

We propose programs such as the DCDA New Hire Sales Training Program on a project fee basis. This provides DCDA with a firm, fixed price for the deliverables proposed. The price to DCDA for all of the items proposed in the preceding pages is $35,500. This includes the course development, video taping, audio transcriptions, transparency preparation, course books for the participants and the instructor guide. All course materials will be provided in hard copy as well as computer-readable media.

The payment scheduled proposed is:

Up-front Commitment Fee: $2,500–to be paid upon signing of DCDA consulting agreement

Completion of the Weekly Milestones committed: $28,000–($4,000 per week) to be paid within 10 days of receipt of the weekly invoice

Final modification: $5,000–to be paid on completion of the pilot training program

The optional items proposed, i.e., direct facilitation of the pilot program and extended competitive analysis are available at the rate of $1,500 per day.

WRITING PROPOSALS

Sample Proposal
Engineering Consulting

Proposal for:

HARRIS Garden Products, Inc.

New Product Design of Yard Utility Cart

By:

BradfordDesign
INCORPORATED

May 2, 1997

WRITING PROPOSALS

Contents

WRITING PROPOSALS

I. EXECUTIVE SUMMARY

This proposal is designed to meet the requirements of Harris Garden Products to develop a new yard utility cart for introduction in the Spring of 1998. This next-generation product will be designed to take advantage of the latest material advances in structural aluminum extrusions and pressure-treated wood products, and will be designed to collapse for storage in garages and yard sheds when not in use.

The overall product design objectives are:

1. Significantly reduce the volume and floor area now required for storage of the present Harris Yard Cart.
2. The collapsible design will be accomplished at a cost premium over the present cart not to exceed twenty percent.
3. The high-quality and rugged design for which Harris Garden Products are known will be stressed in the design of the new collapsible, yard utility cart.

A specific list of Performance Objectives will be met as outlined in the following paragraphs.

Give a brief description here of the client's requirements for the consulting effort. This should succinctly state the top two or three items which give an overall perspective on the work being quoted.

II. CURRENT SITUATION

Harris Garden Products (HGP) continues to be recognized as a leader in the home gardening industry. Growing attention to this market segment has spawned a number of competitive products that are beginning to challenge HGP's market share. This new competition makes it imperative that HGP reasserts its product leadership by introducing a next-generation yard utility cart that brings new, value-added features to the home gardener.

Because of the targeted fall trade show product introduction, it is important that the product development proceed at an aggressive pace and on a timetable which will support this date.

Harris Garden Products' reputation for high-quality, rugged, and dependable products demands that this new yard cart be equal to, or exceed, the performance and features of present competitive products.

This section should contain a synopsis of the factors that highlight and illustrate the client's need for the proposed services.

WRITING PROPOSALS

III. PRODUCT DESIGN OBJECTIVES

Harris Garden Products' key objectives for the design of the new yard utility cart are as follows:

1. The product will be designed to allow for ease of operation by someone with little or no mechanical ability, and require a minimum of effort to assemble.
2. The product components will incorporate the latest advances in structural materials and assembly practices.
3. Incorporation of product value-added features to competitively position this product as superior to all competitive units now on the market.
4. Product design will focus on minimizing parts count and factory assembly labor.
5. The working load rating of 500 pounds will be maintained and increased by a factor of twenty percent if feasible.
6. Cart design will take into account components and design to achieve maximum weather resistance.
7. Product safety will be featured in the design to minimize the risk of operator injury during opening/collapsing and use of yard utility cart.
8. The industrial design of the new yard utility cart will be consistent with the present line of Harris Garden Products.
9. Total supplier tooling expenses for components should not exceed $20,000.
10. Product will be designed and prototyped by September 1, 1997.

This section should list the technical objectives and considerations that must be met to satisfy the customer's requirements for the product or service. Requirements may be written, industry standards, or suggested by the customer's comments.

IV. THE APPROACH—ACHIEVING SUPERIOR PRODUCT DESIGN THROUGH PERFORMANCE OBJECTIVES

A. Evaluate Competitive Products

Before any design work is initiated, we will conduct an exhaustive engineering study of competitive yard utility carts now on the market. We will review units for features, load capacity, ease of assembly and use, parts count, and estimated manufacturing cost and working life.

B. Design Proposal

Various features and construction alternatives will be considered using the "Design Matrix" System, which is proprietary to Bradford Design. Utilizing this industry-acknowledged strength in developing value-added product features, we will propose conceptual representations of design alternatives and recommend a "best" solution.

C. Design Details and Documentation

After an extensive design review and approval by HGP, we will develop drawings and specifications to allow for parts quoting and a product manufacturability review. All documentation will be provided in a computerized format utilizing the Pro-Engineer software package.

This section should contain details of your approach to meeting the requirements of the proposal. Be sure to add information demonstrating the unique things you will bring to the assignment.

D. Prototype Fabrication

Two prototypes will be fabricated utilizing the drawings and documentation developed in step three. To meet the aggressive development timetable, we will manufacture all fabricated parts in our internal prototype shop. During assembly of components, all parts received will be inspected to the documentation package and any interference dimensions or assembly problems noted and corrected.

E. Final Design Release and Approval

After testing and evaluation of prototype units, print package will be updated and presented to HGP for approval. Bradford Design's databank of qualified vendor sourcing for components will be made available to HGP's purchasing staff to support the vendor quoting and selection process.

V. DELIVERABLES OVERVIEW

Bradford Design's goal is to provide Harris Garden Products with a manufacturing-ready design and documentation package. Consistent with this, the following deliverables are proposed:

WRITING PROPOSALS

1. Two (2) sets of drawings at prototype stage for review and critique.
2. Two (2) fully-functional, prototype yard utility carts.
3. Two (2) sets of final revision drawings and one (1) set of complete software files.
4. Listing of product components and estimated purchasing and tooling costs.
5. Listing of recommended vendor sourcing for all fabricated and purchased components.
6. We will be glad to supply, at no additional cost, 3-D illustrations that can be used in your owner's instruction and assembly manual.

Define in as much detail as possible, exactly what the client will be receiving under the terms of the proposal.

VI. RESULTS ENHANCERS

A. Design Review Meetings

In order to ensure that HGP personnel are able to participate in the design development, we will hold biweekly design meetings at Bradford's office. All interested HGP staff are invited to attend.

We will also call two formal meetings for the presentation and review of both the prototype and final drawing packages. We anticipate these meetings to take place during weeks five and ten respectively.

B. Engineering Reports

We will supply an engineering design report concurrent with delivery of the prototype drawing package. This report will detail all of the features considered for incorporation in the product, and it will supply a rationale for those features chosen.

C. Video Taping

We will make a video tape of the yard utility cart performance and load testing, and this will be provided to HGP for use in their sales presentation package.

D. Options

Options that are not priced with this proposal are:

1. Support and illustrations for possible patent application opportunities that may arise during the prototype design review.
2. Development of incoming inspection and production assembly procedures to support manufacturing operations.

Use this section to list those related services you could supply but that were not requested in the original proposal. Try to link the need for these additional activities to items or services detailed within the present proposal.

VII. PRICE PROPOSAL

We propose programs such as the HGP Yard Utility Cart on a project fee basis. This provides HGP with a firm, fixed price for the deliverables proposed. The price to HGP for all of the items detailed in this proposal is $56,500.

The payment scheduled proposed is:

10% Up-front Commitment Fee $5,850–to be paid upon signing of HGP consulting agreement
On-going Weekly Design Activities (11 weeks) $44,000–($4,000 per week) to be paid within 10 days of receipt of the weekly invoice
Final Design and Drawing Acceptance $6,750–to be paid on completion of the design program

The optional items proposed, e.g., patent application support, will be quoted if activities become necessary and are specifically requested by HGP.

It is best to quote on a total program effort, and not on an hourly or daily basis as the client focuses on the deliverables, not on the hourly rate. Try to get an up-front commitment fee and request progress payments which reduce your need to carry a large receivable.

WRITING PROPOSALS

Sample Proposal
Marketing Consulting

Proposal for:

Custom Picture Framing, Inc.

Sales Promotion Campaign

By:

Marketing Services, Ltd.

June 6, 1997

WRITING PROPOSALS

Contents

Section	Proposal Topic
I	Executive Summary
II	Current Situation
III	Sales Promotion Objectives
IV	The Approach–Achieving a Winning Promotional Campaign Through Performance Objectives
V	Deliverables Overview
VI	Results Enhancers
VII	Price Proposal
VIII	Appendix

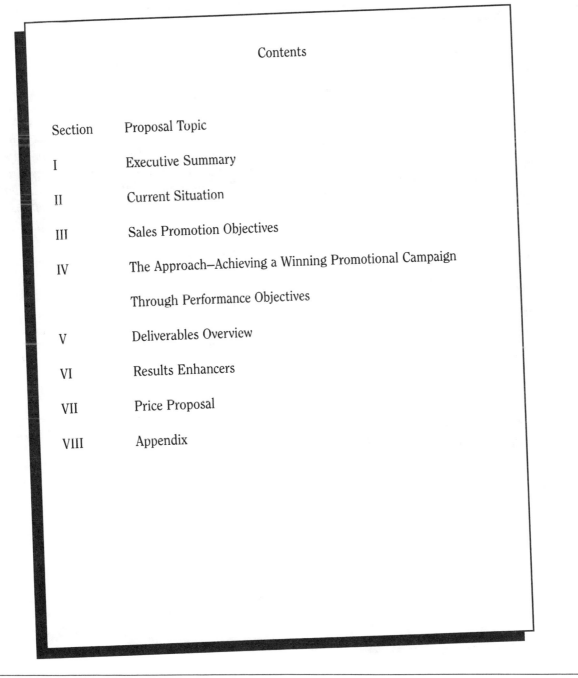

WRITING PROPOSALS

I. EXECUTIVE SUMMARY

Custom Picture Framing, Inc. has recognized that sales in their four regional stores have remained flat during the last year. To break this trend, management desires that a sales promotion campaign be developed that will create sales growth momentum by both bringing back their traditional customer and attracting new first-time buyers.

This proposal is designed to provide several promotional sales program options to Custom Picture Framing, Inc. (CPF) so that they can elect to implement them at their discretion (seasonally), and when the budget allows.

The promotional program objectives are:

1. Define and conduct a market study to determine the products and services of most interest to present and potential customers.
2. Determine the key buying influences for the existing products and services.
3. Develop promotional program options and recommend a yearly sales campaign and budget.

A specific list of Performance Objectives will be met as outlined in the following paragraphs.

Give a brief description here of the client's requirements for the consulting effort. This should succinctly state the top two or three items which give an overall perspective on the work being quoted.

II. CURRENT SITUATION

Custom Picture Framing, Inc. (CPF) continues to be a competitive supplier of picture framing products and services in the local metropolitan area. However, the emergence of competition from large national chains with broad product lines of imported frame products, and less-expensive "do-it-yourself" kits, has given impetus to CPF senior management to create and implement a sales campaign that will stimulate sales growth. These sales promotions must offer alternatives that target various market segments.

The outcome of this analysis will lead to an in-depth exploration of marketing alternatives and a final recommendation for a proposed yearly promotional plan and budget.

This section should contain a synopsis of the factors that highlight and illustrate the client's need for the proposed services.

III. SALES PROMOTION OBJECTIVES

The key activities and objectives for the CPF sales promotion program are to:

1. Define the total available market and identify the target segments to be addressed by CPF's promotional program.
2. Determine the key buying influences for the target markets and customers.
3. Define the product and services to be offered, and explain CPF's product differentiation from that of the competition.
4. Determine price sensitivity for product and services with various target market segments, and recommend an updated price list.
5. Develop promotional campaign options that focus on the various market segments, and include a range of budget options.
6. Propose a promotional strategy and program for the coming year that will result in a minimum growth in sales of ten percent.

This section should list the key objectives and considerations that must be met to satisfy the customer's requirements for the product or service. Requirements may be written, industry standards, or suggested by the customer's comments.

IV. THE APPROACH—ACHIEVING A WINNING PROMOTIONAL CAMPAIGN THROUGH PERFORMANCE OBJECTIVES

A. Review and Define the Total Potential Market and Competition

We will review all competitors offering framing products and services in the geographic area to determine their product lines, pricing, and product positioning. We will develop estimates of their total sales in this category.

B. Determine the Market Segments to Be Served by CPF

We will conduct in-store customer interviews to define the existing customer base, the key influences on their buying from CPF, and their evaluation of the competitive alternatives.

WRITING PROPOSALS

C. Define and analyze the existing product offering

We will perform a comparison of the present CPF product line and services with that of the competition. Customer interviews will also focus on identifying unmet customer product needs and expectations for support services. We will make recommendations for the inclusion of new products and services, and/or the elimination of currently offered product.

D. Review the existing promotional approach and strategy

We will conduct a review of the promotional activities of CPF for the last three years to determine the effectiveness of the individual programs, and their relative strengths and weaknesses. We will also review ongoing promotional programs offered by the competition and develop an estimate of their effectiveness.

E. Develop promotional program options

We will develop a variety of promotional program options by drawing upon the knowledge gained from the review of both past and competitive promotional activities, and the understanding of key buying influences derived from the customer interviews. It is anticipated that this will include a range of options from couponing, direct-mail advertising, special event sales, flyers, and local media advertising encompassing both print and radio.

F. Develop final copy and graphics for promotional programs

For each of the unique programs recommended, we will develop final copy and graphics for review and testing. Traditional CPF logos and tag lines will be incorporated as possible.

G. Evaluate promotional program options

Promotional programs will be run on a trial basis to measure respective effectiveness in terms of customer impact and return on investment. We will institute a system with store personnel that will measure responses to the various programs.

WRITING PROPOSALS

This section should contain details of your approach to meeting the requirements of the proposal. Be sure to add information demonstrating the unique things you will bring to the assignment.

H. Recommend a Promotional Campaign for the Coming Year

Using the information and results gained from the evaluation trials, we will recommend a promotional program for the next year. This program will specifically include a listing of the unique promotional activities and recommended timing and budgets.

V. DELIVERABLES OVERVIEW

Marketing Services is committed to providing the management of Custom Picture Framing, Inc. with a successful formula for boosting sales this coming year. Consistent with this, the following deliverables are proposed:

Define in as much detail as possible, exactly what the client will be receiving under the terms of the proposal.

1. An interim report detailing an analysis of competition and the total market, and explaining the conclusions of the customer survey to identify buying influences.
2. A final Promotional Program Report detailing the promotion options explored, their effectiveness in eliciting new business as determined in the trial evaluations, and the recommended program and budget for the coming year.
3. One (1) set of complete documentation and graphics for each promotional program recommended in the proposal.

VI. RESULTS ENHANCERS

A. Focus Group Critique of Promotional Programs

In order to measure the relative impact and clarity of copy messages, we will conduct a minimum of two focus groups for program evaluation. These meetings will be held at the offices of Marketing Services, and will also be used to confirm that the inclusion of the key buying influences is readily apparent in the promotional materials.

We will hold two formal meetings for the presentation and review of both the Interim and Final Promotional Program reports. We anticipate that these will take place during weeks six and twelve of the expected three month program.

WRITING PROPOSALS

B. Video Taping

A video tape will be made of the in-store customer interviews and two focus groups. These can be used to answer later questions or can be incorporated in promotional programs.

C. Standardized Questionnaires

All customer and competition questionnaires will be supplied in a standardized format so that they may be used again some time in the future and provide consistency for measurement purposes.

D. Options

Options that are not priced with this proposal are:

1. Support and execution of full implementation of the proposed promotional program.
2. Evaluation of demographics and competition in other nearby locales, and recommendation for potential new store sites.

Use this section to list those related services you could supply but that were not requested in the original proposal. Try to link the need for these additional activities to items or services detailed within the present proposal.

VII. PRICE PROPOSAL

We propose activities such as the development of the CPF Promotional Program on a project fee basis. This provides CPF with a firm, fixed price for the deliverables proposed. The price to CPF for this estimated ten-week program, including all of the items detailed in this proposal, is $18,600.

The payment schedule proposed is:

It is best to quote on a total program effort, and not on an hourly or daily basis as the client focuses on the deliverables, not on the hourly rate. Try to get an up-front commitment fee and request progress payments which reduce your need to carry a large receivable.

10% Up-front Commitment Fee: $1,860–to be paid upon signing of CPF consulting agreement
On-going Weekly Development Activities (11 weeks): $15,000–($1,500 per week) to be paid within 10 days of the weekly invoice
Final Design and Drawing Acceptance: $1,740–to be paid on completion of the program

The optional items proposed, e.g., full promotional program implementation, will be quoted if that activity is specifically requested by CPF.

Sample Proposal
Financial Consulting

Proposal for:

Metro Cleaning Services, Inc.

Update Credit and Collection Policies and Procedures

By:

Star Financial Services, Inc.

January 23, 1997

WRITING PROPOSALS

Contents

WRITING PROPOSALS

Give a brief description here of the client's requirements for the consulting effort. This should succinctly state the top two or three items which give an overall perspective to the work being quoted.

I. EXECUTIVE SUMMARY

This proposal is designed to meet the need of Metro Cleaning Services for review and update of their Credit and Collection Policies and Procedures.

The overall objectives for this proposal are to:

1. Review present company Credit and Collection Policies and Procedures for deficiencies
2. Formulate and issue new recommendations for system improvements, focusing on Credit protocol and Receivables collection procedures
3. Train personnel in use of new guidelines

A specific list of Performance Objectives will be met as outlined in the following paragraphs.

II. CURRENT SITUATION

This section should contain a synopsis of the factors that highlight and illustrate the client's need for the proposed services.

Metro Cleaning Services (MCS) has been in business for over fifteen years providing janitorial services to commercial and retail industry. Throughout this period, an informal system of credit approval has been utilized requiring considerable discretion on the part of anyone at MCS responsible for approving new customer credit levels.

Additionally, collection of past-due Receivables has been carried out inconsistently. Receivables are now out to eighty-five days and working capital is becoming tight. Further, the recent write-off of several bad Receivables has signaled that local businesses might be entering a slow business period.

This proposal addresses MCS's desire to aggressively address this situation by instituting new policies and procedures, and bring down the outstanding Receivables to an average of forty-five days.

III. PERFORMANCE OBJECTIVES

Key objectives for the development and implementation of new Credit and Collection Policies and Procedures are:

1. Establish a Credit Policy that specifically defines the procedures for the setting and approval of customer credit levels.

WRITING PROPOSALS

2. Review present collection activities and prepare new guidelines for implementation which will aid in bringing down outstanding Receivables to forty-five days.
3. Work with the accounting department to train all staff in new procedures.

This section should list the technical objectives and considerations that must be met to satisfy the customer's requirements for the product or service. Requirements may be written, industry standards, or suggested by the customer's comments.

IV. THE APPROACH—UPDATING CREDIT AND COLLECTION PROCEDURES

A. Review Present Credit and Collection Policies and Procedures

Meet with all accounting staff to define and review existing system. Determine issues and deficiencies with current system that are creating problems for Credit level approvals and Receivables collection.

B. Develop New Policies and Procedures

Formulate new guidelines for setting credit limits, and define the management sign-off process for approving these limits for new accounts. Develop specific step-by-step procedures for Receivables collection and escalation of efforts for slow payment accounts.

C. Review Proposed Policies and Procedures with Accounting and Sales Staff and Management

Meet with both accounting and sales staff to review proposed guidelines and to address any issues and concerns raised.

D. Formulate Final Guidelines

Update proposed guidelines to incorporate feedback and concerns, and review with senior management.

E. Train Company Personnel in Use of New Guidelines

Meet with accounting staff to train in use of new procedures. Meet with sales department to review how new procedures will be addressed in job bid proposals.

This section should contain details of your approach to meeting the requirements of the proposal. Be sure to add information demonstrating the unique things you will bring to the assignment.

WRITING PROPOSALS

Define in as much detail as possible, exactly what the client will be receiving under the terms of the proposal.

V. DELIVERABLES OVERVIEW

1. Two (2) sets of manuals on Credit and Collection Policies and Procedures.
2. Training and Communications Meetings with the accounting and sales departments.

VI. RESULTS ENHANCERS

A. Delinquent Payment Letters

In support of the new collection procedures, we will provide suggested form letters to use when seeking payment for late accounts. These letters will range from "first reminder" to "final warning."

B. Telephone Training

We will conduct a telephone procedures meeting to train accounting staff in the best approach for dealing with delinquent accounts over the phone.

C. Options

Options that are not priced with this proposal are:

1. Review of internal accounting controls for validity and accuracy.
2. Review of existing cash records for completeness and accuracy and providing system update recommendations.

Use this section to list those related services you could supply but that were not requested in the original proposal. Try to link the need for these additional activities to items or services detailed within the present proposal.

VII. PRICE PROPOSAL

We propose programs such as the MCS Credit and Collections Policies and Procedures Update on a project fee basis. This provides MCS with a firm, fixed price for the deliverables proposed. The price to MCS for all of the items detailed in this proposal is $3,750.

The payment scheduled proposed for this three-week program is:

1/3 Up-front Commitment Fee: $1,250–To be paid upon signing of MCS consulting agreement

WRITING PROPOSALS

Second Week Progress Payment: $1,250–to be paid within ten days of receipt of invoice

Final Payment: $1,250–to be paid on completion of program

Any optional items requested will be quoted if specifically requested by MCS.

It is best to quote on a total program effort, and not on an hourly or daily basis as the client focuses on the deliverables, not on the hourly rate. Try to get an up-front commitment fee and request progress payments which reduce your need to carry a large receivable.

WRITING PROPOSALS

Sample Proposal
Human Resources

Proposal for:

MicroTECH Software Systems, Inc.

Human Resources Support:
Development of Job Descriptions and
Employee Evaluation and Incentive Systems

By:

Employment Specialists, Inc.

October 16, 1996

WRITING PROPOSALS

Contents

Section	Proposal Topic
I	Executive Summary
II	Current Situation
III	Program Objectives
IV	The Approach–Developing Key Human Resource Systems
V	Deliverables Overview
VI	Results Enhancers
VII	Price Proposal
VIII	Appendix

WRITING PROPOSALS

I. EXECUTIVE SUMMARY

MicroTECH Software Systems, Inc. has been undergoing very rapid growth exceeding fifty percent a year for the past two years due to the strong market acceptance of its new modem software packages.

This proposal is designed to provide the Human Resources Department with assistance in coping with the commensurate growth in personnel. In response to your Request for Proposal dated October 4, 1996, Employment Specialists, Inc. is pleased to submit this proposal which addresses and meets the requested assistance.

Give a brief description here of the client's requirements for the consulting effort. This should succinctly state the top two or three items which give an overall perspective to the work being quoted.

Specifically, development of the Human Resources programs requested includes:

1. Development or updating of Job Descriptions for all employees at MicroTECH Software Systems (MSS)
2. Development of an employee Performance Evaluation System
3. Formulation of an Incentive Compensation Program

A specific list of Program Objectives will be met as outlined in the following paragraphs.

II. CURRENT SITUATION

Business growth has required MicroTECH Software Systems (MSS) to add sixty-two full- and part-time employees over the last two years. Because of this tremendous growth, the Human Resources Department has not been able to keep up with its normal support to job descriptions. Further, this increase in employees and new management positions makes it even more important that a formalized system of employee performance reviews be established.

This section should contain a synopsis of the factors that highlight and illustrate the client's need for the proposed services.

MSS management also recognizes that they should now introduce an incentive compensation program in order to keep employees motivated at the level of effort required to continue this successful track record.

Business demands on the Human Resources Department make it imperative that these programs proceed on a timely basis and with a sense of urgency if related problems are to be avoided.

WRITING PROPOSALS

III. PROGRAM OBJECTIVES

Key objectives for the MSS Human Resources programs are:

1. Establish Job Descriptions for all MSS employees that accurately reflect and delineate their full responsibilities.
2. Develop an employee Performance Evaluation System that standardizes evaluation guidelines throughout the company so that all employees are measured and rewarded against a consistent set of standards.
3. Formulate an Incentive Compensation Program that provides significant motivation and reward for superior efforts by employees which are critical to the continued growth and success of MSS.
4. Introduce these new company programs in a manner that maximizes employee support and enthusiasm.

This section should list the key objectives and considerations that must be met to satisfy the customer's requirements for the product or service. Requirements may be written, industry standards, or suggested by the customer's comments.

IV. THE APPROACH—DEVELOPING KEY HUMAN RESOURCES SYSTEMS

Organizational Structure

1. Develop organizational chart.
2. Interview all personnel to ascertain specific tasks, functions, assignments performed by them.
3. Document each job function using written job descriptions and workflow diagrams.
4. Review updated and new job descriptions with senior management and revise accordingly.
5. Distribute final job descriptions to employees and conduct meetings as necessary to gather feedback regarding new duties and responsibilities.

Develop Employee Performance Evaluation System

1. Develop written guidelines for performance measurement and prepare detailed narrative for each evaluation category.
2. Design and provide managers/supervisors with evaluation forms and rating system for comments.

3. Review comments and concerns with employees, supervisors, and senior management.

Develop Incentive Compensation Program

1. Conduct a survey of incentive compensation programs at benchmark companies.
2. Solicit senior management input and development guidelines.
3. Determine standards for eligibility and design measurement techniques.
4. Prepare model for calculation of bonus pools and prepare formalized program description.
5. Review final draft with senior management for approval or modification.

This section should contain details of your approach to meeting the requirements of the proposal. Be sure to add information demonstrating the unique things you will bring to the assignment.

Implementation

1. Review all three programs with senior management for final approval.
2. Develop written copy and handbooks for employee distribution.
3. Hold company-wide meeting to formally introduce program to all employees.

V. DELIVERABLES OVERVIEW

In support of the recent rapid growth of MicroTECH Software Systems, Employment Specialists is committed to providing the Human Resources Department with the following proposed deliverables:

Define in as much detail as possible, exactly what the client will be receiving under the terms of the proposal.

1. Thirty-seven Job Descriptions (estimated), one per job category identified on the organizational chart that will be developed within this contract.
2. Development and formalization of an Employee Evaluation System.
3. Development and formalization of an Incentive Compensation Program.
4. Fourteen (14) Personnel Manuals (one per manager plus two additional), each containing one set of Job Descriptions and a copy of both the Employee Evaluation System and the Incentive Compensation Program.

WRITING PROPOSALS

VI. RESULTS ENHANCERS

A. Benchmark Survey Results

Survey results of the Incentive Compensation Programs offered by competitors and noted benchmark companies will be organized and presented to senior management for background comparison.

B. Employee Attitude Survey

During the process of defining and reviewing employee job descriptions, we will conduct a confidential employee opinion survey to evaluate the impact that growth has had on employees and their workloads, and the level of employee morale in coping with this high-pressure situation. We will provide the results of this survey to senior management.

C. Employee Database

We will develop a confidential, computerized database of all MSS employees and their personnel records, including Job Descriptions, Performance Evaluations, and Incentive Compensation history, and provide the database to the Human Resources Department.

D. Options

Options that are not priced with this proposal are:

1. Training of MSS managers in federal and state legal guidelines for hiring and reviewing employees.
2. Interviewing and preselection of qualified candidates for open job positions.

Use this section to list those related services you could supply but that were not requested in the original proposal. Try to link the need for these additional activities to items or services detailed within the present proposal.

VII. PRICE PROPOSAL

We propose activities such as the MSS Human Resources Support program on a project fee basis. This provides MSS with a firm, fixed price for the deliverables proposed. The price to MSS for this estimated six-week program, including all of the items detailed in this proposal, is $12,920.

The payment scheduled proposed is:

WRITING PROPOSALS

10% Up-front Commitment Fee: $1,292–to be paid upon signing of MSS consulting agreement

On-going Weekly Development Activities (6 weeks): $10,500–($1,750 per week) to be paid within ten days of receipt of the weekly invoice

Final Design and Drawing Acceptance: $1,128–to be paid on completion of the program and delivery of Personnel Manuals

The optional items proposed, e.g., full promotional program implementation, will be quoted if activities are specifically requested by MSS.

It is best to quote on a total program effort, and not on an hourly or daily basis as the client focuses on the deliverables, not on the hourly rate. Try to get an up-front commitment fee and request progress payments which reduce your need to carry a large receivable.

WRITING PROPOSALS

USING THE TEMPLATES TO WRITE YOUR PROPOSAL

The proposal generation templates that follow provide tools which can be effectively used to generate a proposal more easily and in far less time. The foundation for the proposal-writing process was completed when you filled in the information required in the First Six Steps of the proposal generation process.

TEMPLATE NO 1: COVER SHEET

The proposal cover sheet introduces your proposal to your client. It typically includes the client's name, the name of the project or assignment you are bidding on, the name of your firm and the date of proposal submittal. To increase the visual appeal of the cover page, consider scanning in your client's logo and inserting client company name as indicated on the template. Also, use color for your logo after the "submitted by" prefix. The use of color dramatically increases the cover's visual appeal. A color printer can produce these options or you could use an outside service to print this page on a color ink jet or laser printer.

WRITING PROPOSALS

Proposal for:

(Client Company)

(Name of Project or Program)

By:

(Name of Your Consulting Practice)

XXXX XX, XXXX
(month, day and year issued)

WRITING PROPOSALS

TEMPLATE 2: TABLE OF CONTENTS

A table of contents allows readers of your proposal to find the information they want more easily. A busy executive may be inclined to read your Executive Summary and go directly to the Pricing Section. When the proposals are relatively short and simple, perhaps five pages or less, you may consider not using a Table of Contents. Longer proposals with many sections benefit from the ease of access to information afforded by a Table of Contents.

WRITING PROPOSALS

TABLE OF CONTENTS

WRITING PROPOSALS

TEMPLATE NO. 3: EXECUTIVE SUMMARY

The purpose of the Executive Summary is to provide the reader with a one- or two-page capsule summary of the results you will accomplish when you successfully complete the consulting assignment called for by the Request for Proposal. Refer to Table 3 (Summary of the Purpose and Objectives) and extract the information you input regarding the client's major objectives. The impact of the Executive Summary can be enhanced by supporting the statement of results with any organizational, decision criteria, and people issues you have discovered.

WRITING PROPOSALS

I. Executive Summary

The purpose of this proposal is to provide (name of client company) with the consulting services required to (general description of task and time frame involved). Successful completion of this project will (general statement of benefit to the client).

The specific overall objectives to be accomplished are: (list them)

1. ______
2. ______
3. ______
4. ______
5. ______

(Suggest using no more than five major objectives for maximum impact and readability.)

These are the major overall objectives. A specific list of each of the items described in your Request for Proposal is contained in Section ___ of this proposal.

(You can also add any secondary benefits that will result from the success of this project. If your consulting assignment will produce measurable financial benefit to the client be sure to include this information.)

1. ______
2. ______
3. ______
4. ______
5. ______

WRITING PROPOSALS

TEMPLATE 4: CURRENT SITUATION

In describing the client's current situation, provide a recap of the information that the client has shared with you–both in the RFP and in open (not private) conversations you've had with client personnel. In this section, review with the client what he already knows to be true, including those factors that are causing the client to seek an outside consulting resource. This indicates to the client that you understand their needs and reinforces the decision to use an outside resource.

II. Current Situation

There are (number) critically important factors affecting the outcome of the (proposed consulting assignment). These factors are: (list them)

1. __________
2. __________
3. __________
4. __________
5. __________
6. __________
7. __________
8. __________
9. __________
10. __________

(Factor No. 1) is important because (explain relevance of first factor)

(Factor No. 2) relates to the objective to be accomplished by (provide impact of Factor No. 2)

(Factor No. 3) has a results-leveraging effect because (develop importance of Factor No. 3).

Information about these factors and their importance can be included when introducing the factor. This approach is used in the sample proposal to DCDA.

WRITING PROPOSALS

TEMPLATE NO. 5: SPECIFIC OBJECTIVES

This section involves producing an extensive list and discussion of the specific objectives called for by the RFP. If the Request for Proposal you receive has references to meeting mandatory and desirable requirements, this is the section in which to indicate your compliance with each of the items specified in the RFP.

Taking the time to carefully respond in this section can either qualify or disqualify your proposal. Responding in-depth when it is called for will reinforce to the client that you truly understand their requirements. This section could also be used to provide insight into the approach you will be introducing in the next section. Refer to the work you have completed in the second portion of Table 3.

III. Design Objectives

The list of the specific requirements called for by (client company). Request for proposal is provided below along with a statement of compliance by (name of your consulting firm).

I did not use this approach with the example proposal because mandatory and desirable categories were not identified.

For compliance, you may want to indicate "Comply," "Do Not Comply," or "Comply with Clarifications." Be totally forthright, as there can be legal ramifications. Also, make sure the client is open to a "Comply with Clarifications" approach (where you can meet the intent of the specification, and have an alternative to offer).

Item No.	Description	Compliance
1.		
2.		
3.		
4.		
5.		
6.		
7.		
8.		
9.		
10.		

WRITING PROPOSALS

TEMPLATE NO. 6: THE APPROACH

A winning proposal develops the approach around all of the factors associated with the client's current situation and the major purpose and specific objectives to be accomplished. Design your approach to provide sufficient details to the client for your approach to be accepted–without giving away the store. Use the Approach information you've developed in the first section of Table 4 (Approach Summary and Value Add Items) to outline the approach you will use to accomplishing the client's objectives.

WRITING PROPOSALS

IV. The Approach—(Title of Approach)

(Your consulting firm) proposes to meet the objectives and requirements of (client company) by implementation of the following approach. This implementation plan consists of ___ elements. (List each element of your approach, and provide sufficient detail in your description for each element.)

1. (Element 1 ....)
2. (Element 2 ....)
3. (Element 3 ....)

In the example proposal, one approach element was to group the training objectives into four major categories; the second was to structure the course flow for maximum impact.

1. ______________________________
2. ______________________________
3. ______________________________
4. ______________________________
5. ______________________________
6. ______________________________
7. ______________________________
8. ______________________________
9. ______________________________
10. ______________________________

WRITING PROPOSALS

TEMPLATE NO. 7: DELIVERABLES

In this section of the proposal, tell them what you're going to give them. The description of deliverables outlines for the client exactly what services you will be providing. State these deliverables succinctly, but provide enough detail so that your communication of commitment cannot be misinterpreted.

Note: The example proposal lists seven deliverables along with some options that I proposed for the DCDA new hire sales training course.

WRITING PROPOSALS

V. Deliverables Overview

Based on the information provided in your Request for Proposal and from subsequent meetings elaborating upon and further clarifying your requirements, (your company) will provide the following deliverables: (List them)

1. ______________________________
2. ______________________________
3. ______________________________
4. ______________________________
5. ______________________________
6. ______________________________
7. ______________________________
8. ______________________________
9. ______________________________
10. ______________________________

In addition, the following optional services are available (describe in narrative or list form).

WRITING PROPOSALS

TEMPLATE NO. 8: RESULTS ENHANCERS

Fully developing this section of the proposal will set you apart from your competition. This is the area where you position the added value–your "results enhancers" for the client. Use the information you provided in Table 4 (Approach Summary and Value Add Items), review that list of unique differentiators you offer, then add any others that come to mind which will uniquely add value to your approach and proposal.

VI. Results Enhancers

To provide accelerated project completion and reduce development costs, we propose the following items that add value to, and enhance the results we will provide you. These results-enhancers will provide (client company) with (capabilities, material, etc.) not specifically called for in your Request for Proposal.

These are: (list them along with detailed information on how each of these value-added components will benefit your client.)

1. ____
2. ____
3. ____
4. ____
5. ____
6. ____
7. ____
8. ____
9. ____
10. ____

(Optionally, summarize the benefits after completing the list and descriptions above.)

WRITING PROPOSALS

TEMPLATE NO. 9: PRICE PROPOSAL

This area of your proposal provides your client the price that will be charged for the value they receive. As we've discussed before, price your services on a project or results basis instead of daily fees. When you feel it is appropriate, ask for some partial payment of your fee upon agreement to proceed.

VII. Price Proposal

(Name of your consulting firm) propose programs such as the (name the client and the project assignment) on a project fee basis. This provides (client) with a firm, fixed price for the deliverables proposed. The total price to (client) for all of the items proposed in this document, except (list exceptions) is ($$$$$$$). This includes (overall summary of what's provided).

Travel and lodging expenses (are/are not included) and (if not included) are estimated to be ($$$$$$) for (list travel frequency and destinations as appropriate).

Up-front Commitment Fee:	$$$$$-to be paid upon execution of consulting contact
Completion of Deliverable 1:	$$$$$
Completion of Deliverable 2:	$$$$$
Completion of Deliverable 3:	$$$$$
Final delivery:	$$$$$
Total:	$$$$$

Prices are in U.S. dollars and are due net (payment terms) after invoice.

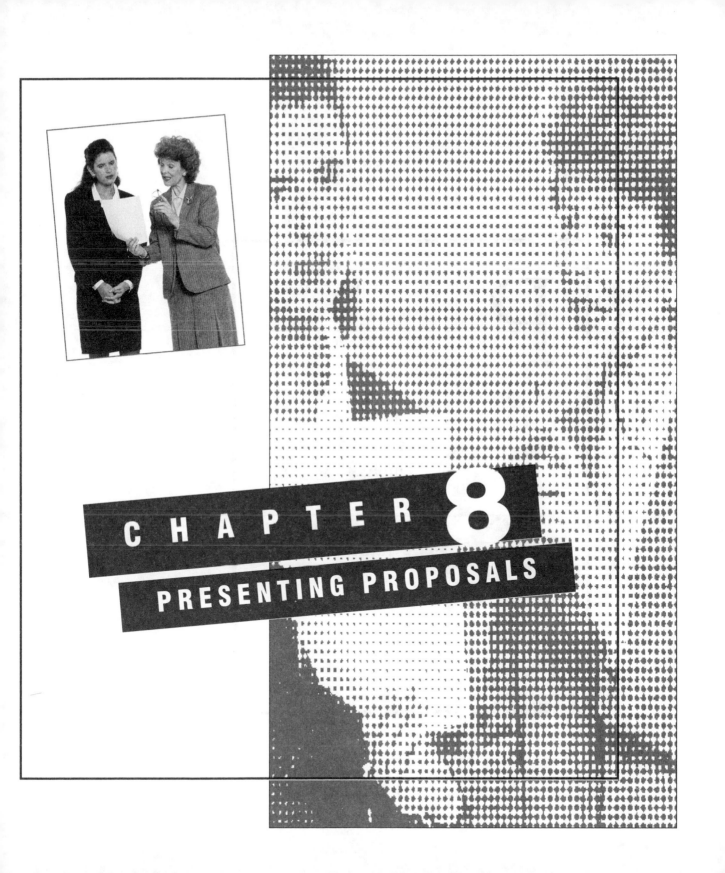

CHAPTER 8
PRESENTING PROPOSALS

Presenting your proposal in person will dramatically increase your chances of winning an assignment. This section shows you how to structure your presentation and how to use sales aids for emphasis. Notice how the sample sales aids are rather simple—but also very clear and effective.

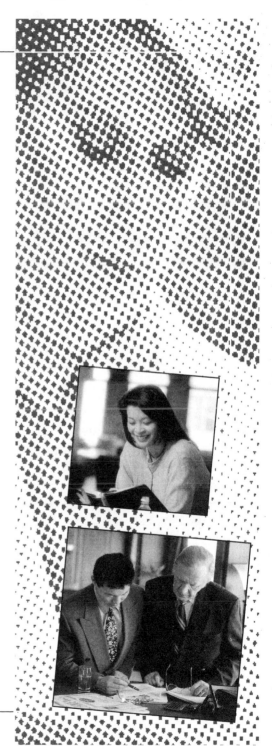

Whenever you have the opportunity to write a proposal, your ability to win the consulting assignment increases dramatically if you can then present your proposal to the client in person. When a proposal is presented in person, it provides an environment for further developing your relationship with a client. This forum allows you to interact with the client and explain the benefits of your approach. You will also be able to determine additional information you can use to make any adjustments necessary to win the business.

Your ability to stand before the people who are responsible for selecting your services and share with them your approach, your added value, and your commitment is probably the most important factor determining if you will win or lose. The presentation could be one-on-one or to a group. Flip charts, summary sheets, or overhead transparencies are some of the media to consider.

Creating the Presentation

Here are some suggestions for creating a proposal presentation:

- Use the proposal flow
- Keep it simple
- Make it hard-hitting, factual, and benefit-oriented

PRESENTING PROPOSALS

Proposal flow

In order to provide maximum impact to your audience, use the proposal flow that has already been developed. The flow was created to provide your client with a logical, persuasive explanation of your solution to their issues and the advantages you provide.

Keep it simple

Design the presentations to logically showcase your approach—don't get mired down in detail. In developing each of the presentation charts, consider a top-down approach, using a few bulleted items instead of highly complex charts or overhead transparencies.

Keep your presentations simple, yet focused on the facts of both the client's need and the benefits you can offer.

Make it hard-hitting, factual, and benefit-oriented

Hard-hitting means focusing on the client's major purpose and your commitment to helping them achieve the results desired. Factual means truthful—any exaggerations will be strongly rejected by your client. Lastly, focus on the benefits—how your client's situation will improve as a result of your involvement.

Use the Sample Presentation as a Model

In the narrative below, the charts used to win the DCDA Peripherals account are presented. The presentation medium was overhead transparencies created on a color ink-jet printer. Each of the transparencies (slides) has a description of its purpose.

DCDA Peripherals, Inc.
New Hire Sales Training Program
by
SalesWinners
INCORPORATED

1. **Slide 1: Title Page**
   Create a title page that describes the client's project or assignment. Show the client company name and if possible, their logo. Outside firms, such as Kinko's will typically scan a logo for use in your PC programs for approximately $5.

PRESENTING PROPOSALS

New-Hire Sales Training Course

Program Outcomes

- Measurably improved knowledge and skills
- High-quality—high course ratings
- Cost-effective

SalesWinners
INCORPORATED

2. **Slide 2: Major Purpose/Objectives**
   State the major purpose or objectives that you will accomplish. These are obtained from the client's written requirements and personal interviews. Beginning with the results brings focus to the meeting. The initial focus is on the client and their issues, not on you and your practice.

Current Situation

Factors affecting outcomes

- No sales training manager on board
- Extensive list of Performance Objectives
- Ambitious and do-able set of deliverables
- Nine weeks to target completion

SalesWinners INCORPORATED

3. **Slide 3: Current Situation**
   Following the purpose/objectives slide with the current situation reminds the client of the difference between where they are and where they want to go. Summarizing the current situation indicates to the client that you understand their needs, and it reinforces the decision they've made to use an outside source.

PRESENTING PROPOSALS

SalesWinners—a 'temp' solution

A track record of successes

- Serve only high-tech companies
- Direct responsibility for results
- Support resources available
- Able to meet schedule requirements

SalesWinners
INCORPORATED

4. **Slide 4: Summarize Your Capabilities**
   After letting your audience know that you understand their situation and what they want to accomplish, tell them about your capabilities. Provide a summary background of your consulting practice. Illustrate a few points about your background to build credibility for solving their issues.

Performance Objectives
A consolidation approach
Organization and capabilities
Positioning
Creating customer solutions
Qualifying and selling
SalesWinners
INCORPORATED

5. **Slide 5: List the Objectives–Provide the Approach**
   Stating the specific objectives that they want to obtain demonstrates that you understand their needs. Then you can effectively provide insight into the approach that you intend to use. In the DCDA example, I mentioned the fourteen Performance Objective points verbally, then used this approach slide. This kept the audience's attention and focused on the consolidation approach I proposed to use to accomplish the objectives that they had in mind.

PRESENTING PROPOSALS

Deliverables Overview

Seven critically important elements

1. Develop course agenda
2. Create pre- and post-testing materials
3. Rework existing presentations
4. Update existing competitive presentations
5. Develop new presentations
6. Provide speaker notes
7. Write instructor's guide

SalesWinners
INCORPORATED

6. **Slide 6: Deliverables**
   This slide tells them what you're going to give them. In this case, there were seven items that I planned to deliver as part of my consulting assignment. This provided the client a succinct summary of what they could expect from me in terms of the deliverables for the sales training course. This reinforced the approach I wanted to use without "giving away the store" in terms of any proprietary information that I might not have wanted to share.

Weekly Project Schedule

With weekly project reviews

1. Co./product info—develop course agenda
2. Framework and video tape presentations
3. Transcribe videos—develop speaker notes
4. First cut—revised and new presentations
5. Augment existing competitive presentations
6. Final presentation review and modifications
7. Pilot development—write instructor's guide

SalesWinners
INCORPORATED

7. **Slide 7: Value-Add No. 1**
   I used a weekly project schedule to build credibility and value to my proposed approach. Providing DCDA with a timeline of deliverables and weekly project reviews gave them the comfort factor they required, especially with the pressures from the Sales Department.

PRESENTING PROPOSALS

Results Enhancers

Items that can make a measurable difference

- Video tape presentations
- Transcribe audio portion for future use
- Use outside resource for in-depth competitive analysis (Option 1)
- Personally conduct the pilot program and future training sessions (Option 2)

SalesWinners
INCORPORATED

8. **Slide 8: Value-Add No. 2**
   I called this value-add slide "results enhancers." I presented my approach for using video and audio devices to capture information for the course development and for future reference. I also introduced options for additional services.

What Does All This Mean?

Price Proposal—The Bottom Line

- Project completed on schedule
- Quality high because of intensity of effort
- Value-adds for higher course evaluation
- Cost-Effective—$35,500 for total effort

SalesWinners
INCORPORATED

9. Slide 9: Price Proposal
This slide provides the price that will be charged for the value received. I proposed the price on a project basis, not on an daily fee basis, so that the client knew exactly what it was going to cost them.

PRESENTING PROPOSALS

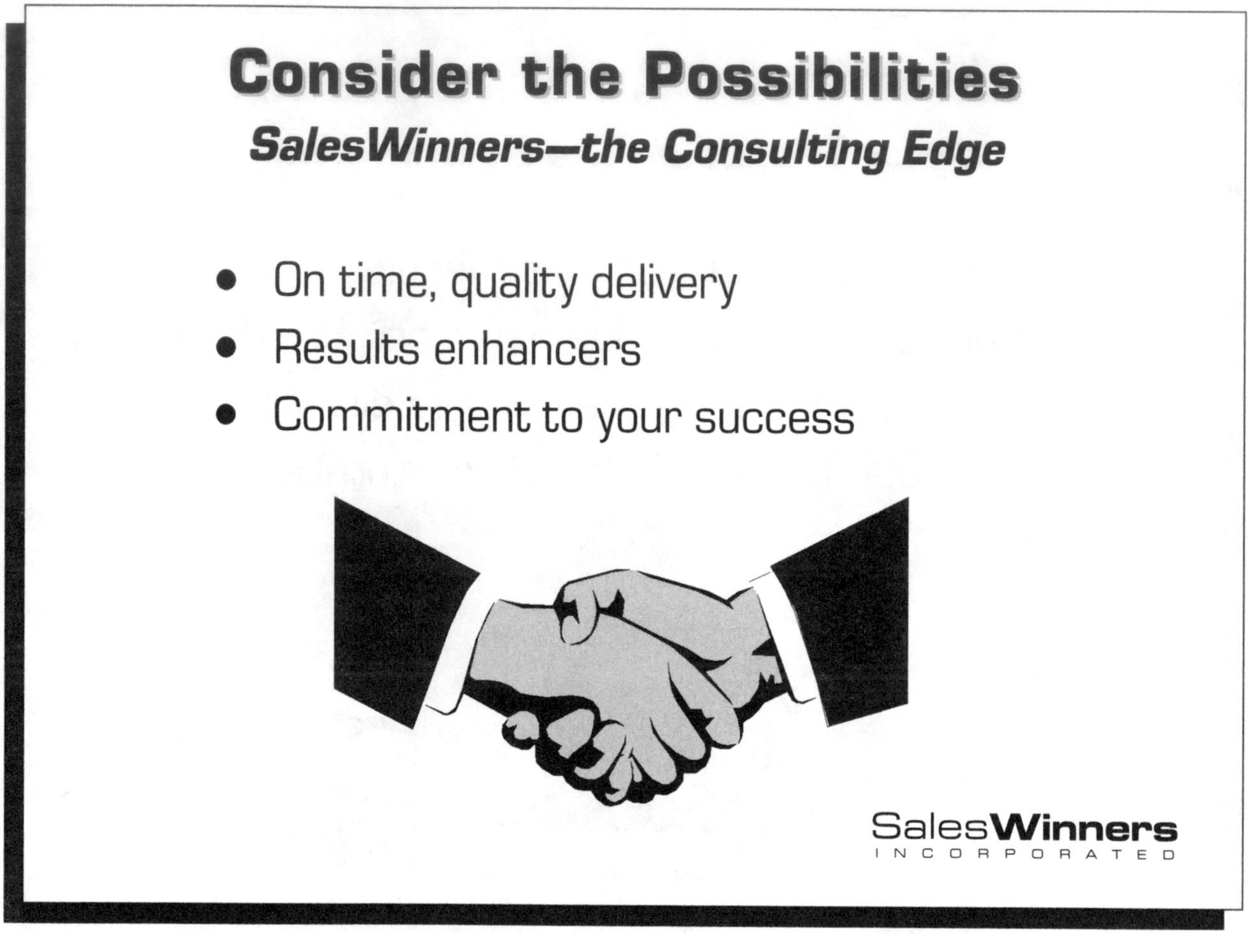
Consider the Possibilities
SalesWinners—the Consulting Edge
On time, quality delivery
Results enhancers
Commitment to your success
SalesWinners
INCORPORATED

10. **Slide 10: Summary**
    This slide provides a summary of the presentation and a reminder of why to choose my consulting practice.

Note: Clip art was selected from New Vision Technologies, Inc. *Presentation Task Force.*

CHAPTER 9
HANDLING LEGAL ISSUES

The consulting field is filled with legal issues that if mishandled could become major problems. This chapter covers contracts, consulting services agreements, non-disclosure agreements, independent contractor agreements, staying out of court, copyright, and trademarks. You will also get important advice on choosing a legal form your business, such as an explanation of the important differences between sole proprietorships and partnerships, corporations, S corporations, and Limited Liability Companies.

The saying "An ounce of prevention is worth a pound of cure" certainly applies to small business law. You need to get a great attorney and rely on his or her advice. You also need to acquaint yourself with some of the most basic legal issues you are likely to run into before you find yourself in the courtroom.

SOLE PROPRIETORSHIP

This form of business is the easiest to start because you need to obtain only the licenses that are required to begin business operation. The sole proprietorship gives you absolute control over your business, more so than other business structures such as partnerships or corporations. Very often, a small business owner will choose to start with a proprietorship. As the business grows, he or she might explore the possibility of forming a partnership or a corporation.

You will need to contact your local county or city clerk's office to determine what is required to operate a business in your area.

The sole proprietor's income from the business is treated as personal income. You can declare this income as part of Schedule C, Profit and Loss from a Business or Profession, with a standard 1040 Federal Individual Income tax return. You will also need Form 1040ES, Declaration of Estimated Tax for Individuals. The IRS will supply you with vouchers for submission of quarterly estimated tax payments. These payments are made in January, April, June, and September.

ADVANTAGES

- You are in business
- Easy to form

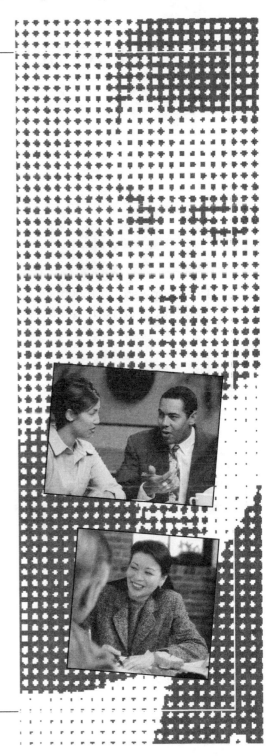

HANDLING LEGAL ISSUES

There are hardly any restrictions and very few forms to fill out. You need only file with your local city or county clerk's office.

- Control of profits
  As a sole proprietor, you control all of the money made by the business.
- Control of decision-making
  You make all business operation calls.
- Flexibility
  You are management, and you can respond more quickly to day-to-day changes and decisions.
- Freedom from bureaucracy
  You experience less government control and taxation.
- Simpler taxes
  You don't have to do a separate tax return for the business, and you don't have to prepare a balance sheet for the business.

Sole proprietorships gives you control over your business.

Disadvantages

- Unlimited liability
  As a sole proprietor, you are responsible for 100 percent of all business debts and obligations. This liability covers all of the proprietor's assets, including his or her house and car. Additional insurance coverage may be needed for personal injury or physical loss that may hamper the continuity of the business.
- Fragile business existence
  The death, physical impairment, or mental incapacitation of the owner can result in the termination of the business.
- Difficulty raising capital and financing
  It is typically more difficult for sole proprietors to raise operating cash or arrange long-term financing because they have fewer assets.
- One view, one way of doing business
  All the decision-making power rests with one individual.
- Less professional appearance

However, with complete control of a company comes complete liability for debt and obligations.

HANDLING LEGAL ISSUES

A sole proprietorship appears less professional than a partnership, and certainly less so than a corporation.

PARTNERSHIP

The Uniform Partnership Act defines a partnership as "an association of two or more persons to carry on as co-owners of a business for profit." Although not required by law, you may have to submit written Articles of Partnership. This would apply, for instance, if you wanted to open a company bank account. These articles would define the contributions made by the partners to the business–financial, managerial, material, or other. They would also define the roles of each partner in the business relationship. All articles should be filed with your secretary of state.

In a partnership, all persons involved are seen as co-owners of the company.

A partnership differs from a corporation in terms of the limited life of the partnership, the unlimited liability of at least one of the partners, the co-ownership of the assets, mutual agency, share of management, and share in partnership profits.

ADVANTAGES

- Easy to form
  Set-up expenses are kept to a minimum, and the legal documentation required to form a partnership is more straightforward and less complicated than that needed for incorporation.
- Direct rewards
  Partners have more motivation, as they directly share in the profits.
- Improved growth possibilities
  Attracting capital for financing a business operating under a partnership is easier than it is for a sole proprietorship.
- Flexibility
  Executing decisions is easier than it would be in a corporation, but more difficult than it would be in a sole proprietorship.
- Freedom from bureaucracy

HANDLING LEGAL ISSUES

This arrangement will give you more freedom from federal regulations and taxation.

DISADVANTAGES

- Unlimited liability of at least one partner
  One or more partner must assume the business risks and purchase considerable insurance to protect the business.
- Instability
  If any one partner decides to quit or passes on, the partnership is dissolved. The business can still operate based on the right of survivorship and the creation of a new partnership. Partnership insurance should be considered.
- Difficulty in obtaining large sums of capital
  Long-term capital may be difficult to find. Using partnership assets as collateral makes it somewhat easier than in the case of a sole proprietorship.
- Firm is tied to the acts and judgment of one partner as agent
  All partners can be held liable for partnership business activities and the commitments of any partner.
- Severing partnership ties
  Buying out a partner can be a difficult process, unless an agreement is reached at the beginning of the partnership.

If one or more people within a partnership leaves, the partnership is dissolved.

TYPES OF ARTICLES FOUND IN A PARTNERSHIP AGREEMENT

- Name
- Purpose
- Domicile
- Duration of agreement
- Character of partners: general, limited, active, or silent
- Contributions by partners: at inception, at a later date
- Business expenses
- Authority
- Separate debts
- Books, records, and method of accounting

Partnership agreements outline the responsibilities, duties, and legal rights of each partner within the company.

- Division of profits and losses
- Draws or salaries
- Rights of continuing partner
- Death of a partner: dissolution and winding up
- Employee management
- Release of debts
- Sale of partnership interest
- Arbitration
- Modifications of partnership agreement
- Settlements of disputes
- Required and prohibited acts
- Absence and disability

The varied types of partnerships reflect the inequality between partners in many situations.

Are There Specific Types of Partnerships?

Yes. This is especially true if the partners are unequal in some way. Examples are:

- Ostensible partner
  Active and known as a partner
- Active partner
  May or may not be ostensible as well
- Secret partner
  Active, but not known or held out as a partner
- Dormant partner
  Inactive and not known or held out as a partner
- Silent partner
  Inactive, but may be known as a partner
- Nominal partner
  Not a true partner, but can be represented in name or by some other representation
- Subpartner
  Not a member of the partnership, but contracts with a partner to participate in the interest of such partner in the firm's business and profits

HANDLING LEGAL ISSUES

- Limited partner
  Assuming compliance with the statutory formalities, the limited partner risks only his or her agreed investment in the business

Partnerships range from full executive involvement in the company to limited investment in the company.

CORPORATIONS

Since the corporation is considered a distinct legal entity with no ties to the individuals who own it as a legal structure, it is a very attractive option for small business owners. Incorporating is, however, a complicated undertaking. It gives you the opportunity to present your firm to the public as a bigger company than it actually is. It also gives you a better shot at obtaining long-term financing, although this is generally not a consideration for a consulting business. Since you are not held personally responsible for the corporation, your personal assets, including your personal bank accounts, may remain untouched if the business fails. There are, however, more regulations and government filings to deal with than there are in sole proprietorships and partnerships.

Before you decide to incorporate, ask yourself:

- How much risk are you willing to absorb?
- If something happened to the principal(s), how long would the company be able to function?
- What legal structure would offer the greatest flexibility in terms of administration?
- How will the laws of incorporating in your state influence your decision on method of incorporation?
- Will you need to raise any capital?
- What is the goal of your enterprise?
- Are you willing to share control of the business with outsiders?
- Is there a tax advantage or incentive for you to incorporate?

Though an attractive option to small business owners, incorporation involves a complicated series of government rules and regulations.

ADVANTAGES

- Limited liability
  If the company is sued, the individual members of the company are protected under the corporate shield. In other words,

they cannot be held liable unless the company is successfully sued for an outrageous act.

- Going concern
  If a principal of the firm passes on or becomes incapacitated for any length of time, the business will continue to exist as a legal entity.
- Selling stock in the corporation
  It is easier to sell small amounts of stock to raise capital.
- Lower tax rate
  In some cases, the tax rate for corporations may be less than it would be for other forms of business structures.
- Professionalism
  Incorporating makes your firm look bigger and more important in the eyes of clients, suppliers, and the financial community.

Disadvantages

- Activities limited by charter and various laws
  Depending upon which state you incorporate in, you may have flexibility or you may have no options whatsoever.
- Extensive government regulations
  Filing reports for federal, state, and local governments can be tedious and time-consuming. Filings can include financial statements, such as a balance sheet.
- Double taxation
  You must pay corporate income tax on corporate earnings. If the earnings are distributed to shareholders as dividends, you must also pay personal income tax on those same earnings.

Corporations protect the individual owners of the company from full liability.

Though a complicated legal structure, with extreme care you can undertake the process without the guidance of legal counsel.

FILING FOR INCORPORATION

Although incorporation is considered the most complex legal business structure, it is possible for a small business owner to incorporate without legal counsel. To minimize legal fees, consider obtaining and filling out all forms for incorporation yourself. Forms and guidelines are available from your state secretary of state's office.

HANDLING LEGAL ISSUES

Prior to filing with the state, you should have your attorney advise you as to whether or not incorporation is the right step for your business. If so, have him or her review your incorporation documentation to ensure that you have included all required information.

A corporation is formed with the authority of a state government. Incorporation allows capital stock to be issued while the principals create an organization. Approval for incorporation must be obtained from the secretary of state's office after filing articles of organization. The secretary of state in the filing state will issue a charter for the corporation stating the powers and limitations of the corporation. Officers of the corporation can be employees of the corporation while owning stock in the corporation. As such, they can be held liable for such items as withholding tax, unemployment tax, Workers' Compensation, and Social Security.

Incorporation forms require the following:

1. **Company name**
   You begin the process of incorporating very simply, by selecting a name for your corporation. The name must have the words "Corporation," "Inc.," "Limited," or "Ltd." contained within to indicate that the liability of the shareholders is limited.
   You need to reserve that name with the secretary of state's Corporate Division office. If you have an out-of-state company, check to see whether or not you can use your company name in that state. In some states you will have to pay a reservation fee, typically around $20, to reserve the name for a 120-day waiting period. Once your name has been accepted by the state, your corporation can officially use that name, however, this does not protect you from being sued for trademark infringement.
2. **Mailing address**
   You must have a mailing address for your company. In some states, a P.O. box is not acceptable unless your business is located in a rural area with no formal street address.

HANDLING LEGAL ISSUES

3. **Period of duration**
Corporations are usually considered to be perpetual, ongoing entities unless otherwise stated. It is highly unusual to specify a date in the future when the corporation will no longer be in existence.
4. **Lawful reason or a specific purpose for the business**
Some states may require that you define your specific purpose in terms of what the company will do to make a profit. A statement such as "and all other legal acts permitted for general and business corporations" may be included as part of this section. Educational or not-for-profit organizations may have to submit additional documentation to support their organizational purpose.
5. **Number of shares to be issued and a statement of par value, if applicable**
If the corporation decides to issue more than one class of shares, or if a class of shares has two or more series, then you must include a statement that outlines various condition. Those conditions may be total number of shares of each class authorized for issue, total number of shares issued for a series, or a fixed number authorized by the board of directors. In addition, a designation of each series or class of shares and the rights, preferences, privileges, and restrictions granted to or imposed on the respective classes must be included in the statement. If the board of directors authorizes a fixed number of shares, the articles of incorporation may also authorize the board to increase or decrease shares without going below the number of shares outstanding.
6. **Number of directors constituting the initial board of directors and their names and addresses**
Typically, in most states, only one director is required. If you are the only director, you will most likely be named president and secretary as well. Individuals can serve dual roles as officers and board members.

7. **Name and address of the incorporator**
   The incorporator is the individual who is the founder of the corporation. If there is more than one individual involved, only one should volunteer to provide his or her name and address as the incorporator.
8. **Date when corporation existence will begin**
   Choose a starting date. This should coincide with the date you expect to formally operate your business as a corporation.
9. **Notarize documents**
   Some states require the signature of a notary public on all incorporation forms.
10. **Name and address of registered agent**
   The registered agent of the company is the individual who is incorporating the business and who received all the formal information about incorporating the business from the secretary of state's office.

Starting a corporation involves the election of directors and officers, the issuing of stock, and the settlement of fiscal matters through the bank and IRS.

STARTING A CORPORATION

Hold an Organization Meeting to Elect Directors and Officers

In some corporations, the officers will consist of one or two individuals–the president and a treasurer.

Adopt Bylaws

The corporate bylaws should spell out, in detail, the methods by which your company will operate. They should specify the time and place of the annual shareholders' meeting, shareholder voting rights, the titles and authority of the officers of the company, and the specific powers granted to the president and the board of directors. Bylaws are not filed with the state and are not accessible to the general public.

Issue Shares of Stock

As part of the incorporating process, a certain number of shares of stock, generally 1,000, need to be issued at a predetermined value. This value is usually $1 per share.

HANDLING LEGAL ISSUES

Adopt Banking Resolutions

Banks use a special form that you must fill out to establish a formal banking relationship and open a corporate account. The form will include special instructions for depositing and withdrawing funds, signatures that will be required on checks or withdrawal forms, borrowing privileges, letters of credit, how the company will repay the bank for any loans that are due, and what assets of the corporation the bank can seize as part of that repayment.

Fix a Fiscal Year

Some companies use a calendar year beginning January 1 and running to December 31; others use from July 1 to June 30 of the following year.

Obtain Your Tax I.D. Numbers from the Internal Revenue Service

Tax I.D. numbers are used for employee withholding on federal and state tax forms. These forms must be filed with the Internal Revenue Service and will be used for filing income tax forms. Tax I.D. numbers can be obtained from the Internal Revenue Service office in your state.

Obtain a Corporate Seal

The corporate seal is typically a round emblem that has the words "Corporate Seal" included in the design. The name of the corporation and the state in which the company does business should also be a part of the seal. Corporate seals are available from your secretary of state's office.

Contact County and Local Agencies Regarding Area Business Requirements and Restrictions

Some county or local government agencies will have restrictions such as zoning laws, requirements for building modifications, and/or regulations regarding fire exits and sprinkler systems. Check with your local governments–some of these regulations will likely apply to your business.

HANDLING LEGAL ISSUES

Communication between directors and shareholders through meetings is essential.

ONGOING REQUIREMENTS OF A CORPORATION

Hold Shareholders' and Board of Directors' Meetings on a Regular Basis

There should be annual shareholders' and board of directors' meetings.

Take Minutes at Board Meetings and Make Them Available to Shareholders

Minutes are very important. They are proof that your firm is acting as a corporation. They provide protection against individuals who may try to "dent" the corporate shield in a legal dispute with the corporation.

Advise Shareholders of Board of Director Elections

All shareholders should be notified of impending elections, including the number of openings, a description of potential candidates for the board, and a sealed ballot to vote for candidates.

Advise Shareholders of Changes in Stock Disbursements

As your company grows, the potential for stock swaps with other companies, mergers, takeovers, and stock splits become a matter for shareholder vote. The corporate bylaws may require a special meeting in the event of a takeover, merger, or other stock disbursement.

File Taxes

Corporations are required to file income taxes as well as quarterly estimated tax payments with the Internal Revenue Service and state and local tax authorities, when applicable.

SPECIAL TYPES OF CORPORATIONS

S Corporations

In some cases, to alleviate a tax burden, individuals may choose to form an S Corporation (formerly known as a

HANDLING LEGAL ISSUES

Subchapter S Corporation). An S Corporation is a corporation for which an election has been made with the Internal Revenue Service for the income to pass through and be taxed directly to the stockholders on a pro rata basis. This allows the small business owner to avoid dealing with the double taxation of profits and dividends. Also, shareholders may be able to offset business losses by the corporation against their personal income, subject to certain restrictions.

In an S Corporation the IRS taxes the stockholders directly.

Some provisions for forming an S Corporation are:

- The corporation must have thirty-five or fewer shareholders who are either individuals, estates, or certain qualifying trusts
- The corporation may have only one class of stock
- Nonresident alien shareholders are ineligible
- All shareholders must consent to an election
- The corporation may not own eighty percent or more of another corporation
- At least seventy-five percent of the company's receipts must be derived from the business rather than from outside investments or passive income
- Former S Corporations that have revoked or had their S status terminated must wait five years before making a new election

LIMITED LIABILITY COMPANIES

The limited liability company (LLC) is a relatively new business structure that is valid in almost every state. It is a cross between a corporation and a partnership. Essentially, an LLC carries the limited liability advantages of a corporation but operates with the flexibility and tax obligations of a partnership. In terms of taxes, it is less restrictive and less expensive than an S Corporation.

S Corporations, at the time of this book's printing, are allowed in all states except Massachusetts, Hawaii, and Vermont. All three of those states have the legalization of the LLC structure under consideration.

The LLC is becoming a very popular form of organization for new, small businesses.

HANDLING LEGAL ISSUES

If you are setting up a partnership or investing with others in a corporation, do everything you possibly can to maintain control.

Carefully plan out the structure of your business before decreasing its value with poor decisions.

STREETWISE ADVICE ON BUSINESS STRUCTURE

You Don't Need to Incorporate

If you are going to be the only employee of your consulting business and you don't envision a significant chance of getting sued or having large debts, then you'd be better off not incorporating—and saving the related expenses.

Keep Control

If you are setting up a partnership or investing with others in a corporation, do everything you possibly can to maintain control. Fifty-one percent of a two-person corporation is worth infinitely more than fifty percent. A minority share in a closely held corporation can be worth very little. The majority shareholder may set salaries, determine expenditures, or sell control—or do just about anything he or she pleases unless the corporate bylaws state otherwise. Similarly, a partnership agreement that gives one partner decision-making power, rendering the other partner powerless, is worthless financially.

Death, Taxes, Disagreements

Don't kid yourself! No matter how harmoniously your relationships with other major investors in a corporation or partnership begin, there will inevitably be disagreements. There might and probably will be major disagreements. You need to clearly figure out what will happen when, not if, a major disagreement occurs.

Think It Through Before You Start

Many small business owners don't give enough thought to structuring their business before plunging into it. One woman gave a fifty percent partnership to another woman who was essentially going to be her secretary in the consulting practice. The value of your share of your business, and your business as a whole, can be dramatically affected by the decisions you make during the formative stages. So weigh the issues carefully.

HANDLING LEGAL ISSUES

CONSIDER YOUR NEEDS FOR "CASHING OUT"

One important factor to consider in setting up a business structure is how and when you hope to take large amounts of money out of the company. It might seem like a dream now, but suppose your plans all work out. When do you want to cash out and how?

If you plan on cashing out by selling the firm to a larger corporation in five years, for example, a traditional C corporation may suit your purposes fine. If you never plan to sell the business, and don't plan to have many employees or assets in your practice, but still want the protection of a corporate "shell" then an S corporation or a limited liability company would serve your needs better.

Loaning money to a corporation that you fully run gives you a greater chance of recouping that money if difficulties arise.

QUESTIONS & ANSWERS ON BUSINESS STRUCTURE

Is it possible to change the type of organization my business is?

Yes, it certainly is. However, there may be significant tax liabilities incurred in changing the structure of your firm. But a knowledgeable CPA or tax lawyer should be able to help you either avoid or minimize that liability.

If you switch to a corporate structure to avoid a legal action, you are unlikely to protect yourself from the ramifications of any incidents that occurred prior to your incorporation.

Can my corporation buy stock in other corporations?

A corporation can buy stock in other companies. It can borrow money from banks or conduct any type of financial transaction permitted an individual. Note, however, that an S corporation may not own more than eighty percent of another corporation.

Can I loan money to a corporation that I own?

Yes. One of the advantages of formally loaning money to a corporation that you wholly own is that you will have a greater chance of recouping your money as a debtor than as a shareholder, should your consulting practice experience difficulties.

Another advantage is that you can pay yourself interest that is tax deductible for the corporation. Remember, though, that you have

HANDLING LEGAL ISSUES

to pay taxes on the interest. The interest you can charge should be at market rate at the time of the loan.

If your loan balance is too high and your equity investment is too low, the IRS can reclassify part of the loan as equity, and your interest payments will become nondeductible dividends. You can pay yourself a salary as well. Make sure that it is within reason. If the tax authorities consider it to be excessive, they will restate the "excess" salary as a dividend and tax it as both corporate and personal income.

If you think that either your loan to or salary from your company is tipping the scales, check with a qualified tax advisor.

If you see your business as having a limited life with low risk you should run it as a sole proprietorship. If you are short on funds, try borrowing from friends before forming a partnership.

Can I buy assets in my own name and then lease them to my corporation?

Yes. This is usually done for two reasons. One is for tax purposes. If you own assets such as computers, buildings, or vehicles, they may be depreciated. Depreciation, under most circumstances, allows you to reduce your tax bill. Check with your accountant to see if your current and nonsalaried income levels allow you to qualify for income offsetting depreciation under the tax laws.

Another reason to personally own assets is to protect them from seizure should the corporation get into trouble. Also, if the personally owned asset is real estate, for instance, you will personally realize the profits from any appreciation in value. Remember, though, if you own the assets, you are in a personally liable position.

Leasing assets to your corporation is one way to get the money, other than salary, out of the corporation. There are special tax rules, however, that prevent you from using leasing as a method to avoid the "passive loss rules" in the tax code.

Is it easier to dissolve a partnership or a corporation?

Legally, it is easier to dissolve a partnership. Remember, a partnership is merely an agreement between two or more people. A corporation, however, is a distinct legal entity. Dissolving it will take a fair amount of time and expense.

The biggest hurdle in dissolving a partnership is arriving at an agreement with the other partner or partners regarding distribution of assets and liabilities and who, if anyone, will continue to run the business.

If you see your business as having a limited life with low risk you should run it as a sole proprietorship. If you are short on funds, try borrowing from friends before forming a partnership.

CONTRACTS

Like most people, small business owners tend to shy away from signing anything. They avoid contracts like the plague. But this is a risky way to do business.

When you are making a major consulting service sale, you need to get the details of the transaction in writing. If you don't, you will inevitably find yourself in the middle of a heated discussion over specific terms. Can sanctions be imposed if delivery per terms isn't met? What if the services rendered are considered unsatisfactory? In many cases, a purchase order and/or a written estimate will provide the answers to these types of questions and serve, in effect, as a contract.

For small, routine contracts, you may wish to have an attorney review the basic consulting contract that you will be using. For larger or unusual services, you may wish to have your attorney review the contract you intend to use, if not draft it. After you have been in business for awhile and have learned a thing or two from your attorney, you will gain the ability and confidence to write many of your own contracts.

For more important contracts, retain the original copy containing the original signatures from all parties. True, in many situations a photocopy or even an agreement without signatures offers adequate proof of a purchase or sale agreement, but nothing can beat an original copy as legal protection.

Any substantive change to a contract should be noted in writing. If it is in the body of the contract, then each change should be initialed by all parties involved. If it is in the form of an addendum, it should be signed by all parties involved. A contract should specify that it represents the entire agreement between the parties and that any changes must be in writing.

Contracts are important legal documents often overlooked by small business owners.

HANDLING LEGAL ISSUES

To avoid court and the legal costs associated with lawsuits, contracts should, generally, have a clause specifying that disputes will be arbitrated. The method of arbitration should be stated and the results of the arbitration should be held binding.

Understanding legal jargon will help you avoid problems in the future with contractual issues.

STREETWISE ADVICE ON CONTRACTS

YOURS VS. THEIRS

Whenever possible, provide the contract yourself. Don't use someone else's. You may save the cost of creating a contract, but you will lose that important control-over-content advantage a contract gives you.

UNDERSTAND IT

Understanding "legalese" may seem like an overwhelming task, if not an impossibility. But if you intend to build a growing consulting business, you need to become comfortable with contracts, their language, and their meaning. You should have your lawyer review every contract you don't fully understand. And you should have him or her carefully and clearly explain any terms or passages you don't completely understand.

As a business person you must understand that every business transaction has implications for your company. Don't sign anything blindly. Get past the legal jargon so that you can fully understand the contracts you are signing and be able to protect the best interests of your business.

STANDARDIZE

Because your consulting business will likely involve a lot of contracts, negotiate hard-to-get customers to adhere as closely as possible to your standard contract. Changing a long contract can take a lot of hard and time-consuming work. Any change in contractual wording requires that the entire contract be reviewed and proofed again. A change in one area can create misleading implications in another area of the contract. And a simple retyping can result in a serious typographical error or omission.

Any substantive change needs to be viewed suspiciously. Are there hidden implications that the other party has insisted upon?

Standardization can save you time, money, and headaches.

SAFEKEEPING

It is so easy to misplace contracts–even crucial ones. Keep copies of your contracts in a fireproof file, or even in your bank safe deposit box. If the contract is particularly important, have your lawyer keep a copy on file as well. Have one or more office copies available for easy reference. Don't use the original as your reference copy!

QUESTIONS & ANSWERS ABOUT CONTRACTS

Do big corporations alter standard contracts for smaller firms?

Yes, it happens frequently. But more often, the smaller firm just signs the standard agreement that it is given. Depending upon how much another corporation wants your service and how agreeable the particular people involved are, you may or may not be able to negotiate deviations from the standard contract.

How can I determine what points are negotiable?

Perhaps you can find another consultant in your industry who has previously negotiated with the firm in question. If not, you have two basic options. One is to make a formal proposal or counterproposal. The other is to have a more casual discussion. For example, you could say, "I'm used to having a deposit with the customer's commitment to a contract," or "For me to train your sales force in this program, I'll have to add an additional fee," and listen carefully to what the initial response is.

How can I avoid going to court if a contract is broken?

The best way to avoid a court battle over a broken contract is to have specific remedies for specific, potential problems written right into the original contract. A cover for a potential missed completion date, for instance, might be, "The payment will be reduced by a certain amount for every week the project is late." On another level, you

HANDLING LEGAL ISSUES

can stipulate within the contract that the entire contract go into binding arbitration, not court, in the event of a dispute.

Do I need to have my attorney read every contract?

After you have been in business for a period of time, you will begin to feel more confident in your ability to read contracts. Until then, however, I would have an attorney review every major contract and explain any passages or clauses in minor contracts that cause you difficulty.

What should I watch out for in contracts?

Watch out for any items that are inserted into your contracts by any other parties involved. These items may significantly alter the meaning of the contract. This is not an isolated occurrence—it happens all the time. Often, but not always, it is done innocently. Nonetheless, you need to be on constant guard against this problem. Don't sign anything that isn't exactly what you thought you were agreeing to.

Have attorneys review major contracts until you feel comfortable enough with the procedure to do so on your own.

Protecting Your Intellectual Property

In the typical consulting practice, you will want to protect many of the proprietary programs and publications you develop in the course of your ongoing business. Because you will frequently be presenting many of your unique business processes, forms, and other proprietary information to clients, you should try to protect your ownership of them. This can be done in a number of ways.

Copyrights

Items protected by copyright law include books, magazines, software, advertising copy, newspapers, music, movies, audio recordings, and artwork. Items not protected by copyright law include concepts or ideas, titles, names, and brands. In the United States, copyright protection automatically extends to any appropriate material. This is the case whether you file for a copyright notice or not.

However, if it is at all practical, you should spend the small fee (currently $20 in the United States) to formally register your copyright if the material is of significant value to you. This will increase

Copyrighting helps to protect your legal ownership of such media as books, magazines, and software.

both the legal protection of your work and the value of any rewards you might recover in an infringement of copyright lawsuit.

You should put a copyright notice on all copyrighted materials. This will decrease the likelihood of infringement. The copyright notice should be placed in a highly visible spot on the property, and it should include the word copyright or the copyright symbol, the first year the work was issued to the public, and the formal name of the holder of the copyright.

© 1998 Adams Media Corporation

To obtain U.S. copyright forms or for more information, contact the Copyright Office, Library of Congress, Washington, D.C. 20559.

Most other countries offer copyright protection that is roughly similar to that offered in the United States. And U.S. copyrighted material will usually be protected in other countries. While a few countries, particularly in Southeast Asia, have long ignored or not enforced copyright protection, the trend has been toward enforcing a strong uniform protection of copyrights worldwide.

TRADEMARKS

Unlike copyrights and patents, trademarks affect all businesses. When you use the name of your business publicly, you are using it as a trademark. When you sell products using a brand name, you are using that brand name as a trademark. The brand name of any service you provide is a service mark or, essentially, a trademark for services. A trademark or service mark may consist of letters, words, graphics, or any combination of these elements.

If you were the first person to use that trademark in commerce, you automatically have some protection for your trademark, even if you did not register your trademark. However, many small businesses get into trouble by doing an inadequate trademark search. They often inadvertently use a name already employed by another firm. You should hire an attorney to do a trademark search for you, especially if you intend to do business on a national basis. Some commer-

cial firms also provide trademark search services and/or offer access to their electronic trademark databases.

Trademarks do not necessarily offer national, let alone international, protection.

Trademarks do not necessarily offer protection across the nation, let alone internationally. Typically, they cover those geographic regions in which the trademark is being used. They also generally don't cover multiple classes of goods or services, but only the class of goods the trademark is being used in. For example, if you operate a local retail business called Big Balloons in the state of New York, it would not necessarily be in conflict with a retail store operating in California under the same name. Similarly, if a Big Balloon Flying School were to open in New York, it would not be in conflict with the Big Balloon store because the type of product being offered is noncompetitive.

If you plan to use your trademark nationally, you should register it with the U.S. federal government. Contact the U.S. Patent and Trademark Office, Washington, D.C. 20231. You can also seek protection for your trademark in individual states, but it is much weaker than federal registration. You will have to seek separate protection from every foreign country you want trademark protection in.

You need to make sure your trademark doesn't bear any resemblance to another firm's.

If you obtain federal registration in the United States, you should use the registered trademark symbol at the end of the mark. But you may not use this symbol until and unless the federal registration has been issued.

Businesship®

You cannot use someone else's trademark. Additionally, to avoid confusion, you need to make sure your trademark doesn't bear any resemblance to another firm's trademark.

In order for trademarks to offer protection, the copy cannot merely be descriptive of your function or product. For example, "Bicycle Store" would not offer trademark protection, but "The Merry Cycle Place" probably would. The validity of a trademark is subject to many variables. One examiner at the federal trademark office may have one opinion regarding the validity of a trademark application, and another examiner may have an entirely different opinion. So if your trademark registration or creation is important to you, consider hiring a specialized attorney.

PATENTS

If you are consulting in technical areas, most clients will want you to sign an agreement before you begin the assignment that all patents coming from your work will be exclusively owned by them. This is usually a fair policy. The patent work will likely be done by their attorney with only minimal effort on your part. However, make sure the contract spells out how you will be reimbursed for this effort.

A patent gives you the right to litigate against anyone who infringes upon it.

In the course of your work, you may also develop patents that you will be free to own yourself. Many people think of patents in connection with inventions. But patents are granted for a wide range of creations. You can be granted a design patent that will protect the "look" of a product or even a plant patent to protect a particular hybrid plant.

For a patent to be effective in the United States, you need to apply for the patent within one year of the first commercial use of the product. But it is recommended that you apply for the patent before the product is placed on the market.

The authority of a patent is limited to the country in which you have applied for that patent. You need to apply for a patent in each country in which you intend to market your product. In most countries, application for the patent must be made prior to placing the product on the market.

Most U.S. patents have a life span of twenty years, commencing with the date of application. Patents cannot be renewed. Design patents offer protection for fourteen years. To be awarded a patent, an invention must be considered novel and nonobvious. And, even though the federal government may award a patent, it may later be revoked if it is found to infringe on another patent.

A patent gives you the right to litigate against another party whom you believe is infringing upon your patent. You must take your case to the court–there is nothing automatic in patent protection. If the alleged infringer is a major corporation, be prepared for rapidly mounting legal expenses. You also need to consider the very real possibility that another individual or company may take

legal action against you for infringing on their patent, even though you hold a valid patent for your product, design, or invention.

A basic patent application fee can be several hundred dollars, depending upon the size of your business. The process is quite complex, and you would be well-advised to spend the several thousand dollars necessary to have the filing done by a patent attorney. If you are awarded the patent, you will need to pay additional fees to the patent office over the course of the patent life in order to keep the patent active throughout its term.

AGREEMENT TEMPLATES

To make it easier to get your consulting business off the ground, this section includes templates and examples from my consulting practice that you can review and modify for your use. These forms have worked for me over the years. Before using any of these forms, have your attorney review them to limit your liability and to ensure that all contingencies are covered.

TEMPLATE DESCRIPTIONS

Some of the most often used forms include:

Consulting Services Agreement

In my experience, the client usually asks the consultant to sign the client's consulting agreement. Most corporations have a consulting agreement in their forms inventory. To help you with smaller clients that may not have agreements on file, or with corporations that would like to review your consulting agreement, an example is provided.

Non-disclosure agreement

Again, agreements of this type typically will be provided by your clients. Because of the intimate insight and knowledge you often gain about your client's business, most customers will expect you to keep all interactions confidential. I have modified a representative client non-disclosure agreement as an example that typifies what you will often be asked to sign.

Independent contractor agreement

From time-to-time, you may require the services of another consultant to help you on a client assignment. In effect, this consultant will be subcontracting his efforts to you. To protect your trade secrets, as well as the confidentiality of your client, you may want to execute an Independent Contractor Agreement with your consultant.

HANDLING LEGAL ISSUES

(Your Company Name or Logo)

CONSULTING SERVICES AGREEMENT

In consideration of the agreement by Blank Corporation ("Blank"), a Delaware corporation, to have ABC Consultants ("ABC"), a (State) corporation serve as a Consultant for Blank, we agree this ________ day of _______, 19 __, that:

1. ABC shall perform those services as requested and directed by a person or person(s) designated by Blank on a mutually agreed to schedule.
2. For performance under this Agreement, ABC shall be compensated per the Fee Schedule included as Attachment B to this Agreement.
3. ABC is not authorized to incur any expenses on behalf of Blank without the prior authorization of a designated agent of Blank.
4. This agreement shall terminate on ______, 19__, unless it is terminated by ABC or by Blank upon two weeks written advance notice. Blank may terminate this Agreement immediately upon ABC's refusal or inability to perform any provision of this Agreement or upon ABC's breach of any provision. Paragraphs 5-8 shall remain in effect despite any termination of this Agreement.
5. ABC will abide by the provisions of the Blank-ABC Confidential Disclosure Agreement executed _____________ (Date) which is included as Appendix A to this Agreement.
6. Upon the termination of this Agreement or upon an earlier request by Blank, ABC will return all Blank property to Blank unless ABC has Blank's written permission to keep it. The product of all work which is performed under this agreement shall be the property of Blank, and Blank shall have the right to use, sell, license, publish, or otherwise disseminate or transfer rights in such work product.

HANDLING LEGAL ISSUES

7. During the term of this Agreement and without further consideration, ABC will assign to Blank, all rights, title, and interest in any copyrightable material which is produced in connection with this Agreement, excluding information previously copyrighted by ABC.
8. With respect to all subject matter, such as ideas, processes, designs, and methods which ABC discloses or uses in the performance of this Agreement; (a) ABC warrants that ABC has the right to make such disclosure of use without liability to others; and (b) ABC agrees to hold Blank harmless for the use of subject matter which ABC knows or reasonably should know any other has rights in, except for that subject matter which ABC discloses to Blank in writing along with the identity of the other before Blank uses the subject matter.
9. ABC shall not assign rights or delegate responsibilities under this Agreement without Blank's prior written approval.
10. This Agreement is made under and shall be construed according to the laws of __________ (State).

Blank Corporation

____

By: (Signature and Title)

Date: ______________________________

ABC Consultants

____

By: (Signature and Title)

Date: ______________________________

HANDLING LEGAL ISSUES

CONFIDENTIAL DISCLOSURE AGREEMENT

Agreement No.: __________ Consultant: (Your Consulting Firm)

Effective Date: (Month, Day, Year) Address: (City and State of Practice)

(Client) and (Consultant) agree to establish a confidential relationship to exchange certain confidential, proprietary, and trade secret information ("Information") in accordance with the terms and conditions stated herein:

Purpose

(Client) will provide Market and Strategic Information together with Current and Planned Product Information to (Consultant). (Your name) will be given access to data on personnel and salaries not publicly available.

All notices required by this License shall be in writing and sent to the parties designated below.

(Client) Attention: (Agreement contact, address)

(Consultant): (Your name and address)

The parties agree that this Agreement states the entire agreement between the parties with respect to its subject matter and supersedes all prior agreements and representations of the parties, oral or written. This Agreement may only be amended in writing and signed by duly authorized representatives of both parties.

(Client)

(Consultant)

By: (Signature and Date)

By: (Signature and Date)

Name: (Print or type)

Name: (Print or type)

Title

Title

1. Identification of Information

1.1 Written

The disclosing party shall identify all written information provided under this Agreement, regardless of the media on which it is contained, by including or affixing a legend stating that the information is confidential and proprietary information of the disclosing party and/or its suppliers prior to disclosure to the receiving party. Samples and prototypes shall be considered written information for purposes of this Agreement.

1.2 Verbal

Information verbally communicated by the disclosing party to the receiving party under this Agreement shall be verbally identified as being confidential and proprietary information of the disclosing party and/or its suppliers prior to or simultaneous with disclosure to the receiving party.

2. Obligations of Confidentiality

2.1 Any information disclosed by either party to the other party shall remain the property of the disclosing party and/or its suppliers. No license rights are granted to the receiving party, directly or indirectly, to use the Information disclosed under this Agreement for any purpose other than for the Purpose stated herein.

2.2 Any information disclosed by either party to the other party shall only be made available to employees, agents, or consultants of the receiving party who have a need to know and who have agreed in writing to abide by the terms and conditions of this Agreement prior to disclosure.

2.3 The receiving party shall not reproduce the information provided under this Agreement in any manner or for any purpose without the prior written authorization of the disclosing party except as stated herein.

2.4 The receiving party shall immediately notify the disclosing party of any disclosure, inquiry, or demand made by any third party regarding the information.

2.5 The receiving party shall protect the information provided under this Agreement by taking all necessary and reasonable precautions to prevent unauthorized disclosure for a period of three (3) years from the date of disclosure.

3. Exceptions to Obligations

3.1 The receiving party shall not be liable under this Agreement for disclosure of information under the following circumstances:

3.1.1 The information required to be disclosed by judicial or governmental action after all available legal remedies to maintain the confidentiality of the Information have been exhausted;

3.1.2 The information is made public through no fault of the receiving party;

3.1.3 The information was known to the receiving party prior to disclosure by the disclosing party and the receiving party provides written notice to the disclosing party to that effect any time after disclosure;

3.1.4 The information is independently developed by the receiving party subsequent to disclosure by the disclosing party.

4. Return of Information

4.1. Any information disclosed under this Agreement, together with any and all authorized copies, shall be returned by the receiving party to the disclosing party promptly upon the disclosing party's written request or upon termination of this Agreement.

5. TERMINATION

5.1 Either party may terminate this Agreement if the other party becomes insolvent, files a Petition in Bankruptcy, ceases doing business, or fails to cure a breach of any term or condition of this Agreement within thirty (30) days written notice specifying such breach.

5.2 The rights and obligations of the parties as set forth in Articles 2 and 3 shall survive any termination of this Agreement.

6. GENERAL

6.1. Should any provision of this Agreement be held by a court of competent jurisdiction to be illegal, invalid, or unenforceable, the remaining provisions of this Agreement shall not be affected or impaired thereby.

6.2. The failure of either party to enforce any term or condition of this Agreement shall not constitute a waiver of either party's right to enforce each and every term and condition of this Agreement.

6.3. This Agreement shall not be assignable by either party without the prior written consent of the other party. Any attempt to assign any part of this Agreement without such consent shall be void.

6.4 This Agreement shall be binding upon and inure to the benefit of the parties' successors, legal representatives, and authorized assigns.

6.5 This Agreement shall be interpreted and governed by the laws of the State of (State).

HANDLING LEGAL ISSUES

STAYING OUT OF COURT

In all but the most extreme cases, you want to avoid going to court either as a plaintiff or a defendant. Think about it. Do you really want to shell out the huge legal fees you are likely to incur? Do you want to have your time tied up for months or even years? Do you want, after all the expense and time, to lose your case? Courts offer uncertain outcomes. Even if you are right and see the situation as clear-cut, you can still lose your case.

You might not be drawing a big salary, but your time and the time of your key managers is valuable. Time spent in court or thinking about a court case is time spent away from growing your business.

Try to avoid going to court—and amassing huge legal fees—at all costs.

The outcome of going to court is extremely uncertain, and a loss could significantly change the way you do business. And, win or lose, a court case will have the same effect on your cash flow–cash flowing out.

The uncertainty of the outcome can be exacerbated by the timing of the outcome. No one can predict how long a court case will last. While a small claims hearing might not take years, the possibility of any other type of case lasting that long is quite real.

If you suspect that you might eventually be forced to pay out a settlement, you might get lulled into delaying the end of a court case. But remember that you need to disclose outstanding suits in your financial statements, and such disclosures may affect your ability to borrow or raise cash. Also, settlements can be subject to interest.

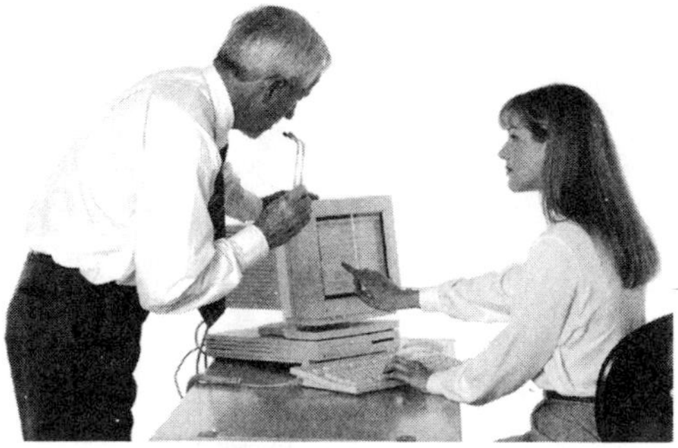

AVOIDANCE

The best way to stay out of court is to avoid problems before they occur. Run your business within the law. Run your business with humanity–make your workplace a fun place to be. Develop good, solid employment policies, especially in the critical areas of hiring, promoting, firing, and sexual harassment.

Use contracts whenever appropriate, with all the key details spelled out clearly in writing. And include in your contracts, whenever possible, a proviso that directs all disputes into binding arbitration, not court.

HANDLING LEGAL ISSUES

Finally, don't be shy about consulting an attorney whenever you have questions about employment or business decisions that may portend a legal risk for you. Spending a few bucks for a half of hour advice here and there is certainly worth saving the major expense of a court battle.

Early Response

In many potentially litigious situations, an early response may avert a legal suit. Often, legal claims arise out of misunderstandings, which good communication can alleviate. For example, if a client has decided not to pay your bill in full as invoiced because he or she was not satisfied with the quality of the services delivered, call the client immediately. Back up your verbal communication with a letter to the client. You need to get them to see the quality issue from your point of view and instill empathy for your situation. Just sending a demanding second notice, without discussing the problem with the client, is begging for court involvement.

Dealing with misunderstandings and small breaches of contract in the beginning will avoid larger problems later on.

If an employee complains about sexually hostile behavior in your workplace, promptly take action to eliminate the behavior. This may satisfy the victim and keep you out of court altogether. But even if the case does end up in court, your attempts to correct or alleviate the problem will count in your favor.

Generally, in any negative business situation, respond quickly and maintain dialogue and rapport with the other party. This policy never hurts!

Settlement Meetings

A face-to-face settlement meeting with the opposing party can help you avoid the courtroom. Any such meeting should be conducted on a peer-to-peer basis. This means company president to company president, for example. Of course, if you are the sole proprietor of a company and the other party is IBM, don't expect the president of IBM to meet with you. But do insist on meeting with someone in as similar a position to yours as possible. For example, if you are trying to resolve a problem with a large client, try to speak with the national manager, not the district manager or the purchasing agent for your account.

HANDLING LEGAL ISSUES

If you encounter problems in attempting a settlement with another party through informal meetings, try a more formal approach. Try meeting in a neutral location with attorneys for both parties in attendance.

The presence of attorneys signals confidence. It sends the message that both you and the disputing party are willing to pursue the matter through the courts if necessary. Through such a meeting, you will be able to ascertain the strength of the opposing party's claim or defense, and hear his or her arguments, much as you would if the case goes to court. Of course, the opposing side will be able to size up your case or defense as well.

Formal meetings, with attorneys present, can help assess the position of the other party, and will demonstrate the seriousness of the issue.

ARBITRATION

If you can't resolve an issue with calls or meetings, consider binding arbitration. In this case, both parties agree on an arbitrator (often a retired judge arranged for through an arbitration organization). Both parties agree that the results of the arbitration will be binding and may be entered into the prevailing court. Be sure to get the agreement to arbitrate in writing.

IN COURT

There are exceptions to avoiding or delaying an appearance in court. Sometimes you will want to get there as quickly as possible. If your rights as a small business owner are being wantonly trampled on by a large corporation, think about going to court. Corporate giants typically figure that a small entrepreneur will back down because he or she doesn't have the funds to do legal battle or will jump at the first pathetic settlement offered.

But do be absolutely sure that you want to pursue your claim through to resolution before you file with the courts. Have your attorney advise you. Find out what the costs might be, what the time element might be, and what the various outcomes, good and bad, might be.

WHEN IN DOUBT

When in doubt or uncertain about any legal issue–don't skimp–hire the best attorney you can afford. Remember, "an ounce of prevention is worth a pound of cure."

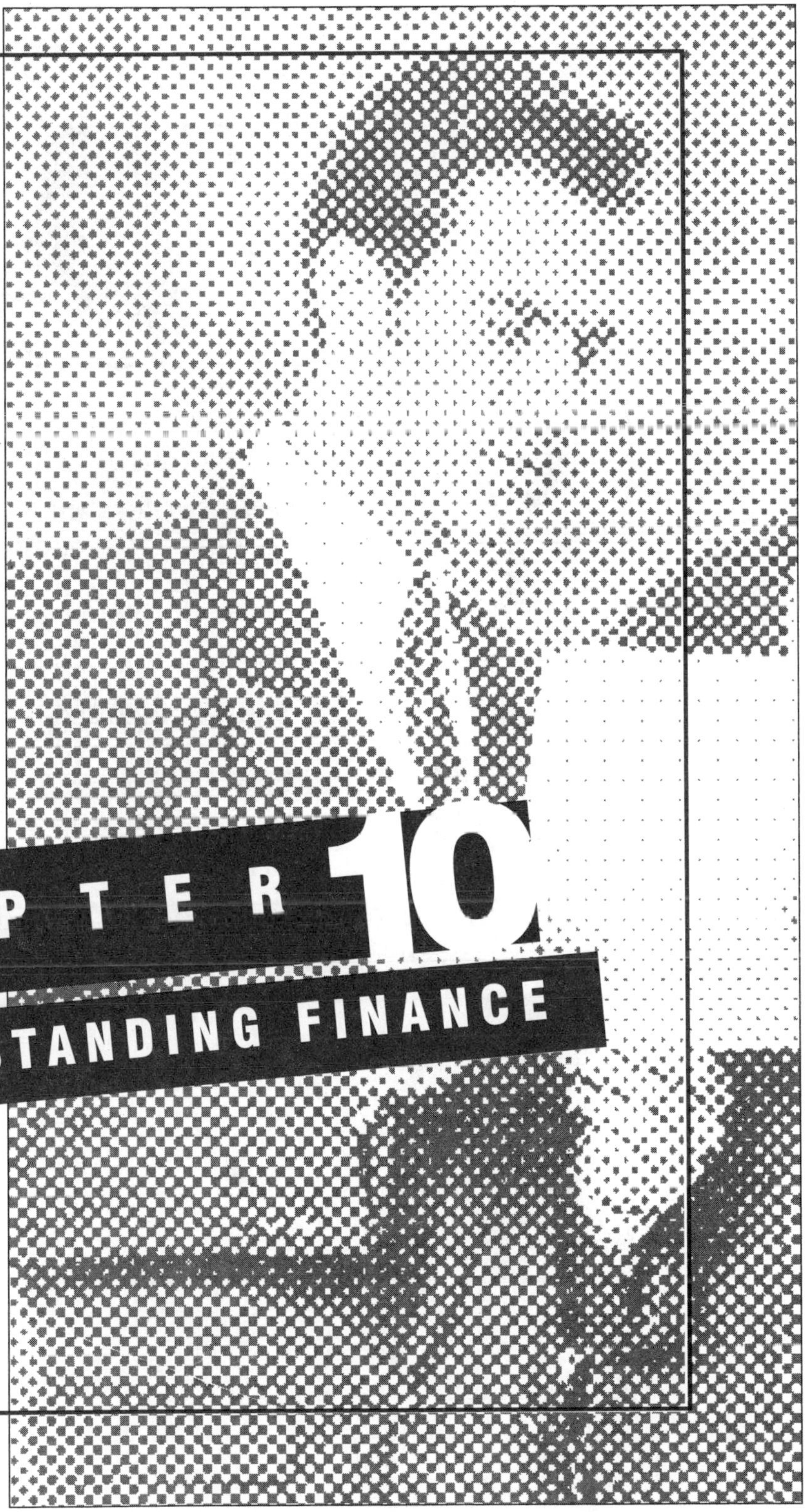

CHAPTER 10
UNDERSTANDING FINANCE

You don't need an MBA or a CPA degree to successfully handle your finances. But you do need to know the basics—that are covered in this chapter. From creating an income statement and a balance sheet to projecting cash flow, here you'll find the critical information you need to control your finances.

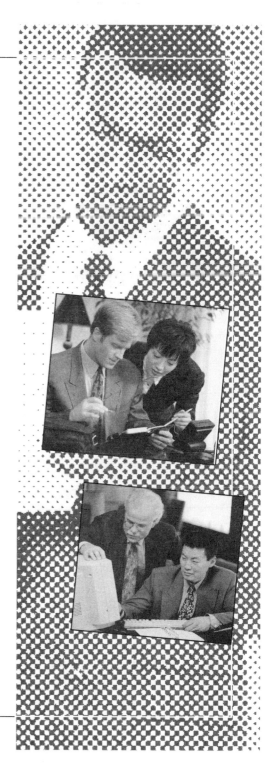

In operating your own consulting business, you will find that the scope of the accounting work to be done is substantially less than if you had started a manufacturing firm or a retail business. Because your product is your services, there is no inventory or cost of goods sold to contend with. If you are beginning as a solo practice using independent contractors to assist you when required, the payroll efforts are substantially simplified.

Typically, you'll have a maximum of three financial statements that you or your accountant will be required to generate. Examples and detailed descriptions are provided later in this chapter. The following is an overview.

According to my accountant, most solo practitioners operating as a simple proprietorship need only be concerned with generating an Income Statement. The Income Statement provides a snapshot of profit and loss and is sufficient for reporting income for tax purposes.

If you incorporate your business, you'll also be required to generate a Balance Sheet for your annual tax return. This statement of assets, liabilities, and stockholders' equity is relatively simple to prepare.

My accountant also recommends that beginning consultants start out with accounting software with double-entry methodology. He has found that consultants who record revenues and expenses using a single-entry method with spreadsheet software sooner or later make a mistake.

Double-entry accounting packages avoid this pitfall. *Peachtree Accounting, Quickbooks* and *M.Y.O.B.* are software titles you may want

UNDERSTANDING FINANCE

to consider. After six years, and more mistakes than I want to remember, I am converting from my single entry *Excel* spreadsheet to *Peachtree Accounting*. (You would think an MBA would have known better!)

Income statements help to track revenues and to see how your business operates over or under budget.

THE INCOME STATEMENT

An income statement provides a snapshot of your profits and losses; it is a summary of profit and loss during a period of time, such as a month, a quarter, or a year. The income statement records all revenues for a business during an accounting period, as well as the operating expenses for your practice.

HOW CAN YOU USE INCOME STATEMENTS?

An income statement is an accounting tool used for tracking your revenues and expenses so that you can determine the profitability of your business. Consultants use these statements to find out what areas of their business are operating within budget or over budget. You can analyze specific expenses to determine if these expenses can be reduced or if the budget can be increased. Looking at several income statements over time can help you determine growth and profitability trends for your business. An income statement is required for tax purposes, and can be shown to potential lenders, such as banks and investors, for setting credit limits or providing you additional funds.

1. **Sales**
   The number recorded for sales is the revenue you have brought into the business. This number is the sum total of the revenues that you achieved in the period of time indicated. Depending on your consulting practice, you will want to record the categories for revenue received, e.g., consulting services, training courses, etc.
2. **Direct Expenses**
   Here you include the direct costs of providing consulting services, such as salaries and payroll taxes for yourself and any other consultants on your staff.

The number of sales recorded is the revenue brought into the business.

UNDERSTANDING FINANCE

3. Operating expenses

The expenses recorded are a summary of your expenses for the period of time described by the income statement. In this simplified sample for a solo practitioner, the following expense categories are used:

- Salary
  This is the salary you paid yourself in the applicable year.
- Collateral and promotions
  Collateral fees are expenses incurred in the creation or purchase of printed sales materials used in marketing your consulting services.
- Advertising
  This includes design and implementation of direct-mail campaigns and other advertising expenses you incur.
- Other sales costs
  These include any other costs associated with selling your services. These costs may include travel, client meals, meetings, equipment rental for presentations, copying, and miscellaneous printing costs.
- Office expense
  These are the expenses of running your office. These expenses could include rent if you are leasing space, or lease payments for furniture. Telephone expenses are recorded. Utility expenses are included, if applicable.
- Depreciation
  Depreciation is an annual expense that takes into account the loss in value of equipment used in your consulting business. Examples of equipment that may be subject to depreciation include copiers, computers, printers, and fax machines.
- Outside services
  As a solo practitioner, you may require outside secretarial services for dictation and typing, and answering service or help from another consultant operating as an Independent Contractor. Expenses for these services are recorded here.

Other sales costs, office expenses, salaries, and outside services are recorded in the income statements.

UNDERSTANDING FINANCE

- Other overhead costs
  Expenses that do not fall into other categories are considered to be other overhead costs. These types of expenses include insurance, office supplies, or business licenses.

4. **Total expenses**
   This is a tabulation of all expenses incurred in running your business, exclusive of taxes or interest expense, if any.
5. **Net income before taxes**
   This number represents the amount of income earned by a business prior to paying income taxes, This figure is arrived at by subtracting total operating expenses from gross profit.
6. **Taxes**
   This is the amount of income taxes you owe to the federal government and, if applicable, state and local governments.
7. **Net income**
   This is the amount of money the business has earned after paying income taxes.

After paying income taxes and expenses, the net income is the money left over for profit.

UNDERSTANDING FINANCE

Income Statement
12 months ending December 31, 1995
for
ABC Consulting

1. SALES	
Consulting services	$95,000
Training courses	55,000
Total Income	150,000
2. DIRECT EXPENSES	
Salary	75,000
Gross profit	75,000
3. OPERATING EXPENSES	
Collateral and Promotion	7,500
Advertising	3,000
Other sales costs	7,500
Depreciation expense	2,500
Insurance	1,000
Office expense	7,000
Outside consultant services	11,000
Outside secretarial services	5,500
4. TOTAL EXPENSES	$45,000
5. NET INCOME BEFORE TAXES	30,000
6. TAXES	14,500
7. NET INCOME	$15,500

UNDERSTANDING FINANCE

THE BALANCE SHEET

A balance sheet is a snapshot of a business' financial condition at a specific moment in time, usually at the close of an accounting period. A balance sheet includes assets, liabilities, and owners' or stockholders' equity. Assets and liabilities are divided into short- and long-term obligations, including cash accounts such as checking, money market, or government securities. At any given time, assets must equal liabilities plus owners' equity. An asset is anything the consulting firm owns that has monetary value. Liabilities are the claims of creditors against the assets of the business.

Balance sheets show the financial status of a business at one time.

WHAT IS A BALANCE SHEET USED FOR?

A balance sheet helps a consultant quickly get a handle on the financial strength and capabilities of the business. Is the consultant in a position to expand? Can the consultant easily handle the normal financial ebbs and flows of revenues and expenses? Or should the business take immediate steps to bolster cash reserves?

Balance sheets can identify and analyze trends, particularly in the area of receivables and payables. Is the receivables cycle lengthening? Can receivables be collected more aggressively? Is some debt uncollectable? Has the business been slowing down payables to forestall an inevitable cash shortage?

Balance sheets, along with income statements, are the most basic elements in providing financial reporting to potential lenders such as banks, investors, and vendors who are considering how much credit to grant the consulting firm.

Balance sheets are useful in analyzing trends in expense, time, and income.

1. **Assets**
   Assets are subdivided into current and long-term assets to reflect the ease of liquidating each asset. Cash, for obvious reasons, is considered the most liquid of all assets. Long-term assets, such as real estate or equipment, are less likely to sell overnight or have the capability of being quickly converted into a current asset such as cash.

UNDERSTANDING FINANCE

2. **Current assets**
   Current assets are any assets that can be easily converted into cash within one calendar year. Examples of current assets would be checking or money market accounts, accounts receivable, and notes receivable that are due within one year's time.
   - Cash
     Money available immediately, such as in checking accounts, is the most liquid of all short-term assets.
   - Accounts receivable
     This is money owed to the consulting firm for services rendered (and for product, if offered) to its clients or others.
   - Notes receivable
     Notes receivable that are due within one year are current assets. Notes that cannot be collected on within one year should be considered long-term assets.
3. **Fixed assets**
   Fixed assets include land, buildings, equipment, and vehicles that are used in connection with the business.
   - Land
     Land is considered a fixed asset but, unlike other fixed assets, it is not depreciated, because land is considered an asset that never wears out.
   - Buildings
     Building are categorized as fixed assets and are depreciated over time.
   - Office Equipment
     This includes office equipment such as copiers, fax machines, printers, and computers used in your business.
   - Vehicles
     This would include any vehicles used in your business.
   - Total fixed assets
     This is the total dollar value of all fixed assets in your business, less any accumulated depreciation.

> Fixed assets include land, buildings, equipment, and vehicles owned by the business.

UNDERSTANDING FINANCE

Liabilities are all debts owed by the business to outside creditors.

4. **Total assets**
   This figure represents the total dollar value of both the short-term and long-term assets of your business.
5. **Liabilities and owners' equity**
   This includes all debts and obligations owed by the business to outside creditors, vendors, or banks that are payable within one year, plus the owners' equity. Often, this side of the balance sheet is simply referred to as "Liabilities."
   - Accounts payable
     This includes all short-term obligations owed by your business to creditors, suppliers, and other vendors. Accounts payable can include supplies and materials acquired on credit.
   - Notes payable
     This represents money owed on a short-term collection cycle of one year or less. It may include bank notes, mortgage obligations, or vehicle payments.
   - Accrued payroll and withholding
     This includes any earned wages or withholdings that are owed to or for employees, but have not been paid.
   - Total current liabilities
     This is the sum total of all current liabilities owed to creditors that must be paid within a one-year time frame.
   - Long-term liabilities

These are any debts or obligations owed by the business that are due more than one year out from the current date.

- Mortgage note payable
  This is the balance of a mortgage that extends out beyond the current year. For example, you may have paid off three years of a fifteen-year mortgage note. The remaining eleven years, not counting the current year, are considered long-term.
- Owners' equity
  Sometimes this is referred to as stockholders' equity. Owners' equity is made up of the initial investment in the business as well as any retained earnings that are reinvested in the business.
- Common stock
  This is stock issued as part of the initial or later-stage investment in the business.
- Retained earnings
  These are earnings reinvested in the business after the deduction of any distributions to shareholders, such as dividend payments.

6. **Total liabilities and owners' equity**
   This includes all debts and monies that are owed to outside creditors, vendors, or banks and the remaining monies that are owed to shareholders, including retained earnings reinvested in the business.

SAMPLE BALANCE SHEET

Balance Sheet - December 31, 1995
for
ABC Consulting

1. ASSETS	
2. CURRENT ASSETS	
Cash	$25,000
Account receivable	10,000
Notes receivable	0
Total Current Assets	**$ 35,000**
3. FIXED ASSETS	
Office equipment	12,000
Less: Accumulated depreciation	(4,000)
Total Fixed Assets	**8,000**
4. TOTAL ASSETS	**$ 43,000**
5. LIABILITIES AND OWNERS' EQUITY	
Current Liabilities	
Accounts payable	2,500
Notes payable (less than one year due)	5,000
Accrued payroll and withholdings	4,500
Total Current Liabilities	**$ 12,000**
Long-term liabilities	
Note payable (beyond one year due)	10,000
Total Liabilities	**$22,000**
Owners' Equity	
Common stock	5,000
Retained earnings	16,000
Total Owners' Equity	**$21,000**
6. TOTAL LIABILITIES AND OWNERS' EQUITY	**$43,000**

UNDERSTANDING FINANCE

DEPRECIATION

The concept of depreciation is really pretty simple. For example, let's say you purchase a computer system for your business. The computer loses value the minute you drive it home from the store. The computer system is considered an operational asset in running your business. Each year that you own the computer, it loses some value, until the computer becomes obsolete and has no value to the business. Measuring the loss in value of an asset is known as depreciation.

Depreciation is considered an expense and is listed in an income statement under expenses. In addition to the computer system you may be using in your business, you can depreciate office furniture and office equipment, as well as any buildings and vehicles you own for the business.

Land is not considered an expense, nor can it be depreciated. Land does not wear out like computer systems or equipment.

To find the annual depreciation cost for your assets, you need to know the initial cost of the assets. You also need to determine how many years you think the assets will retain some value for your business. In the case of a truck, it may only have a useful life of five years before it loses all value.

Depreciation is the measurement of the loss of value of an asset.

STRAIGHT-LINE DEPRECIATION

Straight-line depreciation is considered the most common method of depreciating assets. To compute the amount of annual depreciation expense using the straight-line method requires two numbers: the initial cost of the asset and its estimated useful life. For example, you purchase a computer system for $3,000, and you expect it to have use in your business for five years. Using the straight-line method for determining depreciation, you would divide the initial cost of the computer by its useful life.

Straight-Line Depreciation–Formula:
Initial Cost ÷ Useful Life = Depreciation per Year
$3,000 ÷ 5 = $600

UNDERSTANDING FINANCE

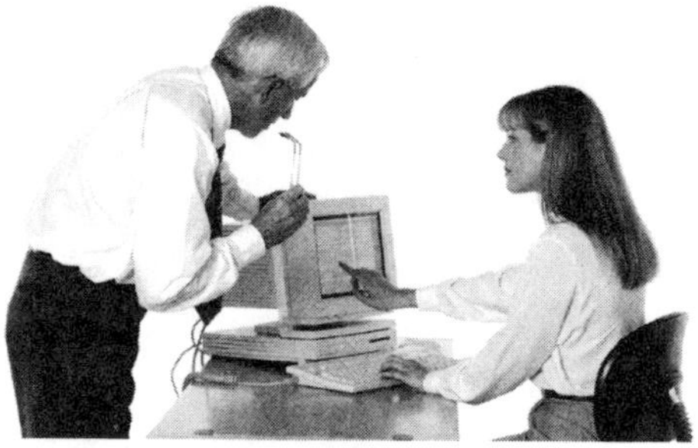

The $3,000 becomes a depreciation expense that is reported on your income statement under operating expenses at the end of each year.

For tax purposes, some accountants prefer to use other methods of accelerating depreciation in order to record larger amounts of depreciation in the early years of the asset to reduce tax bills as soon as possible.

You need to check the regulations published by the Internal Revenue Service and various state revenue authorities for any specific rules regarding depreciation and methods of calculating depreciation for various types of assets.

Book Value

Depreciation is also reflected on your balance sheet as the difference between the "book" or "carrying" value and the initial price of an asset. You determine this by adding up the accumulated depreciation expense and subtracting that figure from the initial cost of the equipment. For example, you purchase a computer for $3,000 in 1995. It has an estimated useful life of five years. The annual depreciation expense is $600. It is now December 31, 1996, and you want to show the book value on your balance sheet. Your entry on your balance sheet would have the following line items:

Cost of computer acquired on January 1, 1995	$3,000
Accumulated depreciation expense January 1, 1995 to December 31, 1996 $600 per year x 2 years	$ 1,200
Book Value = amount of computer cost not allocated to depreciation expense	$1,800

At the end of the fifth year, the book value of the computer system will be zero because the system will have no value.

PRO FORMA INCOME STATEMENTS

A pro forma income statement is similar to a historical income statement, except it projects the future rather than tracking the past. Pro forma income statements are an important tool for planning future business operations. If the projections predict a downturn in profitability, you can make operational changes such as increasing prices or decreasing costs before these projections become reality.

Pro forma income statements provide an important benchmark or budget for operating a business throughout the year. They can determine whether expenses can be expected to run higher in the first quarter of the year than in the second. They can determine whether or not sales can be expected to be run above average in June. They can determine whether or not your marketing campaigns need an extra boost during the fall months. All in all, they provide you with invaluable information–the sort of information you need in order to make right choices for your business.

Pro forma income statements project income for future business operations, and provide invaluable information about future trends and choices.

How Do I Create a Pro Forma Income Statement?

Sit down with an income statement from the current year or use the template from the business plan section. Consider what each item on that statement will be for the coming year. This should, ideally, be done before year's end. You will need to estimate final sales and expenses for the current year to prepare a pro forma income statement for the coming year.

1. **Pro Forma Gross Profit**

   Using the example which follows, let's assume that you expect sales to increase by 10 percent next year. You multiply this year's sales of $500,000 by 110 percent to get $550,000. Then, in this case, you assume there will be no increase in the consulting rates, but you will need 10 percent more work in order to achieve your sales goals. You multiply this year's direct expenses (consultant's salaries and related program expense–let's assume a figure of $200,000), by 110 percent to get $220,000.

   To figure your pro forma gross profit for next year, subtract the pro forma direct expenses from the pro forma

sales: $550,000 minus $220,000 equals your gross profit, or $330,000.

2. **Pro Forma Total Expenses**
   Let's assume operating expenses will increase by five percent. You multiply your historical operating expenses of $220,000 by 105 percent and you get $231,000.
3. **Pro Forma Profit Before Taxes**
   Pro forma profit before taxes is figured by subtracting the pro forma expenses from the pro forma gross profit, or $231,000 from $330,000 for a pro forma profit before taxes of $99,000.
4. **Pro Forma Taxes**
   Pro forma taxes are figured by taking your estimated tax rate, in this case thirty percent, and multiplying it by the pro forma profit before taxes of $99,000. This produces a pro forma tax bill of $29,700.
5. **Pro Forma Profit After Taxes**
   Pro forma profit after taxes is figured by subtracting the pro forma tax bill of $29,700 from the pro forma profit before taxes of $99,000. Your pro forma profit after taxes, in this case, would be projected at $69,300.

Remember that pro formas are essentially best guesses. You should continually update your projections by recalculating your pro formas using any new and actual financial information you have as a base. Doing this on a monthly or quarterly basis will help to assure that your projections are as close to being accurate as possible.

UNDERSTANDING FINANCE

PRO FORMA INCOME STATEMENT FOR 1997
for
MARKETING SERVICES, LTD.

	1996 Historical	Projected Increase	1997 Pro forma
Sales	$500,000	× 110% =	$550,000
Direct Expenses/ Consultants' Salaries	200,000	× 110% =	220,000
1. GROSS PROFIT	300,000		330,000
2. OPERATING EXPENSES	220,000	× 5% =	231,000
3. PROFIT BEFORE TAXES	80,000		99,000
4. TAXES	24,000		29,700
5. PROFIT AFTER TAXES	$56,000		69,300

UNDERSTANDING FINANCE

Pro forma balance sheets help to predict how the business will control its assets in the future.

PRO FORMA BALANCE SHEETS

A pro forma balance sheet is similar to a historical balance sheet, but it represents a future projection. Pro forma balance sheets are used to project how the business will be managing its assets in the future. For example, a pro forma balance sheet can quickly show the projected relative amount of money tied up in receivables, inventory, and equipment. It can also be used to project the overall financial soundness of the company. For example, a pro forma balance sheet can help quickly pinpoint a high debt-to-equity ratio.

1. **Pro Forma Current Assets**
   - Cash
     To obtain your company's estimated cash position, you need to do a careful cash flow projection. Cash flow projections are covered later in this chapter. Let's assume that the projected cash flow for a company called Bradford Design, or the anticipated funds in Bradford Design's checking account on December 31, 19__, will be $50,000.
   - Pro forma accounts receivable
     To estimate the accounts receivable on December 31, you need to take into consideration the average collection time of receivables and the sales projections for prior periods. For example, let's assume that Bradford Design receives payment thirty days after services are performed.

     So, in this case, we need to look at the projected sales for December, which are $70,000. Because it takes thirty days to collect payment, we would expect to have all of December's billings outstanding on December 31. Bradford Design's account receivables would be estimated at $70,000.
   - Pro forma total current assets
     Pro forma total current assets are determined by adding projected cash and projected accounts receivable.
2. **Pro Forma Fixed Assets**
   - Pro forma land

UNDERSTANDING FINANCE

Land is the easiest pro forma asset value to calculate. Because land does not depreciate, it will always have the same value. Just enter the value of the land at its original purchase price. Bradford Design's land holdings are valued at $30,000.

- Pro forma buildings
  Buildings do depreciate. Let's assume we are depreciating the building over thirty years. Bradford Design bought its building for $300,000. Each year the building will depreciate by $10,000. By December 31, 1997, the building will be three years old, so the total depreciation will be $30,000. This will be reflected later in the accumulated depreciation total. Under the building heading, we show the original value of the asset or $300,000.
- Pro forma vehicles
  Vehicles also depreciate. They depreciate over a much shorter period of time than do buildings. Let's assume we are depreciating Bradford Design's vehicles over a seven-year period. The vehicles were purchased for $73,500 on January 1, 1997. Each year the vehicles will depreciate by $10,500. On December 31, 1997, after one year of depreciation, the vehicles will have an accumulated depreciation of $10,500.
- Pro forma total assets
  Pro forma total assets are determined by adding up the pro forma total current assets and pro forma total fixed assets.

3. Pro Forma Current Liabilities

- Pro forma accounts payable
  Pro forma accounts payable are determined by figuring out how much you will spend on supplies during the last months of 1996 and how long it takes you to pay your bills. Because Bradford Design pays its bills in thirty days, it should only have outstanding bills for the supplies it anticipates purchasing in December as of December 31.

Unlike land, buildings and vehicles depreciate over time.

UNDERSTANDING FINANCE

Since Bradford Design estimates a supply expenditure of $30,000 in December, it will have a pro forma accounts payable of $30,000.

- Pro forma accrued payroll
  It should be easy to determine a pro forma accrued payroll. Just check your payroll calendar to find out what employee pay periods will remain unpaid by the beginning of the pro forma balance sheet period. Bradford Design's weekly payroll is $10,000. Since it pays employees on a weekly basis, the pro forma accrued payroll will be $10,000 on December 31.
- Pro forma notes payable
  Pro forma notes payable include all notes or portions of notes that are payable within one year. Bradford Design will include in its pro forma notes payable the portion of its outstanding mortgage that will fall due during 1998 on its year-end 1997 balance sheet. The amount is calculated to be $15,000.
- Pro forma total current liabilities
  To obtain pro forma total current liabilities, you add up pro forma accounts payable, accrued payroll, and notes, or portions thereof, payable, within one year. Bradford Design's total current liabilities are projected to be $55,000.

4. Pro Forma Long-term Liabilities

- Pro forma mortgage note payable
  The size of a pro forma mortgage note payable is calculated by taking the mortgage note payable at the end of the current year and subtracting the principal (not interest) payments that will be made during the upcoming year. To

obtain that portion of the mortgage that will be classified as a long-term liability, you need to subtract what is classified as current liability. In Bradford Design's case, $15,000 is subtracted from the current remaining principal payments of $200,000. Therefore, the long-term portion of Bradford Design's pro forma mortgage note payable is $185,000.

- Pro forma total liabilities
  Pro forma total liabilities are determined by adding up current and long-term liabilities. Bradford Design's pro forma total liabilities are $240,000.

5. **Pro Forma Owners' Equity**
   - Pro forma common stock
     The common stock portion of the owners' equity will not change from year to year unless new stock is issued.
   - Pro forma retained earnings
     Pro forma retained earnings can be tricky to determine. They are the last item to be calculated on a pro forma balance sheet.

Total assets must balance the total liabilities and owners' equity. In Bradford Design's case, we already know that the pro forma liabilities must total $483,000.

Also, total liabilities added to total owners' equity must equal total liabilities and owners' equity. So, you can determine total owners' equity by subtracting total liabilities from total liabilities and owners' equity.

Common stock added to retained earnings must equal total owners' equity. So, by subtracting common stock from total owners' equity, retained earnings can be determined. This completes a pro forma balance sheet.

UNDERSTANDING FINANCE

PRO FORMA BALANCE SHEET FOR 1997
for
BRADFORD DESIGN INC.

ASSETS	
1. Current assets	
Cash	$50,000
Accounts receivables	70,000
Total Current Assets	**$120,000**
2. Fixed assets	
Land	$30,000
Buildings	300,000
Vehicles	73,500
Less: Accumulated depreciation	(40,500)
Total Fixed Assets	**$363,000**
Total Assets	**$483,000**
LIABILITIES AND OWNERS' EQUITY	
3. Current liabilities	
Accounts payable	$30,000
Accrued payroll	10,000
Notes payable (less than one year due)	15,000
Total Current Liabilities	**$55,000**
4. Long-term liabilities	
Mortgage note payable (beyond one year)	$185,000
Total Liabilities	**$240,000**
5. Owners' equity	
Common stock	$40,000
Retained earnings	203,600
Total Owners' Equity	**$243,000**
Total liabilities and owners' equity	**$483,000**

UNDERSTANDING FINANCE

PRO FORMA CASH FLOWS

A pro forma cash flow is created to predict inflow and outflow of cash to your business. It is particularly valuable in predicting when your business may experience a cash shortage. This allows you to determine in advance whether or not you will need to cover your cash shortage by borrowing money, selling more stock in the business, or taking other steps, such as cutting expenses, to improve your cash position.

Pro forma cash flows are useful in predicting a cash shortage for your company.

1. **Starting cash**

   To create a pro forma cash flow, you need to know your current cash position. To demonstrate the steps of building a pro forma cash flow, let's use a hypothetical company, Star Financial Services, Inc. Star Financial will beginning 1997 with $90,000 in its checking account.
2. **Cash sources**
   - Receivables (sales)

     Star Financial consults to small businesses and retailers on a credit basis. Experience has shown that clients pay their accounts to Star Financial thirty days after services are completed. This means that in January 1997, Star Financial will not receive cash from sales made in January, but will be collecting on sales made in December 1996. Those sales totaled $30,000, so that amount is entered in the January sales column of the cash flow.
   - Total cash sources

     This is a totaling of all cash received from all sources. Receivables from sales to retailers constitute the only source of cash for Star Financial. Your cash sources may be more involved.
3. **Cash uses**
   - Consulting salaries

     Star Financial pays the same amount each month for consultants' salaries–$15,000. And this amount is paid almost immediately–on a weekly basis.

UNDERSTANDING FINANCE

- Operating expenses
  The operating expenses for Star Financial are $10,000 per month.
- Income taxes
  Income taxes for most businesses fluctuate from month to month because both state and federal taxes are paid as estimates on a quarterly, not monthly, basis. Star Financial paid its estimated tax installments in December and doesn't have any tax payments due in January.
- Total cash uses
  This is a totaling of all cash expenditures. In the case of Star Financial, in the month of January, this amounts to $25,000 derived from cost of goods and operating expenses.

4. Net change in cash position

This figure is derived by subtracting the estimated cash uses from the estimated cash sources. For Star Financial there is a net change in cash position of +$5,000.

By adding the net change figure to the starting cash figure, you will have the starting cash figure for the next month or time period for which you are calculating a cash flow. In this case, Star Financial will begin February with $95,000.

UNDERSTANDING FINANCE

1997 PRO FORMA CASH FLOW
for
STAR FINANCIAL SERVICES, INC.

	January	February
1. STARTING CASH	**$90,000**	**$95,000**
2. CASH SOURCES		
Receivables	$30,000	
Total cash sources	$30,000	
3. CASH USES		
Consultant salaries	$15,000	
Operating expenses	$10,000	
Taxes	$ 0	
Total cash uses	**$25,000**	
4. NET CHANGE IN CASH	**$5,000**	
ENDING CASH	**$95,000**	

STREETWISE ADVICE ON PRO FORMAS

Multiple Scenarios

Some people suggest that you make several sets of pro formas—most likely, best and worst case scenarios. For a consulting business that likely will not have to raise a large amount of capital, I recommend that you carefully assemble one set of pro forma forecasts based on the most likely case. Developing pro formas is a tedious process. In creating one set of forecasts, you will probably remain more sensitive to your assumptions and their validity regarding sales forecasts, receivable collections, and delivery schedules.

Most banks or investors will be very happy to see one set of well-done forecasts. It is also a lot easier for you to track your business' performance against this one most likely scenario.

Pro formas are more useful when based upon the most likely case, rather than the best or worse scenarios.

Sales Forecasts

Accurately predicting sales is one of the most important factors in making projections. However, making sales assumptions carries a high risk of inaccuracy.

Use last year's sales as your starting point for sales projections. If you are a start-up business, use your break-even sales point for sales projections. Estimate sales by breaking them out for different client types and/or markets. Estimate the impact of price increases, marketing plans, competitors, and any other major factor that could possibly have an effect on your sales potential. To double check your sales forecast assumptions, seek the advice of someone else you can trust, perhaps a close associate or your accountant.

Break-even Forecast

Especially when starting a new business, people tend to underestimate how long it will take to build sales. For a new business it's very difficult for anyone to estimate sales. So I suggest that you estimate what sales level you need to break even. Then, if you are not hitting this break-even level, you can immediately take steps to put the business back on track (such as cutting expenditures) before you get into trouble (such as running out of cash).

TOOLS, NOT PROPHECIES

First, think of pro formas as tools for running your business and only second as predictions of the future.

The true strength of pro formas lies in your ability to make changes in them before their scenarios occur. If profitability looks too low (and it usually does in your first pass through your pro formas), take steps to improve it. Are your rates too low? Can you cut any expenses? Do you offer any services that are not profitable that you could eliminate?

In a growing business, start a new pro forma every year.

QUESTIONS & ANSWERS ON PRO FORMAS

How often should I create pro formas?

If your business is growing, start from scratch once each year. Additionally, the cash flow pro forma should be updated on a monthly basis. The cash flow is the most critical pro forma statement. If you run out of cash, you are effectively out of business!

If you anticipate major changes during the year, you may want to update your profit and loss pro formas at that time. Balance sheets really need to be updated only yearly if you are concerned about violating any bank loan agreements you have made that references your balance sheet.

Is it really worth the time to create pro formas?

Yes! To do it right will take a lot of time. But it is certainly time well spent. Pro forma profit and loss statements will allow you to see whether or not all of your hard work will, in all probability, lead to profits. Pro forma balance sheets tell you whether you will be depositing money in the bank or using it to keep your business running. Pro forma cash flows provide an early warning for cash flow problems.

Which pro forma is the most important?

Cash flow! It's nice to project a profit, and knowing you have a solid balance sheet can make you feel good, but if you run out of cash, your business will be dead in the water!

Just about all small businesses will feel a cash crunch sooner or later, and for most businesses it will happen sooner, later, and fairly

UNDERSTANDING FINANCE

regularly. But if you keep your cash flow projection up to date, you can take steps to avoid cash shortages before the problem becomes acute. Otherwise, you will go merrily along your way until one day you may find you have no money in the bank, your credit is exhausted, your payroll is due, your key subcontractors are howling for payment, the IRS is calling, and clients are still paying their bills slowly. Remember, cash crunches happen all the time in successful, profitable, growing businesses too!

Cash flow pro formas are the most important to keep updated.

Are there any tricks for quickly updating a cash flow pro forma?

Since any pro forma takes quite a while to carefully update, there may be times when you need a shortcut to get a ballpark estimate. I would first revise sales estimates and changes in collection cycle (the amount of time it takes you to get paid by your clients) and any costs that directly change with sales (such as the rates you pay subcontractors or your own staff).

COLLECTING YOUR FEES

What becomes evident in reviewing your financial statements is that collecting your accounts receivables in a timely fashion provides more of your assets in the form of cash. Here are some tips for working with the client to make sure you are paid on time.

Discuss Payment When the Agreement is Signed

Even though your payment terms may have been clearly spelled out in your proposal, mention these payment terms when the client consulting agreement is signed. If this transaction takes place through the mail, mention the importance of your payment terms in the letter of transmittal. This lets the client know your expectations up front, and provides the opportunity to offer alternatives.

Invoice Immediately

With every deliverable on a consulting assignment, invoice upon providing the deliverable. This usually will provide faster approval and processing than if you send the invoice later by mail. It makes good business sense for your client to accept your deliverable and sign off at the same time.

UNDERSTANDING FINANCE

Consistently Follow up

If your payment terms are net ten days after invoice, follow-up after ten days plus a reasonable mail delivery time to find out the status of your payment. Many times the check is in process and is going through the client's normal accounting cycle. Your call acts as a gentle reminder to the client to pay as mutually agreed to. If payment is still not received within two weeks after it is due, send a second reminder. You may want to consider copying this reminder to someone higher in the client organization, depending on the politics involved. I recommend using a tickler file or your software contact manager to remind yourself to follow up.

Work with Your In-house Champion

When you were selected for the consulting assignment, you most likely developed a good relationship with one or more of the people on the client's staff. If your invoice is still 'stuck' in their accounting department and you cannot get a commitment on when the bill will be paid, talk with one of your allies to push the invoice through their system. Work with the highest level possible in the client organization. Clout counts for a lot. Two years ago, one of our invoices languished for an extended period of time with a client who was experiencing financial difficulties. A call at vice presidential level resolved the issue quickly, and payment was sent to me the next day.

Keeping abreast of late invoices will prevent a lack of cash flow.

Have Legal Resources Available

You hope it doesn't come to this, but sometimes you may have to bring legal resources to bear to resolve a payment issue. That has not happened once in our six years of consulting, but I am prepared for this situation should it arise. Whether a solution is attained when you and your lawyer sit with the client and his lawyer, or it goes to small claims court, do not be bashful about using an attorney to assist you. Make sure you have considered the client's point of view and that you have delivered against your contract before seeking legal recourse.

UNDERSTANDING FINANCE

Use payroll services in order to avoid the complicated process of employment taxes.

TAXES

Why can paying taxes be fun? Because they are more fun than going through an audit! And audits can be more fun than having your assets seized for failure to pay taxes! You should look at an exorbitant tax bill as a measure of your success.

Unfortunately, while income taxes will be the largest burden by far on a profitable firm, plenty of other taxes also need to be paid even if you aren't making any money at all.

EMPLOYMENT TAXES

Whether you have one employee or a hundred, you will be way ahead of the game if you get an outside firm to handle your filings and payroll taxes. So, before you do anything else, get yourself a payroll service to take all of the time, hassle, anxiety, and risk out of the payroll process.

Employment tax rules are extremely complex. If you try to handle them yourself, you are bound to make a costly mistake–and you'll pay interest and penalties. If a payroll service makes the mistake, typically, it will pay.

As an employer, you have a tremendous fiduciary responsibility to collect and withhold taxes from employees on virtually every paycheck you issue. Throughout the United States, you must withhold an appropriate amount for federal income and other earnings-related taxes. Many states and some municipalities also require the payment of an income or other tax on earnings.

Your employees must fill out a federal W-4 form and a Form I-9 from the Immigration and Naturalization Service. States that do not use the same income basis for determining tax liability as the federal government does, may require that employees fill out state filing forms.

You or your payroll service must determine the appropriate amount to be withheld for each individual. If you withhold too little from your employees' incomes, you will be penalized by the governments involved. The federal government also requires that you withhold your employees' share of federal Social Security and Medicare taxes. Tables for calculating federal withholding taxes are available from the Internal Revenue Service at: 1-800-TAX-FORM

State withholding tables may be obtained from your state income tax department.

Budgeting for Your Share of the Payroll Taxes

The employer is also responsible for a share of their employees' unemployment, Social Security, and Medicare taxes. The amount that you pay will depend on many factors: salaries, your firm's balance, if any, in your state's unemployment insurance account, dates of hire, and a host of other considerations. As a quick and dirty rule of thumb, allow thirteen percent on top of your gross payroll to cover your share of the payroll taxes.

The employer is responsible for their employees Social Security, Medicare, and unemployment taxes.

Timing of Employment Tax Payments

If you are a growing company, paying employment taxes yourself can be very frustrating. Employment tax rules change as the size of the company increases, and that includes both your liability and the time frame in which the taxes must be paid. Following are two general guidelines:

- New employers pay federal withholding taxes on a monthly basis. As the business grows, the frequency increases to semi-weekly. For the largest businesses, taxes are due within twenty-four hours of each payroll.
- Each state has its own rules for frequency of payment. Generally, payments are not required more frequently than are federal taxes. But be sure to check with your state tax office.

Collecting Sales Taxes

In most states and in many cities, you must collect sales taxes on applicable sales. Generally, sales taxes apply on the sale of just about anything to just about anyone.

Exceptions are sales to resellers, such as wholesalers or retailers, who have valid state resale certificates. Ask to see the resale certificate of any wholesaler or retailer with whom you conduct business. Another exception is sales made to tax-exempt institutions, such as public schools and libraries. In some states, sales taxes apply only to products, while in other states, sales taxes apply to services as well.

A particularly gray, frustrating, and rapidly changing area is the collection of sales tax by firms that sell products or taxable services in states where they do not maintain a clear physical presence. Physical presence is clear if you have an address, store inventory, or maintain an employee, such as a sales representative, within a state. But individual states have taken out-of-state companies to court for the collection of sales tax based on the presence of mail-order catalogs within their state. Results on these suits have been mixed. But the definitions of physical presence are changing and bear watching.

If you are making taxable sales in other states, you should check with your accountant or legal advisor for an up-to-date opinion on your particular situation. The safest route, of course, is to simply collect sales tax in every state where you sell products or services.

Check with your accountant for the safest way to collect sales tax from out-of-state businesses.

Use Taxes

Use taxes basically mean that a business that buys items from out-of-state vendors, which are not collecting sales taxes, must pay the tax themselves to the taxing authority. Some states are particularly aggressive about collecting such taxes and won't hesitate to take an entire industry to court or push gray areas of the law in an effort to collect every last red cent they can.

As a consulting business, chances are almost all of your billings will be for services, and this tax will likely not apply often.

Income Taxes

In the United States, your business, if incorporated, must file and pay federal income taxes, state income taxes in most states, and local income taxes in some areas.

If your business is incorporated, you may elect to become an "S" corporation (formerly known as Sub-Chapter S) for federal income tax purposes. As an S corporation, your company will not pay direct taxes in most cases. Instead, income and losses are passed on to stockholders. Therefore, the individual stockholders pay the income tax.

UNDERSTANDING FINANCE

Some states treat S corporations in the same manner as does the federal government and tax the stockholders. Other states do not recognize S corporation status, and tax the corporation directly.

Remember that the federal corporation tax returns (regardless of S corporation election) are due one month earlier than individual returns—on the fifteenth day of the third month after the end of the company's year. For example, if your fiscal year ends on December 31, your filing date is March 15. The payment for a corporation with an S election is still part of the individual return due on April 15. Be sure to check the section on estimated taxes to know when estimated tax payments are due.

If your business is a sole proprietorship or a partnership, the income is taxed directly to the owner or partners for federal income tax purposes. Most states follow the same rule. However, a few jurisdictions tax the business entity directly. Check with your tax consultant for the rules and regulations that apply to your business.

Remember, you need to file tax returns and pay a minimum tax in some areas, even if your business has yet to earn a profit.

> Federal and some state tax authorities require that you pay an estimated tax on next year's earnings.

ESTIMATED INCOME TAXES

At the beginning of your second year in business, you may be in for a little surprise. Not only do federal, and some state and local tax authorities require payment of income taxes on the first year's earnings, but they want you to start paying taxes on next year's earnings. Yes—before the year has ended!

Estimated federal corporation taxes are due when the annual tax is expected to be at least $500. Payments of twenty-five percent each are due on the fifteenth day of the fourth, sixth, ninth, and twelfth months of your fiscal year. If you are on a calendar fiscal year, for instance, estimated payments are due on April 15, June 15, September 15, and December 15. Each state has its own minimums and payment schedules, often varying from the federal ones.

If you are self-employed or in a partnership, you also will have to pay income tax estimates. They need to be figured into the total estimated tax the individual owes.

UNDERSTANDING FINANCE

Property taxes on commercial property is much higher than on residential property.

Property Taxes

Of course, you will have to pay real estate taxes on any real estate that you or your business owns. Also, many commercial and industrial leases are written so that the lessee, not the lessor, is responsible for taxes. Sometimes the lessor will pay what is referred to as the "base-year taxes." This means the lessor pays tax equal to the taxes of the base year—often the year before the lease was signed—set as the base year; then the lessee pays any increase.

For most localities, the tax rate on commercial and industrial property is significantly higher than the rate applied to residential property. Furthermore, many communities assess the value of businesses, particularly those with nonlocal owners, at ridiculously high levels to minimize the tax burden on local voting citizens. This practice is so widespread that there is a whole group of attorneys who specialize in suing towns and cities in an attempt to receive fair tax treatment for their business clients. These clients are often national chains.

If you feel that your tax assessment is too high, but the amount owed is not huge, file a request for a new assessment before hiring expensive, specialized legal help.

Personal Property Taxes

In addition to taxing real estate, localities impose personal property taxes on just about everything else a business owns, including equipment, furniture, and inventory. The percentage of the estimated value is usually quite small, but the total dollar amount can add up if you own a lot of property.

Inventory and Tangible Property Taxes

Many states place a tax, based on a small percentage of actual value, on tangible property held within their state, including inventory housed on a certain annual date. This date is usually the last day of the year.

Other Taxes

Your business may be subject to additional taxes. Some of these types of taxes are applicable only within certain industries. For example, most localities levy specific taxes on lodging establishments, some on amusement facilities, and others on restaurants.

STREETWISE ADVICE ON TAXES

Not Your Bank

Too many small businesses view their tax bills like trade debts and delay paying taxes during cash crunches. Invariably, they regret this decision. You can usually delay vendor payments, pay up later, and have all forgotten. When you don't pay the tax authorities, they seek penalties and interest. These penalties were designed to be severe enough to discourage you from treating the government like a financing company. Furthermore, it is a lot easier for the tax authorities to seize your assets for tax delinquency than it is for a trade vendor to do so!

Work with the IRS

While it is true that tax collectors are bound by many rules and regulations, they are often quite flexible to deal with. If you have made an honest mistake, have really run out of money, or haven't filled out the proper form, you might be able to avoid penalty or even interest payments. You just need to find the proper way to channel your request.

Decisions and Taxes

While taxes are a heavy burden on any successful business, you are generally better off if you avoid making business decisions based on their tax implications. Avoiding taxes can mean avoiding profits!

Tax Preparation

Have an outside accountant do your taxes. Even though you might have a great conceptual understanding of tax regulations and filing procedures, someone who files hundreds of tax returns a year will be able to do yours more efficiently than you can. And they should be up on the very latest in rules and allowances—many of which you may not be aware of. It will save you time, if not money, in the long run.

Delaying the payment of taxes can accrue stiff penalties and interest.

UNDERSTANDING FINANCE

Keeping good records today will save you time and worry when it comes time for an audit.

DON'T UNDERREPORT INCOME

No matter how determined you are to be aggressive with your tax return, don't underreport your income. The IRS is increasingly suspicious of taxpayers, especially small business owners, who seem to have lifestyles that cannot possibly be supported by the incomes they report. You could find yourself the subject of a "lifestyle audit."

CONSIDER A NEW FISCAL YEAR ELECTION

If your business experiences its strongest profitability toward the end of the year, you might be better off ending your fiscal year mid-year. This would delay your income tax payments on year-end profits, as well as your higher estimated income taxes toward the next year's bill.

QUESTIONS & ANSWERS ABOUT TAXES

Can I deduct the cost of my home office?

The rules on home office deductibility seem to change constantly. The Internal Revenue Service is very careful about the proper deduction of home office expenses. By deducting your home office, even legitimately, you increase your audit chances. To deduct a home office, the office must be used exclusively as the principal place for operating your business. The U.S. Supreme Court has ruled that more than fifty percent of the total time spent operating your business must be spent in the home office. This is a problem for consultants who spend a significant amount of time at client locations.

How should I prepare for a tax audit?

The best time to prepare for a tax audit is now. It is much easier to keep good records today than to try to recreate them two or three years later.

Usually a tax audit will specify the year being audited. Be sure to have all your records for the specified year organized and accessible prior to the audit. An auditor will expect you to instantly support any questioned items. Try to determine in advance which items the auditor intends to question, and have ready answers. Remember, the auditor's questions will stem from information you supplied on your tax return. Are your office supply expenses extremely high? The auditor may want you to substantiate these expenses with invoices and/or canceled checks.

I suggest that you have your outside accountant present during the audit. Ask him or her for advice relevant to your situation. If you are nervous, consider having the accountant be your representative and don't attend the audit in person.

Can I delay filing my tax return?

Any corporation, S corporation, partnership, or individual can get an automatic extension of time to file a tax return simply by filing the appropriate federal and/or state form. Any tax due, however, must be included with the extension on the original date due. All taxes paid after the original date due are subject to interest charges. Inadequate payment with the extension request can also lead to additional penalties.

Although a tax return has been extended, all estimated tax payments remain payable as per the regular schedule.

What if my estimated tax payments appear to be too low at a later date?

If you find during the year that your income tax liability is going to be greater than the estimated taxes you have paid will cover, you should revise any remaining payments to account for the increase. It is best to make any catch-up payments with the next payment due.

Though it is possible to delay filing a tax return, all payments must be made before the end of the extension.

GUIDELINES TO DETERMINING INDEPENDENT CONTRACTOR STATUS

There is no hard and fast rule regarding who does or doesn't qualify as an independent contractor. The IRS examines each situation individually. Here are some of the standard considerations they use as guides:

- Does the hiring firm or the independent contractor determine when, where, and how work is performed?
- Is the hiring firm providing the independent contractor with training?
- How do the independent contractor's services integrate into the business?

UNDERSTANDING FINANCE

- Are the services rendered by the independent contractor performed personally by him or her?
- How does the company hire, supervise, and pay the independent contractor?
- What is the continuing relationship between the independent contractor and the firm that has hired him or her?
- Does the hiring firm set the working hours for the independent contractor?
- Does the hiring firm require the independent contractor to work full-time?
- Does the independent contractor work on the hiring firm's premises?
- Is the work order or sequence of work performed set by the hiring firm?
- Does the hiring firm require written or oral work progress reports from the independent contractor?
- Does the hiring firm pay the independent contractor by the hour, week, or month?
- Does the hiring firm pay travel and other business expenses on behalf of the independent contractor?

UNDERSTANDING FINANCE

- Does the hiring firm supply the tools and equipment necessary for the independent contractor to perform the task?
- Does the independent contractor have a significant investment interest in the hiring firm?
- Does the independent contractor realize profits and losses from the hiring firm?
- Does the independent contractor work for more than one firm at a time?
- Does the independent contractor make his or her services available to the general public?
- Does the hiring firm have the right to discharge the independent contractor?
- Can the independent contractor terminate his or her arrangement with the hiring firm without liability?

General rule of thumb: If you are being used as a consultant to avoid employment taxes, you are probably headed for trouble. If you have doubts about your role as an independent contractor, clarify the situation first with your client. The potential for financial risk is significant should that status be deemed inappropriate by the tax authorities.

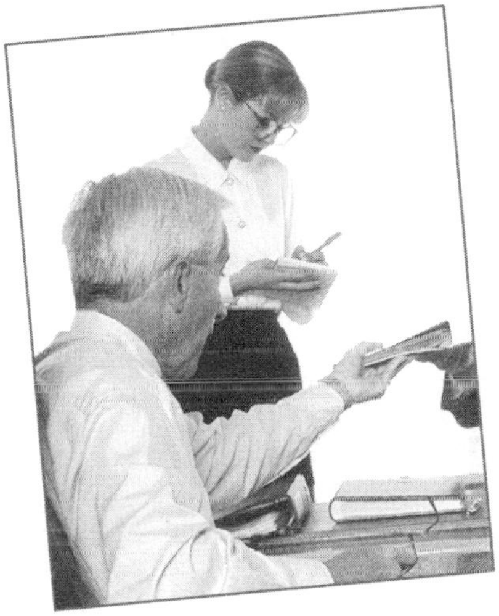

CHAPTER 11

STREETWISE ADVICE

This brief chapter focuses on important issues that you are likely to encounter in getting your business off the ground. Learn from the voice of experience. Study this astute, insider-advice on how to avoid and resolve problems and issues you may encounter.

TEN STEPS TO CONSULTING SUCCESS

The following are ten elements for succeeding in your consulting business:

Be Persistent

Total commitment to your decision to pursue a consulting career is absolutely essential. If you "dabble," you're dead. It is almost impossible to succeed with a half-hearted commitment.

Commitment is the number one success ingredient. It's easy to get discouraged. At times the gaps between assignments can seem excruciatingly long. Hang in there. Use the time between assignments to market your services as never before, and invest some time in personal development.

Focus on the Client's Needs

What you can do for the client is not nearly as important as what he or she needs. Taking extra time up front to qualify a client's needs in depth will make a major difference in the quality of the perceived results you will provide.

It's all too easy to focus on your past experiences and successes. Your client doesn't care about them unless they have a direct relationship to the problems and issues he or she is facing.

Develop Your Unique Selling Proposition

In the first few seconds of a face-to-face meeting or over the telephone, you have the opportunity to share with the client why your services should be considered. Being able to crisply articulate your USP directly determines your positioning in the client's mind.

What do you say when people ask you what to do? Pretend that you are riding up in an elevator with the person who will be deciding whether to use your services, and you have two minutes or less to get your points across. Develop a two minute "elevator pitch" with punch and polish. Practice it until you have a compelling story to tell.

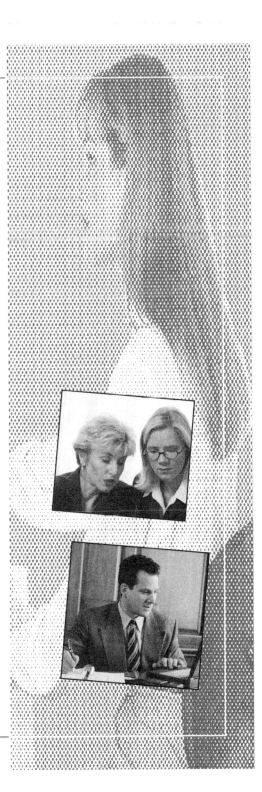

STREETWISE ADVICE

> Professional-looking consultants are able to ask for professional-range fees.

Project a Professional Image

You are initially judged by how you look and sound. First impressions, including telephone impressions, can set the stage for developing a relationship–or not! Your appearance comes across in how you dress, your logo, your literature and promotional material, and the quality of your proposals and presentations.

Investing in your image helps to determine the fees you will be able to obtain. If your promotional material looks unprofessional, it is difficult to command the fee structure commensurate with a consulting professional. Don't be extravagant–just project professionalism. The investment is worth it. You'll be able to project the image of an established consulting practice, not the newly arrived Lone Ranger.

Have Financial Reserves Available

Actively marketing and building your consulting practice can result in a fast burn rate of your start-up money. Make sure you have enough to cover your living expenses as well as the planned expenses for your business for at least six months, or even better, have a year's cash reserves available.

Also, plan for the unexpected expenses and cash flow issues. Know in advance that your net ten day payment terms do not necessarily mean that your client will pay in ten days. Consider all the costs of running your business when calculating your rate of expenditure. Many business plans (including mine) did not cover all the bases. It's important to allocate enough funds when you are starting out to create the image you want for your business.

> The more people you know and are in contact with, the more successfully your business will grow.

Develop and Expand Your Contacts

Consulting is a people business, and the more that you can tap existing or newly-developed contacts, the faster your business will grow. The people you know from your corporate career can be an excellent resource base when you are starting your business. These existing contacts may be able to use your services directly or provide valuable referrals.

STREETWISE ADVICE

I was fortunate when starting out as a consultant because I was quickly able to land a substantial contract with a former business associate. The degree of success you have in the first years in consulting depends upon the number of quality business contacts you have in place when you start your business. Your success beyond the start-up period of your business depends heavily on your ability to establish new contacts.

Never Miss the Opportunity to Spread the Word

Engage in those activities that will provide free publicity and increased awareness of your consulting activities. Get yourself published by submitting articles to periodicals. Consider publishing a newsletter that you can send to existing contacts and prospective clients. Accept speaking engagements to widen your circle of influence.

Since beginning our consulting practice, we have published a newsletter on more or less a quarterly basis. We are now consistent in publishing quarterly, because we have found that we win one new client with each newsletter published. As a result of two articles that were published in regional publications, we've been able to persuade clients to go with us as a "published expert" in our field.

Publicize as frequently and as consistently as possible.

Focus on Results

Results are the driving force behind your clients' motivations to use your services. Consulting has evolved from being an advice profession to being one more focused on producing results for the client. Structuring your approach for client-specific benefits and results will help you win more business and command a higher fee structure.

I believe this point is so vitally important that we will not accept consulting assignments without working with the client to identify the specific results desired. I have walked away from time-for-money exchange situations. Exchanging your time for the client's money is meaningful only when the client's benefits are clearly understood and targeted.

STREETWISE ADVICE

Get Testimonials

Most consultants get results for their clients. Not enough of them capitalize on their results to get referrals and testimonials. Because of the people-centered nature and the importance of credibility and trust in consulting, take the time and effort to get quotes, testimonial letters, and referrals from your clients. What someone else says about you is far more important than anything you can say about yourself.

I learned this the hard way. In our six years of experience I am aware of only one instance where my client was not entirely satisfied. I've offered references when pursuing new business, but I was not, until recently, proactive in asking clients to write to me and tell me that they were satisfied and why. This written quotable information makes credibility issues go away when talking with a new client.

Provide More Value than Expected

Don't you become a more satisfied customer when you receive more value than expected? For example, the extra floor mats with the car or a courtesy call to make sure that you are satisfied? Of course you do, and it's no different with your clients. Any extras you can add to the assignment that have perceived value but take very little of your time can guarantee a long-term relationship with that client.

I do this on each consulting and training assignment I accept. Perhaps it's an extra training session they had not expected, or handling some additional work that was not in the original scope of work. This helps to create a bond between my clients and me.

Any extra efforts that you provide for the client can only benefit you in the future.

QUESTIONS & ANSWERS ABOUT GROWING YOUR BUSINESS

When will you know you should hire some help?

That question presupposes that you will–which is not necessarily true. It's a question of financial benefit–and I would tend to use the services of independent contractors for as long as humanly possible to avoid the regulation complexities of hiring and firing people these days.

STREETWISE ADVICE

If you hire only one person, who should that person be?

The person who contributes the most to your bottom line.

What if your business is growing so much that you feel the need to hire another expert/consultant like yourself? Should you hire them as an employee, or make them a partner or something like that?

When I get this urge I lie down until the feeling goes away. I would never consider a partnership unless the sum of our results was three times what I could do on my own.

How can you network and get more clients at the same time you work on projects for existing clients? How do you manage to strike that balance?

That's what the consulting business is all about. No matter how much work I have on hand, I still produce a quarterly newsletter, and I use my contact manager faithfully to stay in touch with existing and potential clients. I also conduct direct-mail campaigns and stay active in professional organizations to make sure I have enough raw material to work with. Weekends are great for the written part of this activity.

A balance has to be struck between the maintenance of current clients, and the recruitment of new business.

What are some ways to ensure that you will get repeat business from a client and he will give you referrals?

Make sure he is a totally satisfied customer–then ask him. I use the approach that my clients are my clients for life. I continually look for ways that they can improve their business and offer my services (or not) accordingly. I ask if I can include the client's name on my referral list. For the training part of my business, I request written evaluations that I can quote from.

Try to satisfy your client completely, and use their input to improve upon your performance.

QUESTIONS & ANSWERS ABOUT STARTING AND RUNNING A CONSULTING BUSINESS

The following are fifteen questions and answers your may hear (or consider for yourself) about starting and running a consulting business.

What factors can contribute to abandoning your corporate career and starting your own consulting practice?

The situation is different for different individuals. The following factors may come into play:

STREETWISE ADVICE

- Discouragement with the job environment
- You want freedom and independence
- The opportunity for advancement no longer exists
- You no longer enjoy going to work
- You have been reengineered out of your company

Starting your own consulting practice is a great way to gain your own freedom while working for a goal of your own making.

What sorts of surprises can you expect when you are beginning?

Your world has dramatically changed. Many of the skills you thought you possessed require updating and improvement to succeed as a consultant. Plus, there's a seemingly inexhaustible list of new skills to be learned. You are now operating from an influence basis instead of a position of authority.

What are the greatest sources of satisfaction?

Freedom and independence are only two of the sources of satisfaction. Consulting is a stimulating profession because you are continually learning from a variety of client assignments. In addition, your financial success is directly linked to your consulting successes and reputation.

What are the most difficult areas in beginning a consulting career?

The rhythm and predictability of a position in the corporate world is gone, and that includes the weekly or biweekly paycheck. The lack of a predictable income is perhaps the greatest challenge faced by beginning consultants.

Despite the lack of predictable income, consulting offers the opportunity to earn an income that reflects your success and reputation.

What new skills will you have to learn?

Let's assume the skills you have developed over the years are current and applicable to your consulting practice. Marketing your services may then be the largest area for skill development for a beginning consultant. In addition, continual skills development in your area of professional competence is required to better serve your clients.

What are the areas of greatest difference between running a consulting practice and having a career in a corporate environment?

You have no other departments to depend upon. No one makes decisions for you or provides you with guidance. In consulting, you

STREETWISE ADVICE

make your own reality. That means doing whatever it takes to get the job done, and overcoming any obstacles that come up. You rely totally on your abilities to get the job done, rather than depending on the performance of other people and departments in a corporation.

What sorts of ongoing challenges can you expect?

A steady income flow is a continual challenge. Another is the shift in your business from a dependence upon existing industry contacts to development of a totally new set of relationships. These new relationships and clients will be completely outside of the comfortable business associations you developed over the years.

Don't you occasionally get tempted to return to the corporate world?

Some consultants do. I don't. I am totally committed to my business. Starting my own consulting business was the best career and personal decision I ever made. Some consultants do get tempted to return to the old way, perhaps because of the steady pay or benefits. When this happens, I wonder whether they were really cut out for the business to begin with.

What can you do to assure a steady income stream?

A steady income flow means managing the lead and contact resources you have as an ongoing process, not a series of events. No matter what distractions, money, and comfort you can derive from an existing consulting contract, make the effort to continually hustle and prospect for new opportunities.

What sorts of hours can you expect to put in to be successful?

Don't bother to count the hours. Consulting assignments can consume the amount of time and effort you may have put forth in graduate school. That means long hours, weekends, and holidays. The good news is that these "burst" conditions exist during the peak efforts associated with a given assignment. On other occasions, you can schedule a well-earned break for yourself.

What can you expect to be your best source of leads?

Personal contacts and referrals will be your best source of leads for the life of your consulting business. "Word of mouth" advertising will work well for you, but it must be cultivated. Periodically and sys-

> Consulting demands a strong commitment to the business that can lack in the corporate world.

STREETWISE ADVICE

tematically stay in touch with your industry contacts and anyone who has ever given you consulting business. Call them. Send them articles that may be of specific interest. Do what's necessary to stay in touch. Sooner or later the rewards will come.

How important is a business plan to consulting success?

The benefit of putting a plan on paper is the direction it provides to your consulting activities. Periodic plan review provides useful feedback on your progress against the plan, especially the income goals you have set for yourself. To me, the most important part of the business plan is the "Who am I, where am I going, and why?" section. Being true to your mission makes success a whole lot easier.

Plans are important to have in order to keep your business and your goals on track.

How important to success is ongoing professional development?

One of the major reasons that clients hire you as a consultant is because of what you bring to the party. You have acquired some of these capabilities and skills over the years. To stay on the cutting edge, taking the time for personal and professional development is mandatory.

What can you do to minimize unnecessary expenses?

I've known consultants who started out with the best of everything; car, office, computer systems, plain paper fax machines–the works. Their prospective clients did not seem to care. Only spend money that will help you build your business. That means maintaining a professional image with no frills. You will benefit your clients.

When do you know you've arrived?

That's simple. You know you've arrived when you are fully scheduled because people are consistently and continually calling you for your services and you are hard-pressed to keep up with the demand.

QUESTIONS & ANSWERS ABOUT MANAGING DIFFICULT CLIENTS

This is a difficult one for me. I'm in my seventh year of business, and I have never had what I consider to be a difficult client. In all cases, I've taken the time and expended the effort to make sure I had rapport with the people at all levels of an organization that I'm dealing with. I've always been paid for my work–sometimes a little slower

STREETWISE ADVICE

than I would like, but I've been paid. When I sense during the sales process that a client may be difficult, I'll walk away from the business–it's not worth the aggravation.

What are the most typical client problems you're likely to encounter?

From my own experience–slow pay. I once had a company that was in severe financial straits that was only paying their most important creditors (parts for manufacturing). I enlisted the aid of two of my champions within the organization, and my bill was finally paid.

What if the client refuses to pay after you've already completed some/most/all of the work for him or her?

I'd first find out at the top levels of the company why they are not paying and then enlist the legal resources required.

What if the client expects you to do something outside your areas of expertise? Should you hire an expert subcontractor or try to do it yourself? If you do hire someone else, should you be responsible for paying them or should the client?

In most cases I'd sub the work, and it would be transparent to my client. Therefore, I'd pay for the work subbed out. The client expects me to have ownership of my commitment to him. If it requires expertise I don't have, it's my responsibility to get it.

> If your client expects services that you don't have, it's your responsibility to get them.

What should you do if you sense a potential conflict of interest with a client?

If there truly was one, then I'd not take the business. For example, I was asked to perform some competitive analyses for a computer firm to position their products against others in their industry. For a period of two years after completing that assignment, I did not try to undertake a similar task with another computer company.

What if you have already begun work with the client?

If you know what you are doing, this is highly unlikely. If it does happen because of ignorance on your part, discuss it with the client.

What are some forms of conflicts of interest that consultants are likely to encounter, and what are the best ways to avoid them?

One that comes to mind is taking similar assignments for competitors in the same industry. Sales training is one area where a con-

STREETWISE ADVICE

flict would be unlikely–it's somewhat generic and far different in scope and impact that in-depth positioning, organizational restructuring, or marketing strategy. The best way to avoid this is to not chase these opportunities to begin with–or if you have a number of people in your consulting practice–assign one person to one account and another to the second.

QUESTIONS & ANSWERS ABOUT TROUBLESHOOTING

What should you do if things just aren't clicking? Change your specialty? Change your marketing strategy? Just give up and go back to a regular job?

One of the by-products of running a business is the feedback you get. There's not just success or failure–there are all shades of difference in between. I believe that to survive and grow, a consulting practice has to continually evolve. Little did I know six years ago that telesales and telemarketing would play such an increasingly important role, and I've added that area of expertise to my business. That's a case of adding (not changing) a specialty. We've also added direct mail as a critically important dimension of our marketing thrust, and it's made a major a difference in our results. Persistence is key–if you are a true consultant, you'll never go back to a regular job.

To survive and grown, consulting firms have to change and evolve with the industry.

What are your thoughts on subcontracting? Is that a good area to explore if you are having trouble getting your own clients? Or does subcontracting just undercut your own business?

I have subcontracted to other consulting firms in the past and have independent contractors who work with me. Subcontracting to someone else has actually helped me grow areas of expertise without undercutting my own business.

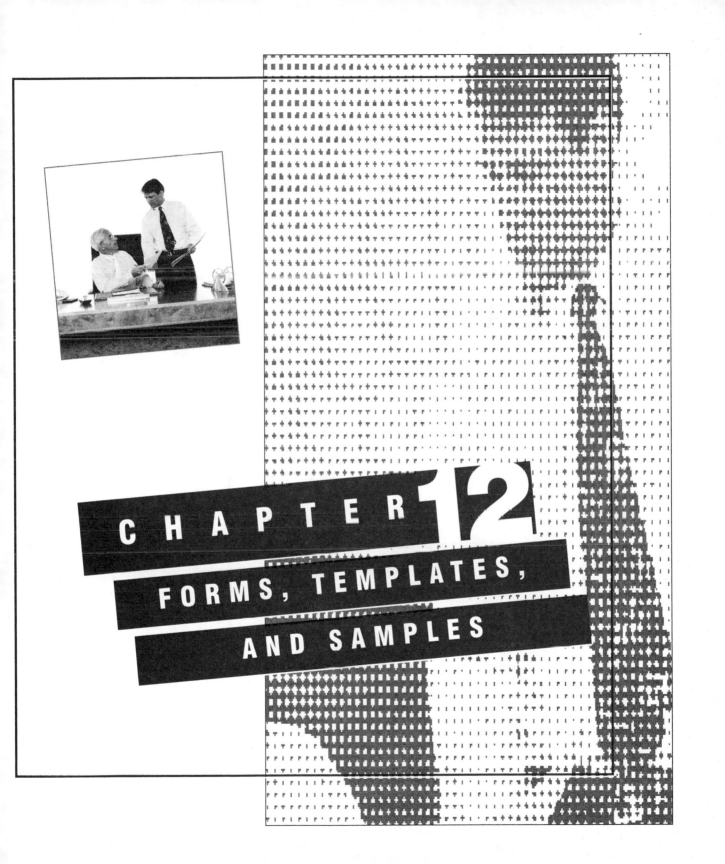

CHAPTER 12

FORMS, TEMPLATES, AND SAMPLES

While it's nice to be given advice on what to do, it's often more effective to see samples or templates. Some of these forms or letters you may want to use as is. Others you may want to use more as inspiration to create your own business forms or letters.

WHAT'S INCLUDED

INVOICES

This is the one form that is enjoyable to complete because it results in revenue for your business. The faster you generate the invoice, and the quicker your client pays, the better your cash flow position. You may want to consider the following:

1. Insert a scanned image of your logo and print the invoice on a color ink jet printer to improve the appearance.
2. Keep the payment terms as short as your client will agree to.

The sample invoice provided was developed using Microsoft Publisher, and the template shown is in a word processing format.

PROMOTIONAL FLYERS AND BROCHURES

In your consulting practice, you should have a promotional document to give to your prospective clients that describes what you do and what you can do for them. These flyers and brochures need not be expensive masterpieces. Your computer's word processor and graphics programs can be used to produce visually appealing statements for your business. Other programs and preprinted color forms can be inexpensively ordered from paper and supplies vendors such as *Papers Direct.*

A template for your word processor is provided for your use, along with three examples of the evolution a single-page flyer. We use this flyer as a direct-mail piece and handout to promote one of our training courses. We began with a simple Microsoft *PowerPoint* version with a pie-chart graphics insertion printed on a color ink-jet printer. Version 2 replaced the pie chart with a more visually interesting scanned photograph of training participants and the equipment we use. Versions 1 and 2 were relatively inexpensive.

Instead of a few dollars to develop and print, Version 3 cost approximately $2,000 for layout and printing of 2,000 copies. The effect is more

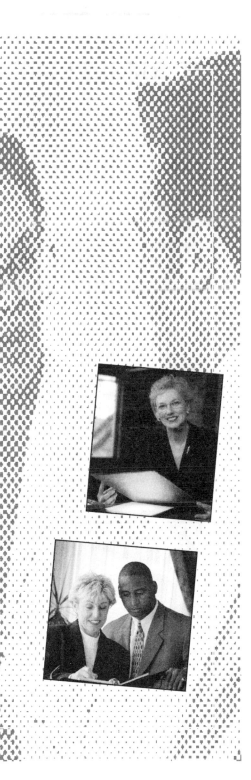

professional, and the cost is minuscule compared to the production of a full-fledged color brochure. The template provides an insert for your logo at the top. In hindsight, that's the approach I would have used with the examples provided; the client would then have had the name of the consulting firm, a picture of the service provided, and a summary description–all in one field of view.

OTHER BUSINESS FORMS

This section includes examples of many of the typical forms you will want to use every day in the running of your business. The exact form you use isn't nearly as important as the necessity to create clear records of the various business functions. Make sure you use forms to collect information on such things as expenses, travel, purchases, etc. You may also need to use these records to substantiate billings when you pass these expenses on to your clients.

Additionally, you will want to formally notify customers of all important contract performance items and can best do this through use of such forms as invoices, purchase orders, and past due notices.

Make sure you use template forms for such things as expenses, travel, and purchases.

FORMS, TEMPLATES, AND SAMPLES

INVOICE

Your Company (or insert your logo)
Street Address
City, State, Zip
Phone Number

Date

Bill To:

Name of Contact
Title
Client Company Name
Street Address
City, State, Zip

Ship To:

Name of Contact
Title
Client Company Name
Street Address
City, State, Zip

INVOICE NO.	CONSULTANT	TERMS	TAX ID (OR S.S. #)
xx-xxxx	your name	Net x days	xx-xxxxxx

QUANTITY	DESCRIPTION OF CONSULTING SERVICES	UNIT PRICE	TOTAL

BALANCE DUE ▶

FORMS, TEMPLATES, AND SAMPLES

Promotional Flyer Template

Insert scanned photo or clip art of your consulting practice service applications or customers

(Statement of Customer Benefit or Description of Service)

Description/Support Statement No. 1 (Describe an aspect of your consulting service and the results or benefits the client can expect. These descriptions support the statement of customer benefit or summary of your services, above.)	**Description/Support Statement No. 4**
Description/Support Statement No. 2	**Description/Support Statement No. 5**
Description/Support Statement No. 3	**Description/Support Statement No. 6**

(Your Address and Phone Number)

FORMS, TEMPLATES, AND SAMPLES

Telesales Excellence

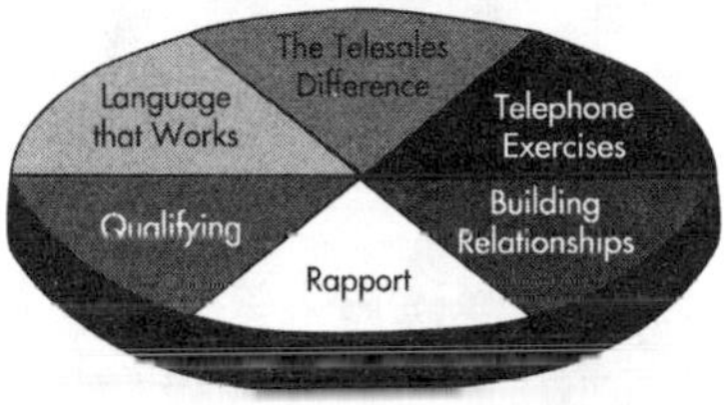

Six Steps to Superior Performance

The Telesales Difference

Telesales and telemarketing are substantially different from face-to-face selling. Understanding the five critically important differences and how to use them makes a measurable difference in results. Participants learn these principles and how to practically apply them in real-world telephone activities.

Telephone Exercises

Learning by doing. Participants use headsets for learning and reinforcing skills (AudioPacer units). They also learn to build more effective voice patterns by seeing their voice on a CRT screen (VoiceMapper). The coaching provided here creates a positive and noticeable difference in the participant's voice quality.

Building Relationships

"Slamming appointments"—or building relationships—the distinction makes a major difference in your short-term and long-term results. Participants learn the five key elements of developing stronger business relationships with prospects and customers.

Rapport

Trust is a key element in any efforts conducted by phone. People share information more readily with those they can easily relate to—and from people who are like them. Participants learn to understand their prospect's "map" and how to instantly and effectively respond.

Qualifying

Gathering quality information about how prospects make buying decisions is critically important. How this information is gathered is 5.4 times as important as the words used to gather information. Participants learn how to use their voice more effectively to dramatically improve their qualifying performance.

Language that Works

Using language that makes the most of telephone communications is key. Using pre-suppositional language patterns are particularly effective. Participants learn seven of these powerfully effective patterns and how to use them.

SalesWinners INCORPORATED

■ 2139 University Drive ■ Suite 425 ■ Coral Springs, Florida 33071 ■ 555-752-7878

FORMS, TEMPLATES, AND SAMPLES

Telesales Excellence

Six Steps to Superior Performance

The Telesales Difference

Telesales and telemarketing are substantially different from face-to-face selling. Understanding the five critically important differences and how to use them makes a measurable difference in results. Participants learn these principles and how to practically apply them in real-world telephone activities.

Telephone Exercises

Learning by doing. Participants use headsets for learning and reinforcing skills (AudioPacer units). They also learn to build more effective voice patterns by seeing their voice on a CRT screen (VoiceMapper). The coaching provided here creates a positive and noticeable difference in the participant's voice quality.

Building Relationships

"Slamming appointments"—or building relationships—the distinction makes a major difference in your short-term and long-term results. Participants learn the five key elements of developing stronger business relationships with prospects and customers.

Rapport

Trust is a key element in any efforts conducted by phone. People share information more readily with those they can easily relate to—and from people who are like them. Participants learn to understand their prospect's "map" and how to instantly and effectively respond.

Qualifying

Gathering quality information about how prospects make buying decisions is critically important. How this information is gathered is 5.4 times as important as the words used to gather information. Participants learn how to use their voice more effectively to dramatically improve their qualifying performance.

Language that Works

Using language that makes the most of telephone communications is key. Using pre-suppositional language patterns are particularly effective. Participants learn seven of these powerfully effective patterns and how to use them.

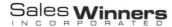

Sales **Winners**
INCORPORATED

■ 2139 University Drive ■ Suite 425 ■ Coral Springs, Florida 33071 ■ 555-752-7878

FORMS, TEMPLATES, AND SAMPLES

STATEMENT

To: Account #

From: Date: / /

DATE	INVOICE #	ITEM/DESCRIPTION	AMOUNT

PLEASE PAY THIS AMOUNT ▶

FORMS, TEMPLATES, AND SAMPLES

CREDIT RECORD

Name:
Account No.:
Home Address:

Home Telephone:
Business Address:

Business Telephone

Credit Line	Date

ORDER #	PAYMENT DUE		PAYMENT REC'D		BALANCE	FIRST NOTICE	SECOND NOTICE
	AMOUNT	DATE	AMOUNT	DATE			

1st overdue call:	
2nd overdue call:	
3rd overdue call:	

FORMS, TEMPLATES, AND SAMPLES

MONTHLY EXPENSE REPORT

From: / / To: / /

Name: ______________________ Position: ______________________

DAY	TRAVEL	AUTO	MEALS	LODGING	ENTERT.	OTHER	DAILY TOTALS
1							
2							
3							
4							
5							
6							
7							
8							
9							
10							
11							
12							
13							
14							
15							
16							
17							
18							
19							
20							
21							
22							
23							
24							
25							
26							
27							
28							
29							
30							
31							

Total Mileage [ ] X [ ]

Subtotal [ ]

Mileage Costs [ ]

TOTAL [ ]

FORMS, TEMPLATES, AND SAMPLES

PAST DUE NOTICE

Date: / /

Account No.:

Your account is past due. Please remit the amount specified below.

INVOICE NUMBER	ITEM/DESCRIPTION	AMOUNT DUE	PAYMENT DUE

AMOUNT DUE ▶

PURCHASE ORDER

To:

Our Purchase Order Number must appear on all invoices, cases, packing lists, and correspondence.

Date:
Order No.:

Date Wanted:
Terms:
Ship Via:

QUANTITY	ITEM/DESCRIPTION	PRICE	AMOUNT

Authorized Signature ______________________

FORMS, TEMPLATES, AND SAMPLES

CASH DISBURSEMENT RECORD

Date From:

Date To:

Prepared By:

Checked By:

DATE	CASH PAID TO	ITEM/DESCRIPTION	DISBURSED BY	ACCOUNT CHARGED	AMOUNT PAID

FORMS, TEMPLATES, AND SAMPLES

RECEIPT

Date: Receipt No.:

Received From: ______________________ Total Due

Amount: ______________________ This Payment

Signed: ______________________ BALANCE DUE

RECEIPT

Date: Receipt No.:

Received From: ______________________ Total Due

Amount: ______________________ This Payment

Signed: ______________________ BALANCE DUE

RECEIPT

Date: Receipt No.:

Received From: ______________________ Total Due

Amount: ______________________ This Payment

Signed: ______________________ BALANCE DUE

FORMS, TEMPLATES, AND SAMPLES

SAMPLE SOLICITATION LETTERS

The TaxWorks
10 Audubon Road
Wakefield, MA 01889

June 2, 1997

Mr. Martin Scweek
Chief Financial Officer
PiecePart Enterprises
4506 Industrial Way
Lowell, MA 01830

Dear Mr. Scweek:

What if the coming tax season were easier? What if you knew for certain that you were going to get the best possible tax allowances for PiecePart Enterprises?

That's why I am writing to you. The TaxWorks specializes in measurably reducing the tax burden of small companies like yours. For example:

"Because of The TaxWorks superior knowledge of the current tax laws, I was able to lower my effective Federal Tax rate by 7.9%. That's profit dollars to our business."

–John Williams–CFO, Emmett Industries, Chelmsford, Massachusetts

The difference in financial results is the analytical tools that The TaxWorks provides–on-line access to tax accounting rules combined with a unique preparation template that keeps your costs–and your tax payments–down.

For further information, send the enclosed postage-free business reply card to receive your Special Report on *Tax Tips for Small Businesses* along with our information package. Or, call me directly at (800) 555-5555 so we can discuss your specific tax issues.

Sincerely,

E. N. Scrooge

President

P.S. If you contact us before June 30, we'll conduct a free tax consultation over the phone for your company.

FORMS, TEMPLATES, AND SAMPLES

Strategy 90
1234 Commercial Boulevard
Ft. Lauderdale, FL 33123

June 2, 1997

Mr. Tom McClelland
Vice President of Marketing
MB Cope Software Systems
5990 Sunburst Boulevard
Ft. Lauderdale, FL 33313

Dear Mr. McClelland:

How will you know for certain that your company will be on target for its business objectives in the year 2000?

Effectively developing and implementing the strategic vision of your company can make all the difference, and we at Strategy 90 have helped companies like yours achieve their strategic objectives.

"Because of Strategy 90's proven methods for strategic plan development, we were able to reestablish our company's core competencies and meet and exceed our revenue and profit goals."
–Roger Holt–President, Holt Products Company, Orlando, Florida

Planning with crystallized objectives–and putting an action plan in place for each area of your company–that's the unique service that Strategy 90 provides. In other words, we help you make it happen–with the most cost-effective process available in the market today. Computer technology, yes–but a lot more!

For further information, send the enclosed postage-free business reply card to receive your Special Report on *Ten Strategic Planning Mistakes–and How to Avoid Them* along with our information package. Or, call me directly at (800) 555-5555 so we can discuss your strategic objectives.

Sincerely,

John McNell
President

P.S. If you contact us before June 30, we'll provide a free 90-minute strategic planning consultation.

FORMS, TEMPLATES, AND SAMPLES

Travel Partners
157 Eastern Avenue - Suite 7000
Manchester, NH 03104

June 2, 1997

Mr. Richard Barrs
President
MediSense Systems, Inc.
10 Cambridge Center
Cambridge, MA 02142

Dear Mr. Barrs:

How would you like to save a minimum of 12.5% on airline and lodging costs?

That's what we can do for you–because our travel service volume gives us the best discount in the industry. And we pass our savings on to you.

"Travel Partners enabled us to reduce our travel expenses by 15.4 percent last year, and the numbers are even more impressive this year. I recommend them highly"
–Murray Cayford–CFO, Johnson Computer Products, Inc., Nashua, NH

Our volume discount on travel accommodations are passed on to you–we guarantee to lower your costs! In addition, Travel Partners offers a wide range of meeting and conference capabilities–again at the best prices in the industry.

For further information, send the enclosed postage-free business reply card to receive your Special Report on *Getting More from Your Travel Dollars* along with our information package. Or, call me directly at (800) 555-5555 so we can discuss your strategic objectives.

Sincerely,

Vincent Lopez
President

P.S. If you contact us before June 30, we'll book your next travel request at a 15% discount!

FORMS, TEMPLATES, AND SAMPLES

Custom Financial Services
2100 Atlantic Boulevard
Margate, Florida 33071

June 2, 1997

Mr. Victor Baron
President
MediSense Systems, Inc.
10 Cambridge Center
Cambridge, MA 02142

Dear Mr. Baron:

How would you like to save a minimum of 11.5% on your outside accounting services?

We can do that for you and more–because of our straightforward, proven, highly effective accounting methodology.

"Custom Financial Services took the trouble to understand our business–and are handling our financial reports in a highly competent manner. Their methods are superior, and they are a trustworthy firm to deal with."*–Bill Mooseley–CFO, Century Software Products, Inc., Marlboro, MA*

We employ unique interactive computer templates that enable us to develop financial reports that are custom-tailored for your business. This reduces your accounting service costs and assures reports that are error-free.

For further information, send the enclosed postage-free business reply card to receive your Special Report on *Financial Reporting Tips for Small Businesses* along with our information package. Or, call me directly at (800) 555-5555 so we can discuss your accounting service objectives.

Sincerely,

C. Theo Money
President

P.S. If you contact us before June 30, we'll provide a free 90-minute consultation for your business.

FORMS, TEMPLATES, AND SAMPLES

SalesWinners
INCORPORATED

June 2, 1997

Mr. David Burts
Vice President of Sales
The Software Excellence House, Ltd.
1400 Abernathy Parkway, Suite 1500
Orlando, FL 32104

Dear Mr. Burts:

How to increase telesales results by 24%–and get a coach for free!

What's been your experience with training programs before? Did some group or some person come to town, share some selling tips with your people, and get them interested? Then, after he or she left town, did your people return to their old ineffective ways of selling?

We can change all that for you–by delivering highly effective training that measurably increases your telesales results. Here's a comment from one of our customers:

"Because of SalesWinners training, I was able to increase the effectiveness of my telesales group by 34.6%. That's a phenomenal increase, and SalesWinners made the difference for us!"

–Bart Lawlor–Vice President of Sales, Market Penetration Enterprises, Newton, Massachusetts

What do we do that's different? We provide top-notch training combined with a 90-day one-on-one follow-through with each member of your group. This follow through reinforces skills and measurably increases your sales results.

For further information, send the enclosed postage-free business reply card to receive your Special Report on *Five Telesales Success Factors* along with our information package. Or, call me directly at (800) 555-5555 so we can discuss your strategic objectives.

Sincerely,

David Kintler
President

P.S. If you contact us before June 30, we'll also include our publication *Telephone Sales Openings that Work.*

INDEX

INDEX

INDEX

INDEX

INDEX

INDEX

INDEX

INDEX

INDEX

DAVID KINTLER

David Kintler is President of SalesWinners, Inc., a consulting firm which he founded in October, 1990. SalesWinners provides sales training, competitive positioning, and marketing consulting to Fortune 1000 companies–with an emphasis in the business-to-business telesales arena.

Prior to founding SalesWinners, Mr. Kintler held positions as Vice President of Sales and National Sales Manager for several leading computer industry companies. He has over 25 years of sales and marketing management experience in computer systems, software, CAD/CAM, and image processing.

Mr. Kintler has a Bachelor's Degree in Mechanical Engineering from the University of Louisville and a Master's Degree in Business Administration from the University of Cincinnati. He is active with the Society of Professional Consultants and Sales and Marketing Executives of Greater Boston, and is a guest lecturer at the New York Institute of Technology and Lynn University in Boca Raton, Florida.

Mr. Kintler can be contacted at:

SalesWinners, Inc.
Coral Springs, FL 33071
(954)752-7878 or (888)WIN-SALE

BOB ADAMS

Bob Adams is former president of Adams Media Corporation, a Harvard MBA, and a widely recognized expert on business techniques.

OTHER TITLES IN THE STREETWISE® SERIES:

Streetwise® Achieving Wealth Through Franchising

Streetwise® Business Letters

Streetwise® Business Valuation

Streetwise® Complete Business Plan

Streetwise® Complete Business Plan with Software

Streetwise® Complete Publicity Plans

Streetwise® Crash Course MBA

Streetwise® Customer-Focused Selling

Streetwise® Do-It-Yourself Advertising

Streetwise® Finance & Accounting

Streetwise® Financing the Small Business

Streetwise® Human Resources Management

Streetwise® Independent Consulting

Streetwise® Landlording & Property Management

Streetwise® Low-Cost Marketing

Streetwise® Low-Cost Web Site Promotion

Streetwise® Managing a Nonprofit

Streetwise® Managing People

Streetwise® Marketing Plan

Streetwise® Maximize Web Site Traffic

Streetwise® Motivating and Rewarding Employees

Streetwise® Project Management

Streetwise® Restaurant Management

Streetwise® Retirement Planning

Streetwise® Sales Letters with CD-ROM

Streetwise® Selling Your Business

Streetwise® Small Business Start-Up

Streetwise® Start Your Own Business Workbook

Streetwise® Structuring Your Business

Streetwise® Time Management

Available wherever books are sold.
For more information, or to order, call 800-872-5627 or visit www.adamsmedia.com.
Adams Media, 57 Littlefield Street, Avon, MA 02322